Riot!

Tobacco, Reform, and Violence in
Eighteenth-century Papantla, Mexico

"The author masterfully provides us with new insights into significant themes related to the post-1759 Bourbon Reforms and their impacts on the delicate power balance between colonial rulers and subordinate populations at the local level and beyond in New Spain. This relatively short but well researched, written, and reasoned work will significantly add to scholars' and students' understanding of economic, political, and social tensions in Mexico's late colonial racially and ethnically complex society." Dr. Patrick Carroll, retired professor of history at Texas A&M University, Corpus Christi and author of many works on Blacks in Colonial Mexico, including *Blacks in Colonial Veracruz*

"While not shying away from the grim realities of colonial exploitation, Frederick explores the causes and complexities of Totonac rebellions in eighteenth-century Mexico with a keen eye and a lively tone. A succinct and readable study, Riot! is ideal for graduate seminars and other discussion settings." Matthew Restall, author of *The Black Middle: Africans, Mayas, and Spaniards in Colonial Yucatan* and *Seven Myths of the Spanish Conquest*

Riot!

Tobacco, Reform, and Violence in
Eighteenth-century Papantla, Mexico

Jake Frederick

sussex
ACADEMIC
PRESS
Brighton • Chicago • Toronto

2 4 6 8 10 9 7 5 3

First published in Great Britain in 2016, reprinted in paperback 2019, by
SUSSEX ACADEMIC PRESS
PO Box 139, Eastbourne BN24 9BP

Distributed in North America by
SUSSEX ACADEMIC PRESS
Independent Publishers Group
814 N. Franklin Street
Chicago, IL 60610

British Library Cataloguing in Publication Data
A CIP catalogue record for this book is available from the British Library.

Library of Congress Cataloging-in-Publication Data
Names: Frederick, Jake, author.
Title: Riot! : tobacco, reform, and violence in eighteenth-century Papantla, Mexico / Jake Frederick.
Description: Brighton : Sussex Academic Press, 2016. | Includes bibliographical references and index.
Identifiers: LCCN 2016020691 | ISBN 9781845198169 (hbk : alk. paper)
| ISBN 9781789760187 (pbk : alk. paper)
Subjects: LCSH: Totonac Indians—Mexico—Papantla de Olarte—History—18th century. | Totonac Indians—Government relations—History—18th century. | Tobacco workers—Papantla de Olarte—History—18th century. | Riots—Mexico—Papantla de Olarte—History—18th century. | Papantla de Olarte (Mexico)—Social conditions—18th century. | Papantla de Olarte (Mexico)—History—18th century.
Classification: LCC F1221.T6 F74 2016 | DDC 972/.6202—dc23
LC record available at https://lccn.loc.gov/2016020691

MIX
Paper from
responsible sources
FSC® C013056

Typeset & designed by Sussex Academic Press, Brighton & Eastbourne.
Printed by TJ International, Padstow, Cornwall.

Contents

List of Illustrations

Acknowledgements

Any list of those who deserve my gratitude must begin with my advisor and friend Matthew Restall. No student or scholar could hope to have a more inspiring, more attentive, or more supportive mentor. Though I count myself among dozens of scholars whose careers have been furthered by Matthew's consideration, I flatter myself that, as one who helped hang the basketball net in his driveway, I hold a special place.

This project was launched with the generous support of a Fulbright-García Robles scholarship and funding from the Pennsylvania State University department of history. As I made my way from location to location in search of material on Papantla's history I was fortunate to receive assistance and support from the staff of the Archivo de Indias in Seville and the staff of the Archivo General de la Nación in Mexico City, particularly the insights of Roberto Beristein. I was also fortunate to access the varied holdings of Harvard University through a grant from the David Rockefeller Center for Lain American Studies. My study of the demographics of Papantla would not have been possible without the facilities of The Family History Center of the Church of Jesus Christ of Latter Day Saints. Lawrence University has been supportive with both time and money to help this project along. The great generosity of Lawrence alumni Jean Lampert Woy '65 and Richard Woy '64 has been vital in seeing this project to completion.

Over the course of researching and writing this book I have been fortunate to receive wide ranging support, from scholarly insights, proofreading and editorial advice, encouragement when the writing was slow, to direct orders to sit down and type. The following colleagues and friends all contributed to completion of this project– Phil Rutherford, Randall McNeil, Peter Blitstein, Tatiana Seijas, Ben Vinson III, Emilio Khouri, Antonio Escobar Ohmstede, Michael Ducey, Sheenizah Shah, Alex Kurki, the rotating members of Writing Boot Camp, and David McGlynn, who never lets evidence stand in the way of optimism. I am also thankful to and the anonymous reviewers who provided extensive advice to improve this work.

I cannot begin to articulate my gratitude to my family, for all they have done to make this possible. I can only hope that they are all aware that I could not have completed this by myself. Lastly, for her boundless patience, love, and support, I thank Katherine Moody.

For Kate

Introduction

In one of the former prison cells lining the walls of Galería Cuatro in the Archivo General de la Nación in Mexico City, what was once the center cell block of the Lecumberri Prison, is a leather-bound volume labeled *Indios 3*. It is one of thousands that fill this wing of the archive devoted to Mexico's colonial past. Inside *Indios 3*, among its hundreds of pages of centuries-old records, is a half page of script written by a Spanish official, don Luís de Velasco Mendoza. The note records the arrest of two men in association with an uprising in November 1590, in the town of Papantla, Veracruz. The document asserts that two Totonac natives, Martín García and his unnamed brother, had been jailed for "bringing about revolt," and inciting "fights, debates, and quarrels." The Garcías were apparently inflaming the Totonac of Papantla against the leading figures of the local native *cabildo* (town council).[1] The brothers had undermined local respect for the *gobernador* and *alcaldes* (the senior officers of the native *cabildo*) and incited others to join in opposition to these elected officials of the Totonac community. Velasco had previously warned the brothers to accept the rule of the local *cabildo*, but despite this effort, the two continued to sow discord in Papantla. Seeing no other recourse, Velasco arrested the brothers and then referred their case to the *corregidor* (Spanish regional administrator) of Tonatico and Zozocolco (50 kilometers southwest of Papantla).[2] This brief notation is the entirety of the record of the unrest of 1590.

The brevity of the above account is frustrating, raising far more questions than it answers. What happened to the brothers García? Were they given stiff sentences? Perhaps they were whipped, or sentenced to serve on the galleys. What were their objectives? Was Velasco accurately reading the situation? Were the brothers really attempting to undermine the authority of the Totonac *cabildo* officials, or could they have been revolting against the local Spanish magistrate? Why were these two men sowing discord within the Totonac community? It is quite possible that Velasco himself was dissembling, blaming the revolt on native factionalism to disguise his own role in raising the ire of the local populace. We are left to speculate about the kinds of disputes that may have been unfolding in the community at the time, and to imagine how such a conflict might have played out.

Of course speculation on such thin evidence is perilous, and we are forced to concede that unless new documents surface, we will never know what happened. However, that does not leave the events of November 1590 entirely mysterious. This short account does tell us several things. It shows that in sixteenth-century Papantla, the Totonac were not a homogenous bloc with uniform goals and interests. There was a political elite among the Totonac population, the *cabildo* officers. No less clear is that some factional dispute was present, wherein at least some residents apparently disapproved of who held those positions of authority in the *cabildo*, or perhaps how they were using that authority. If the Spaniard Velasco is to be believed, this event was a demonstration of conflict between two sets of natives. On one side there were the elected officials of the *cabildo*, while on the other side were the brothers García and whatever followers they may have garnered. It also appears that there existed in Papantla some reservoir of anger among the native populace; otherwise incitements by the Garcías to provoke unrest would have fallen on deaf ears and they could not have "brought about revolt." It is also evident that, to the Spanish official, native unrest was a threat that had to be dealt with delicately but firmly. Velasco had first warned the brothers, but when that failed to resolve the problem he jailed them and then forwarded their case to higher authorities. Whether or not this was an internecine fight between two native factions, and unrelated to the actions of the Spanish magistrate, in a town where the vast majority of people were natives living under the colonial administration of a very small number of Spaniards, it was necessary to show moderation when dealing with native discontent, yet critical to preserve some rule of law. In this half page we see hints of the complexities of life in Papantla in 1590. We also see certain characteristics of unrest that would be repeated on occasions of revolt much later in Papantla's history. Factionalism within the Totonac population, the deployment of native hostility for political ends, and the outsized influence of Spanish perceptions of violent conflict, would all appear during clashes in Papantla more than a century and a half later.

Between the 1590 event and the reign of Charles III (1759–1788), Papantla and much of the rest of Spain's American holdings experienced what many scholars have termed the *pax colonial*. This era, between the end of the conquest (a date that varies considerably by region) and the last half of the eighteenth century, has been noted for its relative lack of significant violence in the colony.[3] Following the absorption into the colony, native communities under Spanish dominion generally reached a relationship of stability. For much of the colonial-era communities within Spanish rule operated in such a way that, despite native exploitation and grievous iniquity, open uprising was abnormal. This is not to suggest that Spanish America was a particularly peaceful place. The colonies never wanted for violence, and the term *pax colonial* has been subject to considerable and valid criticism. Even in the absence of open insurrection the Spanish colonies were home to violent abuses of subordinate populations, of slavery and institutionalized racism, of frontier warfare moving ever outward from colonial centers for decades if not centuries, and other forms or violence.[4] Yet no matter the level of unrest during what has been dubiously called "the colonial *siesta*," scholars have identified a notable increase in violent uprising across the colonies during the last half of the eighteenth century.[5] Very few of these events were large-scale revolutionary efforts such as the Tupac Amaru uprisings of the 1780s in the southern cone of South America. Though unrest was frequent in the eighteenth century, it was typically much more local in scope, with attacks on Spanish magistrates, priests, or even native officials predominating. This book argues that while the increased unrest of the eighteenth century was principally centered on local concerns, these events were not local in origin. Rather, they were the outcome of colony-wide changes propagated by the Bourbon reforms, which in turn restructured local power relationships and destabilized long-standing mechanisms that had preserved local order. By examining outbursts of violent unrest in Papantla in the eighteenth century it becomes possible to more fully understand how colonial policy intersected with local populations, and to see how power was managed at the village level.

During the last half of the eighteenth century, the Spanish crown embarked on the most thorough restructure of its American colonies since the era of the conquest. Collectively known as the Bourbon reforms these new policies touched on all facets of colonial administration. Economic, political, religious, military, and social policies, sought to reassert crown control over colonies that had become too unprofitable for, and too unresponsive to Iberia.[6] These reforms touched all aspects and regions of Spanish America, and have been the focus of numerous scholarly studies. This book considers how one of these new policies affected a particular Mexican community. Specifically, this work examines how the predominantly Totonac native community of Papantla, Veracruz responded to the crown's monopolization of tobacco. The 1764 creation of the royal tobacco monopoly changed the local economy in Papantla and in so doing disturbed a fragile balance that had developed over centuries, leading to a fundamental reshaping of power relationships among natives, and between natives and local Spanish officials. As a result, Bourbon-era Papantla became a much more violent place than it had been in earlier generations. Though the tobacco monopoly was by no means the only cause of unrest—local conditions, traditions, and political relationships were also key determinants of discontent—it was the catalyst that pushed natives from non-violent discontent to uprising.

Through six eighteenth-century uprisings, I examine how Totonac perceptions of their own political abilities, their increasingly difficult economic environment, and their sense of justice changed in the wake of reform. Ultimately, the violence of the last half of the eighteenth century demonstrates how, for the Totonac subjects of Spanish rule, colonialism—even in the last decades of Spanish dominion—was an ongoing process of negotiation.

When native riots began to proliferate during the waning decades of Spanish control in the Americas, that violence displayed patterns seen in the unrest described in the 1590 event. The population of Papantla reacted like other communities across the colonies following the imposition of the Bourbon reforms, challenging local leaders when crown policy had made economic survival more difficult. These later events often followed a fairly consistent pattern and, fortunately for the historian, are generally far better documented than the November 1590 revolt. Yet even with more testimony and more detailed accounts of the uprisings, we are still left with many of the same questions. If we are to answer these questions we need to peel away the layers of accusations, complaints, and denials. We must contextualize such events within the social, economic, historical, and even geographic background of the basic landscape of discontent in late colonial Papantla.

The Bourbon era was by design a time of great change for the Spanish American colonies. As new regulations changed the political, military, economic, and even religious landscape, many colonists reacted with anxiety to living in a world that was shifting away from old, well-understood systems of rule. Economic reforms that monopolized certain areas of trade while liberalizing others caused particular unease among the leading figures of the colonies, and those anxieties helped fuel the movement for independence that culminated in the wars of the early nineteenth century. When the crown permitted more than a dozen Spanish cities to begin trading with a variety of ports in the colonies, thus breaking Cádiz's monopoly on Spanish American trade, the new open commercialism benefitted Spaniards far more than it did *criollo* (people of Spanish ancestry born in the New World) merchants. Monopolization of tobacco, mercury, cane rum, playing cards, and gunpowder further restricted available avenues for creole commerce, leading some to chafe against the new changes. As Jay Kinsbruner has argued, "the economic reforms of the late colonial period made it patently clear to many influential colonists that they needed to design their own economies."[7] Much has been written examining this concern on the part of creole elites. What is somewhat less understood is the way these changes affected local power relationships in native communities across the colonies.

For Papantla, the most prominent local effect of the new Bourbon policies was the monopolization of tobacco. From a metropolitan standpoint, the monopolization of tobacco was one of the most successful of the economic reforms, eventually generating more wealth for Spain than any other single revenue source, save the silver tithe.[8] So too was the impact on Papantla tremendous, yet in quite a different way. When the monopoly was put into effect in New Spain, legal tobacco cultivation was restricted to a few specific regions in the Gulf Coast area. Papantla fell outside of those regions where the crop could continue to be legally grown. Thus, for Papantla, tobacco monopolization meant the outlaw of cultivation. This prohibition, the first real consequence of the Bourbon reforms to affect Papantla, helped set the stage for a number of violent conflicts during the last half of the century. By criminalizing the cultivation of this crop, which held not only a commercial value, but also cultural significance to the Papantla Totonac, the Bourbon crown disrupted a delicate balance that had existed between the Totonac and Spanish residents in the community.

By the eighteenth century, despite a low level of Spanish settlement in the community, the Totonac had for centuries endured economic exploitation at the hands of Spanish magistrates. As with all native communities in New Spain, peace between these groups was maintained through a negotiated equilibrium of native exploitation versus native autonomy. When the tobacco monopoly was created and the Papantla harvest was collected and publicly incinerated in late 1764 or early 1765, the Papantla Totonac rose up in violent unrest and burned the local municipal offices. Although the rioters responded to this new crown policy with violence, importantly, they did not actually challenge the crown; they focused their ire on the local magistrate. When the crown created an intolerable situation, the native community deflected their resentment away from the king and onto the local official. This legislation, while wholly successful for the crown, meant great economic and even social dislocation for the Totonac of Papantla. A traditional means of income had been closed off, and thus economic life became more difficult. In consequence, the local relationships among the Totonac and between the Totonac and local Spanish officials began to change. As these new relationships developed, the boundaries of power shifted in Papantla. Totonacs began to fight openly against exploitation by local magistrates, and fight among themselves for authority in the community. At a most basic level, the initiation of the tobacco monopoly in Papantla forced a renegotiation of the colonial power schema.

To set the stage for exploring the increasing violence of the last half of the eighteenth century in Papantla, the first chapter of this book looks at the history and geography of the community. At the time of European contact, The Totonac were the most recent settlers of a region that had hosted numerous other peoples in the past. In the early decades of colonization, the town went largely unregarded by Spanish settlers, who sought success in areas with higher populations or with more readily exploitable resources, such at Mexico City, Oaxaca City, or the mining regions of Guanajuato. Totonac society in Papantla only became truly attractive to Spaniards when vanilla was recognized as a commercially valuable crop in the eighteenth century. The geography and climate of this region made it perfect for vanilla cultivation, and would one day lead Papantla to hold the moniker "the town that perfumes the world." Those same conditions also favored tobacco. These two crops would become definitive in shaping the late colonial history of Papantla.

Chapter Two expands on the demographic history of Papantla by looking at the racial diversity of this community. Papantla was somewhat unusual in that it was home to a 200-man militia unit composed of people of mixed African ancestry. This militia troop was the centerpiece of an Afro-Mexican population in Papantla that was many times larger than the Spanish community. The challenges facing these militia soldiers are indicative of the difficult position that people of African descent occupied in the racially stratified society of New Spain. Militia soldiers were granted certain rights and a level of honor in a highly honor-conscious society by their position as defenders of the empire, yet these men were discouraged by socio-racial dictates from mixing with the Spanish minority in Papantla. Spanish regulation also sought to keep blacks from mixing with natives; however, these militiamen did find partners among the native population with whom they took wives, had children, and presumably formed friendships. In the eighteenth century, as they were increasingly called upon to defend the interests of the *alcalde mayor* and other Spaniards in town, they were drawn into a difficult position between their social world, which was connected to the Totonac population, and their formal role as an arm of Spanish rule.

The third chapter investigates an uprising in Papantla in 1736. This conflict, which drew out for months as natives fled into the hills surrounding the town, permits an examination of native concerns as they existed prior to the Bourbon reforms. This event offers a baseline from which the violence of the latter part of the century may be judged. In this case, we see examples of conditions that would become familiar in the uprisings of the last half of Papantla's eighteenth century. Most notably, the town was divided across all lines. There was conflict between the lieu-tenant curate and his flock. Free-colored militiamen were called upon to fight local Totonacs. Native leaders threatened their own community members to enhance their own positions, and local Spaniards were quick to presume that violence by any native against any Spaniard was at its heart an insurrectionary movement. Following consideration of the 1736 event, the chapter goes on to discuss collective violence more generally, so that we might consider the various conditions that lead communities to violence.

The fourth chapter looks at the uprising of 1764/65 and the response of the community to the creation of the tobacco monopoly. This event marks the beginning of a shift in Totonac attitudes toward the rule of local magistrates. In the subsequent twenty-two years, the Totonac of Papantla would rise up four more times. It is at this point that the Bourbon reforms began to have a clear and tangible effect on the Totonac of Papantla. This chapter contextualizes this influence with a discussion of the Bourbon reforms as a colony-wide program. It outlines the motivations for this fundamental shift in the colonial relationship, and describes the various aspects of the overall reform program. By understanding what motivated the reform process, we can more fully understand how the reforms affected different facets of colonial society. In the case of Papantla, we can then consider specifically how the monopolization of a local commodity restructured native/Spanish relations, and led natives to turn to violence far more often than they had in the past.

Chapter Five investigates an uprising in 1767, one of three that year, and scrutinizes Totonac testimony about the frustrations that underlay these outbursts. Of particular interest to understanding how the attitudes of the Totonac community changed under the new Bourbon economy is how they testified about economic exploitation by the local magistrate. Numerous Totonac witnesses criticized the *alcalde mayor* for forcing local natives to engage in commerce only with him, a practice known as the *repartimiento de mercáncias*. The chapter then examines the *repartimiento* in Papantla and posits that, while the nature of the *repartimiento* did not change in the last half of the eighteenth century, Totonac attitudes toward it did. In 1767, the *repartimiento* was nothing new. It had been part of a long-standing practice by which the local magistrate would exploit the native population to whatever degree he could without jeopardizing the peace of the community. In the past, this exploitation had at times led the local native *cabildo* to complain to the bishop in Puebla or to the viceroy in Mexico City. But after 1765, violence was also a very likely response from natives, who could no longer accommodate the exploitation of local leaders.

The new economic environment of the Bourbon colony led to stresses elsewhere within the colonial system of control. Chapter Six looks at the uprising of 1787, the most violent in Papantla's colonial history, and the native factionalism that underlay the event. We see the workings of the native *cabildo* structure and the ways in which native elites readily formed political bonds with Spaniards to serve their own ends. This event highlights numerous intrigues within the power structure of Papantla, including corruption and sexual misconduct on the part of the *alcalde mayor* and one of his allies. This uprising also demonstrates the extent of native power within colonial system. Through native mobilization of the legal system and through rioting, the Totonac would force the removal of two successive Spanish magistrates in two years.

Don Luis de Velasco Mendoza's brief note from 1590 gives us just the faintest picture of an early conflict in Papantla. Yet, even such a brief account touches on themes that recur more than a century later. Exploring unrest in eighteenth-century Papantla allows us some access to what life was like in the town even in times of relative calm. By looking at these fractures in the peace, fractures that occurred consistently in the same weak points in the social fabric of this community, we find clues about what pressures and strains always existed in communities like Papantla.

Bourbon efforts to expand control and exploitation of the colony added just enough pressure to crack the fragile apparatus of colonial rule.

This study employs uprising as both a theme and a vehicle. Collective violence in colonial Mexico generated enormous volumes of documentation. Included in these records are sources that describe how and why uprisings took place. These documents are also a primary vehicle for discovering what concerns weighed on the minds of local inhabitants and what choices they felt they had in response to challenges to their well-being. At a fundamental level, these documents tell us who the Papantecos were. In the investigations of collective violence in Papantla, witnesses describe not only their actions during a given event, but also their daily lives. They described tilling their fields, transporting cargoes to neighboring communities, and going fishing. They offer us glimpses of the landscapes of their lives, and they reveal the animosities that spurred conflict.

A Note on Sources

Through trial testimonials, military correspondence, and legal cases, I have attempted to distill the causes and effects of riot in a late-colonial Mexican community. Beyond these records of exceptional events, I have examined parish records, land disputes, petitions, and other sources. I have tried to reconstruct the conditions that led to repeated violence in a Mexican village through material examined at the Archivo General de la Nación and the Biblioteca Nacional, in Mexico City, the Archivo de Indias in Seville, the Lamont, Houghton, and Langdell Libraries at Harvard University, the parish records of Papantla (provided by the Church of Jesus Christ of Latter Day Saints), and numerous secondary sources.

An historical investigation is in many ways similar to a modern criminal investigation. The investigator must repeatedly ask, why was this document written? Who was served by the claims contained within it? Because the majority of the original source material in this work is drawn from criminal investigations I have had to be particularly aware of possible biases in the documentation. I have strived to distill what seem to be the most accurate accounts possible by cross-referencing testimonies and by using my own judgment to evaluate the veracity of certain statements. However, I do not claim to be able to see beyond all biases, including my own. I believe that my interpretations of the events detailed in this work are accurate. I leave it to the reader to act as jury and decide what verdict to hand down in the cases presented here.

A Geographic and Historical Biography of a *C'achiqu'ín*

The Landscape

In the hot and rugged Tierra Caliente of northern Veracruz, between the wall of the Sierra Madre Oriental to the west and the undulating coastal plain stretching east to the Gulf of Mexico, Papantla sits as a historic border town between two major ethnographic regions. Twelve miles north of Papantla the Rio Cazones represents the southern limit of the region known as the Huasteca, an area of tremendous biodiversity encompassing parts of the modern states of San Luis Potosí, Hidalgo, much of northern Veracruz, as well as small parts of Puebla and Queretaro. The region is named for the Huastec people, who have occupied the area since the first millennium BCE. The Huastec are "linguistically allied to the Mayas," and are credited by some archeologists with bringing Maya culture as far north as Tamaulipas.[1] Prior to European colonization, the region was also home to native populations of Otomíe, Nahua, Tepehuán, Teenek, Totonac, and Pame peoples.[2] Extending from the coastal lowlands to the dry, cool slopes of the Sierra Madre Oriental, the Huasteca is home to nearly every type of plant found in Mexico.[3] At the southern border of this region is the Tecolutla River basin, with the Rio Cazones to the north and the Rio Nautla to the south. Papantla, along with the nearby ruins of the ancient city of El Tajín, dominates this area, which forms the northern limit of the ethnographic region of Totonacapan. For at least 900 years the area has been home to the Totonac ethnic group, speakers of the Totonac language. Totonacapan extends inland to Zacatlan in the Sierra de Puebla and south to

---

C'achiqu'ín is Totonac for "town."

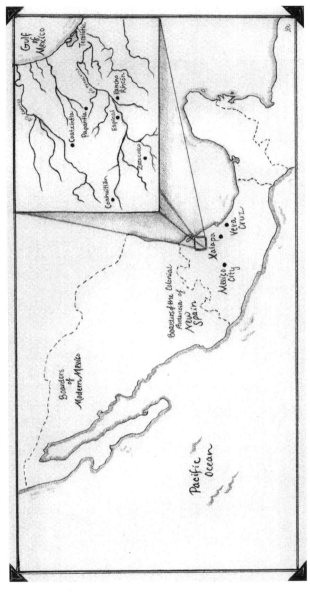

Figure 1.1 L. B. Ames, *Map of Mexico with Papantla Region Inset*, 2016. Ink on Paper, 7 x 13, author's personal collection.

Cempoala.[4] Being right along the frontier of these two areas, Papantla is something of an ethnographic border town, at times included in studies of the Huasteca, but distinct in its Totonac heritage.[5]

Papantla sits on another border as well, a geologic confluence, where tertiary, volcanic, and superior cretaceous stone all unfold onto the surface landscape, forming steep and short hills, averaging roughly 200 meters above sea level.[6] The town clings to the hillsides and fills the gullies of terrain that has aptly been described by historian Emilio Kourí as a "landscape of nooks and crannies."[7] Waters falling down the steep eastern slope of the massive Sierra Madre Oriental carve *arroyos* around the numerous hills that crowd the Tecolutla Basin. Surrounding Papantla these *arroyos* collect into the Tecolutla river, which, having settled into the relatively gentle slope of the coastal plain, meanders south of the town on its way to the Gulf. The area is wet, with nearly 1,200 millimeters of rain each year, two-thirds of which fall during the rainy season between the months of June and October, draining rapidly through the limestone and chalk soils.[8] In the first half of the twentieth century, Papantla averaged just sixty clear days per year. In June the average temperature is thirty-two degrees. The combination of heat and humidity make this an extremely verdant environment, with tropical forests of large papery leaved plants covering the terrain in lush year-round growth.[9] Since its first settlement, through the nineteenth century, the thick vegetation and heaving terrain rendered travel through this area very difficult.

The density of growth does not, however, mean that Papantla is particularly fertile. Like many jungle environments, the topsoil is thin. The nutrients of the land are tied up in vegetation, and successful agriculture demands concerted effort on the part of the local populace.[10] It is only through farming technologies such as swidden, or slash-and-burn, agriculture and double-cropping, that indigenous peoples made the Tecolutla Basin and the area around Papantla into a productive region for such staple crops as corn.[11] Pre-Columbian farmers cleared and then burned forest plots to create cultivable areas. Corn was harvested twice a year, in April and October. Local farmers also cultivated beans, peppers, fruits, vegetables, cotton, and tobacco.[12] While the *milpas* (individual or family farming plots typically given over to corn) were productive, the verdant nature of the region enforced a strict work regimen on farmers, who needed to continuously tend their fields, weeding and fighting off encroaching forest growth.[13] However, the soil in the Papantla region could only sustain limited agriculture. *Milpas* carved out of the forest suffered significant declines in productivity each year, and soon had to be left uncultivated while the soil replenished its nutrients. This agricultural limitation meant that people of the area could only farm about one-fifth of their land at any given time, while the rest lay unused in various stages of recovery. As a result, each family required about twelve hectares of tillable land to sustain themselves and their communities.[14] The area therefore has historically maintained a low-density population, a condition that prevailed throughout the colonial era. The Totonac population tended to reside near their fields rather than in concentrated villages. As late as the nineteenth century, observers noted the tendency of the Totonac to only rarely visit town. This was first and foremost a rural region of small-scale agriculturalists. Throughout its history, the environment surrounding Papantla kept the population thinly settled, lacking "true cities or even sizeable towns until well after 1900."[15]

The Papantla Totonac did benefit from considerable animal diversity in the area, much of which formed part of the local diet. The locals hunted martens and rabbits, and caught fish in the Tecolutla River.[16] The region also had a particularly large variety of birds, being at the confluence of two major north-south migratory routes. Residents ate wild parrots and macaws, and raised turkeys.[17] Prior to European incursion and extensive cultivation, the area was also home to deer and peccary, and at higher elevations jaguars prowled the forests. Following the arrival of Europeans, new animals entered the ecosystem. Juan de Carrión noted in 1581 that the area already supported an abundance of Spanish chickens. As early as 1610 there was a cattle ranch within the parish of Papantla, though ranching never became a significant commercial practice.[18] Spaniards also conducted some small-scale horse ranching in the lowlands of the Tecolutla Basin.[19] By 1787, geographic chronicler Antonio de Alcedo noted that the area around Papantla had become home to numerous pigs, another Old-World import.[20]

The Indigenous Past: From El Tajín to Santa María de Papantla

The 1785 "discovery" of the ruins at El Tajín, thirteen kilometers west of Papantla, by a patrol of the *resguardo de tabaco* (tobacco guard), stimulated an interest in the ancient inhabitants of the area that has never abated.[21] The occupation of the area that would one day be the site of Tajín began at least as early as the second millennium BCE. Construction of the city's ceremonial centers began sometime around CE 100. Following the decline of Teotihuacan in the Valley of Mexico in the sixth century, Tajín expanded in size and importance. Recent scholarship dates El Tajín's apogee between 650–1,000 CE.[22] At its height, prior to the twelfth century, the ancient city boasted more than 160 structures and an estimated population of between 15,000 and 30,000, much higher than that of Papantla at any time during the colonial era.[23] It remains unclear who exactly were the builders of El Tajín. Totonac presence at the site appears only to have corresponded to the last period of Tajín's occupation, between CE 900 and 1100. Between CE 1100 and 1200 Tajín went into decline, finally being abandoned by the thirteenth century.

Legendary Totonac history provides various—and at times somewhat extravagant—accounts of the Totonac past. The earliest records of Totonac history are drawn from the works of Franciscan friars Bernardino de Sahagún and Juan de Torquemada. These chroniclers recorded a tradition claiming that the Totonac originally migrated to the area from somewhere in the north. They then occupied Teotihuacán for a time, building both the temples of the Sun and Moon.[24] Sometime thereafter they made their migration to Veracruz. After the fall of Tula in CE 1165, the Toltec people migrated to the area of Totonacapan, suggesting that the Totonac could make the ever-popular claim of being descendants of the supposed model for civilizational achievement in central Mexico, the Toltec.[25] Mid-twentieth century accounts closely matched those recorded by Torquemada in his 1615 *Monarquía Indiana*. During interviews conducted in the 1950s, anthropologists Isabel Kelly and Angel Palerm found that Totonac lore asserted that Tajín had originally been a Totonac site (a claim unsupported by archeology), which was then abandoned as the result of an invasion of Chichimec and Teochichimec peoples who then subjugated the Totonac.[26] Though some legendary claims, such as Totonac construction of Teotihuacán lack evidentiary support, other features of Totonac lore are supported by archeological study. Archeologists have found that the supposed timing of these legendary invasions agrees well with the collapse of Tajín in the twelfth century; and linguistic evidence also supports possible Chichimec and Teochichimec influence on the Totonac. Papantla itself appears to have been founded around CE 1200, likely as a result of forced migration from farther west. Nahuas from central Mexico also settled in Totonacapan, predominantly in the highlands of the Sierra Madre Oriental, but also in pockets in the Gulf Lowlands. Consequently, by the sixteenth century, Papantla was a bilingual center of Totonac and Nahuatl speakers.[27] The Totonac population of the colonial era was likely a fusion of several repeated migrations into the area. In the worlds of Kelly and Palerm, the population of Totonacapan "probably in blood, in culture, and perhaps language," shows the influence of many successive waves of invaders into the area.[28]

After the founding of Papantla at the beginning of the thirteenth century, this northern area of Totonacapan appears to have enjoyed two centuries of relative autonomy, subject to no outside dominion. This isolation was probably the result of power struggles taking place to the west in the Valley of Mexico, the relatively low population of the region, and its lack of particularly valuable commodities. However, once the Mexica established dominance over the Valley of Mexico and the Triple Alliance (Aztec Empire) formed in the 1420s, Totonacapan faced invasion from the outside yet again.[29] Moctezuma Ilhuicamina (1440–1469) initiated campaigns in the Huasteca and in southern Totonacapan, extending Aztec power to the Gulf Coast. Mexica tribute demands were severe and contributed to a long-term animosity between the Totonac and the

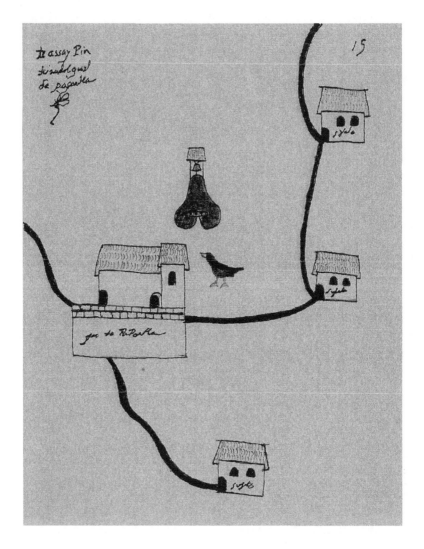

Figure 1.2 Map of Papantla, 1581. Drawn by the author from the original, reproduced in José García Payón, Descripcion del pueblo de Gueytlalpan (Zacatlan, Juxupango, Matlaltan y Chila, Papantla), escrito por el alcalde mayor 30 de mayo de 1581. (Xalapa, Mexico: Universidad Veracruzana, 1965), 68.

Mexica.[30] The uninviting terrain of the Tecolutla Basin appears to have exempted Papantla from the expansionist interest of the next three emperors. This autonomy came to an end with the ascension of Moctezuma Xocoyotzin (1502–1520). Moctezuma Xocoyotzin turned away from the Huasteca and aggressively attacked Totonacapan. During his reign, many Totonac centers fell to Aztec dominion, including

Papantla in the north and Cempoala in the south. The Mexica conquest of Totonacapan was unlike the earlier incursions of the Chichimec and Teochichimec, which had been followed by settlement of the invading peoples. Beyond garrisoning troops and emplacing a Nahua governor, the Aztecs showed little interest in settling the area.[31] Nonetheless, this new subjugation would have profound effects in the near future. Aztec conquest of Totonacapan was a military endeavor focused on the extraction of wealth. The Totonac were forced to pay tribute that included cotton, corn, *chiles*, salt, feathers, jaguar and deer skins, turquoise, jade, vanilla, chocolate, and slaves.[32]

Just as the Totonac were enduring the increased predation of the Aztec Empire, Spaniards were making their presence known on the Mesoamerican coast. It is likely that word of the Spanish incursion spread soon after the arrival in Yucatán of castaways from the wreck of a ship returning to Santo Domingo from Darién in the Isthmus of Panama in 1511. In 1517 Francisco de Córdoba led an exploratory expedition as far as Champoton in western Yucatan. In late summer 1518 Juan de Grijalva ventured along the Gulf Coast as far as north as Tampico. By the time of Cortés's 1519 expedition, Spaniards had more or less accurately surveyed the entirety of the Veracruz coast. Such investigations did not go unnoticed by the Totonac. Although there is no evidence of direct contact between the Totonac and Spaniards before the arrival of Cortés in Totonacapan, the Totonac were aware of the presence of this new force before Cortés's landing, as the Mexica had been receiving reports of Spanish presence along the coast well before Cortés made landfall at Veracruz.[33] When the Cortés's expedition did land, the Totonac of Cempoala greeted this mission relatively warmly, no doubt partly as a result of the rancor that the Totonac felt toward their recent conquerors, the Mexica.[34] According to Bernal Díaz del Castillo, the *cacique* of Cempoala complained bitterly to Cortés about Moctezuma's depredations.[35] By capitalizing on Totonac discontent over the increasing demands of the Mexica, Cortés secured the Cempoala Totonac as his first native allies in the conquest of the Aztec Empire. The Totonac experience of the conquest was thus unusual (albeit not unique) in that they voluntarily became part of the Spanish empire without direct experience of Spanish assault.[36] 150 kilometers farther north of Cempoala, the Papantla area appears to have come under Spanish rule early the following year, well before the fall of Tenochtitlan.[37] It was likely at this point that the town was refounded as Santa María de Papantla.

Colonial Papantla

Though the Totonac forged a relatively amicable relationship with the Spaniards during the conquest, the Spaniards showed little interest in the region surrounding Papantla. In the immediate wake of contact, the Spaniards made an effort at missionizing among the Totonac, but those endeavors were limited and predominantly focused on areas other than Papantla. Christianity first came to the Totonac with Cortés in Cempoala in 1519. After orchestrating an alliance between the Cempoala Totonac and his own mission of conquest, Cortés insisted on putting an end to traditional Totonac religious observation, including idol worship and human sacrifice. Before continuing his march toward Tenochtitlan, and over the protestations of the Cempoalans, Cortés sent soldiers to the top of the city's central temple, where they destroyed the idols and had the temple walls cleansed of blood. Cortés subsequently directed the instruction of native priests in Christianity, and oversaw the baptism of eight maidens who had been awarded to Cortés by his new native allies. The Franciscan missionary Juan de Torquemada later memorialized the event as "the first act of the Christian religion in New Spain."[38] Four years later in 1523, Franciscans missionaries arrived, and ten years after that, in 1533, the Augustinians. However, the sparse settlement of northern Totonacapan meant that missionaries had to traverse great distances over difficult terrain to bring their message to the people of the Papantla area.

The challenge of accessing the relatively small and dispersed population of natives was soon made much worse by cataclysmic population loss among the Totonac at the hands of Old-World diseases. As the port of entry for Spaniards coming onto the continent, the Gulf Coast suffered repeated waves of devastating epidemics. In 1520, smallpox arrived from the Caribbean on board the ships of Pánfilo de Narváez's expedition to arrest Cortés. Noble David Cook, in his history of disease and the conquest noted that by 1531, Veracruz was being called the "tomb of the Spaniards" because of the concentration of disease in the city.[39] Though Spaniards succumbed to disease, it was the unexposed populations of natives, rather than the Spaniards, who suffered the truly horrifying effects of successive epidemics. By 1549 typhus was in Veracruz and the surrounding environs, and before another decade had passed influenza had infected the city. The tropical conditions of the Tierra Caliente fostered the spread of these diseases, and according to N. D. Cook this region suffered particularly high mortality.[40] In 1815 Colonel Juan Camargo y Cavallero reported that "there is no doubt that more people die in Veracruz than in any other part of the kingdom."[41] One early estimate of the population of Papantla and its surrounding district claimed that it had supported 60,000 natives in 1519. In 1550, Papantla and its 15 *estancias* were home to only 1,684 people.[42] Though initial population estimates across the Americas were frequently gross overestimations—the figure of 60,000 people is assuredly exaggerated—it is clear that Papantla, like the rest of the Tierra Caliente suffered devastating demographic collapse in the generations following the conquest. Shelburne Cook and Woodrow Borah identified a population of only 423 individuals in Papantla in 1568.[43] Such terrible losses among an already sparse population further frustrated the efforts of missionaries to proselytize among the Totonac.[44] By 1567 the Franciscans ceased their work among the Totonac.[45]

Throughout the sixteenth century Papantla was without its own resident priest. In the 1560s Papantla was receiving sacerdotal services from a *"sacerdote de pie"* (a priest who worked on his feet, rather than in a church), based in Chincontepec over thirty leagues (roughly 120 kilometers) away, who was able to visit the town no more than six times per year. When father Juan de Torres visited Papantla in 1570 to teach the catechism in Nahuatl, he found no religious building in the town at that time. By 1581 Papantla had been incorporated into the ecclesiastical jurisdiction of Puebla, which was fifty-four leagues (over 200 kilometers) away over poor roads.[46] Papantla would not receive its own priest until 1610.[47] Though Papantla was, by the eighteenth century, the seat of one of the three parishes in the Tecolutla Basin, very few clergy were ever active in the region.[48] Robert Ricard, in his study of the Christianization of New Spain, suggested that the logistical challenges to missionizing amongst the Totonac were particularly acute, and he grouped the Totonac with the Tarascans of Michoacan as peoples whose Christianity remained particularly inflected by persistent pagan practices, due to the difficulty of bringing the catechism to these people.[49] Adrián Salas and María Esther Martínez argued that as late as the eighteenth century "the religious cult among the Totonac was particularly entrenched," and the Totonac of Papantla worked expressly to hide idolatrous practices by concealing specifics of their worship from Spaniards.[50]

Spanish laity were no more drawn to Papantla than the clergy, and Spanish settlement took place quite slowly. Potential settlers found the Tierra Caliente insalubrious, and preferred the much more familiar climate farther to the west in the Valley of Mexico. In 1581, an observer described Papantla and its surroundings as "somewhat sickly for it is very hot."[51] Not only did Spaniards find the region uncomfortable, but the area also lacked other compensations that might draw the adventurous, such as rich mineral deposits or a dense and hence readily exploitable population. The thick forest and uneven terrain further discouraged Spanish interest. Transportation and communication were difficult, making utilization less efficient and profitable than other regions of the colony.[52] Though the area along the Tecolutla River provided some early lumber commerce, the river mouth was shallow and surrounded by reefs and sandbanks, with only a narrow canal too small to permit sizeable vessels. Some Spaniards, *mestizos*, and *mulatos* (people of mixed African and Spanish ancestry) established fisheries along the river, but by and large Spanish settlers showed relatively little interest in the Tecolutla Basin.[53] When Fray Alonso de Mota y Escobar visited Papantla in 1610, he found only 300 native tributaries and just five Spanish men, three married to Spanish women and the other two to *mulatas*.[54]

For the Spanish, the Tecolutla basin was largely uncivilized terrain. Michael Ducey has written of Spanish discomfort with the *monte* (a Spanish term describing a hill or forested land, but more broadly suggesting primitive and wild terrain). Spanish tradition going back to medieval Iberia drew a connection between civilized society and urban living. In the colonies, the space beyond the precincts of cities and villages was alien and threatening. Ducey points out that elite Spanish attitudes envisioned the unrestrained growth of the tropical forest as stifling societal development by providing fruits to those who planted without care or sophistication. The dense landscape corresponded to underdeveloped humanity. At the same time, the impenetrable nature of the vegetation hid the machinations of unassimilated native culture. Ricard suggested that the pyramids of Tajín went undiscovered by Spaniards until the 1780s because the natives were able to deploy the uninviting landscape to help shelter these massive representations of their persistent idolatry. Certainly the Spanish residents of Papantla considered the *monte* to be an area where the colonial order failed and recalcitrant natives violated the precepts of Spanish civilization.[55] What few Spaniards there were in the area confined themselves to the central precincts of the jurisdiction of Papantla.

Largely isolated from Spanish commerce, prior to the eighteenth century Papantla developed into a center of primarily local importance. Papantla was a colonial *cabecera* (head town), meaning that it was the administrative center for an area that included numerous smaller communities.[56] Its colonial population likely never exceeded 11,500 inhabitants.[57] Even that number is somewhat misleading, as it wrongly conjures an image of urban concentration. As noted above, throughout the colonial era the agricultural population of the jurisdiction was quite spread out. Furthermore, Papantla was off the beaten path of the regular overland trade routes, lying, as it does, well north of the *camino real* (the Veracruz-Mexico City road).[58] "The Tecolutla Basin; it turns out," writes Kourí, "was not on the way to anywhere."[59] Thus Papantla was the leading community in a fairly diffuse and almost entirely indigenous region. The few non-Indian settlers who did come to the area participated in relatively meager trade activities. At the southern periphery of Papantla's jurisdiction some non-indigenous settlers engaged in trade along the Tecolutla River for wood and salted fish that would be sold either to Guachinango to the north, Veracruz, or to the small Spanish population in Papantla itself.[60] Generally speaking, Papantla experienced little interaction with outside commerce. Prior to the mid-1700s, when vanilla became a valuable export resource, Papantla had little to connect it with interregional trade. Kourí argues that this commercial disconnection never abated during Spanish dominion: "Well into the 1800s, this area remained in virtual geographic and commercial isolation, practically absent from the regional and international networks of trade and transportation that developed across much of Mexico in the wake of colonial rule."[61] As had been the case prior to the invasions of Moctezuma II, and for the missionaries in the sixteenth and seventeenth centuries, the landscape around Papantla discouraged outside incursion. The economy around Papantla was primarily focused on domestic production centered on the *milpa*. Throughout the Tecolutla Basin, families provided for themselves, cultivating necessities, and engaging in only modest trade.

As an area with an overwhelming native majority, political life in Papantla was focused on the *pochguin*, (the Totonac term for the building housing that housed the Totonac town council). Colonial rule came to Papantla in the same dual republic system that governed the rest of the colony. In the early decades of the colonial exercise, the crown developed the two-tiered *república* system in which Spaniards and other non-indigenous people fell under the authority of the *república de españoles*, and natives were administered within the subordinate *república de indios*. Spanish authority in Papantla resided in the office of the *alcalde mayor* (Spanish district magistrate). This position came from the Iberian *cabildo* system, in which the alcalde mayor was the senior officer of a town council that included *alcaldes* (judges and councilman), *regidores* (councilmen), and an *escribano* (scribe or notary). This body was responsible for judicial and political administration. In the Americas only a minority of communities had full Spanish *cabildos*, which were in charge of administration of the non-native population. In most colonial towns the Spanish population was too small to merit the entire cabildo structure.[62] In these locales one would find a Spanish *alcalde mayor* and his designated lieutenant. In Papantla, by the eighteenth century, there was an *alcalde mayor*, and a lieutenant often selected from the officer corps of the local militia. Military authority was administered through the captain of the free-colored militia, and the church was staffed by a curate and lieutenant curate. In a town like Papantla, in which the majority of the population was native, the Spanish *alcalde mayor* served not so much as the head of a town council, but as a political and judicial leader unto himself, administering the population through orders disseminated via the native *cabildo*.

The *república de indios* and the institution of the native *cabildo* was developed as an arm of colonial rule that co-opted native elites to aid in colonial political administration. Initially staffed by native nobility, the institution of the native *cabildo* allowed the Spanish colonizers to deploy native systems of authority to enact colonial aims. The *cabildo* was both the political voice of the native community and simultaneously a vehicle for Spanish administration. Native *cabildo* offices included a *gobernador* (highest indigenous official), and a varying number of *alcaldes*, *regidores*, and an *escribano*. In the earliest phases of colonization, *cabildo* positions were filled by those who had held positions of leadership prior to Spanish conquest. In addition, the office of sacristan, a native resident with responsibilities for the upkeep of the church building and sacred objects, and outside the *cabildo* structure, was also filled from this same group of locally powerful individuals. Eventually *cabildo* officers were chosen by election. In Papantla, the officers of the *cabildo* were elected by *vocales* (*cabildo* members with voting rights) representing the eight native barrios. The electors themselves were comprised of native authorities known as *maguines* (a Totonac term meaning "leaders"). These individuals marked a political boundary between the internalization of the Spanish political institution of the *cabildo* and the persistence of the Totonac indigenous political tradition. Positions within the *cabildo* conferred political authority within the native community, and provided opportunities for economic advantage. The positions of *gobernador* and *alcalde* were particularly valuable, as they had control over the community coffers.[63] As a consequence, positions within the *cabildo* were often passed around among families of prominence in the community.

The native *cabildo* was the vehicle through which tribute was collected. In 1520 Papantla's tribute obligations shifted from the Aztecs to the Spanish. The first *encomendero*, Andrés de Tapia, received corn, blankets, and poultry equivalent to 1,720 pesos from the Papantla Totonac. His heirs maintained the right to Papantla's tribute through the early seventeenth century, when it appears that the *encomienda* ceded back to the crown.[64] The *cabildo* also held responsibility for assuring that the native community complied with the orders of the Spanish *alcalde mayor*. While the *cabildo* was a mechanism through which Spanish interests were achieved, it was also empowered as a means to address the concerns of the native community. Following the Iberian model, the *cabildo* was granted the right to directly petition the king, or more often, the viceroy. Frequently the *cabildo* filed petitions on behalf of the community in disputes with other native communities or against the local Spanish magistrate. Thus, the *cabildo* provided a legal mechanism for addressing native frustrations.

Though the Papantla Totonac operated within the structure of the Spanish *cabildo* system, Totonac cultural and economic traditions persisted through the first two centuries of colonial rule more so than elsewhere in the colony. This endurance of Totonac culture was abetted by Papantla's economically disadvantageous location. Because Papantla lay outside of the major route between the coast and the capital, without any particular resource to draw Spanish settlers, Papantla experienced far less hispanization than many areas of colonial New Spain. In the eighteenth century, some natives would be identified in legal documents as *ladinos* (natives who spoke Spanish), yet very often native residents spoke only Totonac, including those serving as officers of the *cabildo*. As noted above, the area lacked either the mineral wealth or the population concentrations to draw significant Spanish attention. It also lacked any significant agricultural draw. Papantla was north of that part of Veracruz that was given over to sugar production in the colonial period and thus fell outside the zone of regularized large-scale agriculture where plantations predominated.[65] This neglect served in many ways to preserve Totonac culture much more than in areas attractive to Spanish exploitation. Hence, through the eighteenth century, Papantla's native population remained predominantly subsistence agriculturists. Yet they did grow two crops, vanilla and tobacco, which by the 1700s would draw increasing Spanish attention. The Totonac of Papantla had long historical relationships with each of these plants, relationships that would change dramatically in middle of the eighteenth century. The Spanish attention directed at vanilla was centered on the expansion and exploitation of the crop for international trade. The attention eventually directed at tobacco would be based on its control and eradication from the region.

The Papantla geography is particularly well-suited to the growth of vanilla, which requires significant rain but depends on a dry season to permit flowering.[66] Prior to the mid-eighteenth century, vanilla was almost never cultivated, but was instead collected from wild plants growing in the surrounding hills. Totonac peasants would collect the odorless green pods to sell in town as a small supplement to their subsistence. The buyers, who by the late 1700s were customarily Spaniards and mestizos, would then carefully cure the beans in the sun, allowing them to dry over a long period.[67] During the curing process the beans would turn brown and develop their characteristic rich smell.[68] By the seventeenth century, vanilla had developed into a valuable export commodity, and New Spain became the almost-exclusive provider of vanilla to Europe. There it was consumed with chocolate, prescribed as medicine, and employed as an aphrodisiac.[69] Initially, Papantla played only a supporting role in the production of vanilla for export, which was dominated by the towns of Misantla and Colipa, northeastern Oaxaca, and southern Veracruz; but by the middle of the eighteenth century, Papantla vanilla would gain commercial significance, and the town's connection to broader trade in the spice would expand.[70]

By the 1760s, the market for vanilla had become profitable enough for the Totonac to begin for the first time to cultivate the plants. Vanilla grew well in the *acahuales*, which were abandoned agricultural fields undergoing the first stage of regrowth as they recovered fertility.[71] Cultivation was time-consuming, and as the value of vanilla rose, the risk of theft increased. Poachers would sneak into fields, cutting the beans just prior to planned harvests. Even before the practice of cultivation began, competition for the spice was so fierce that collectors would fight to be the first to collect the beans. This meant that the beans were often harvested before they were mature, decreasing the value of the finished product. In 1751 the residents of Misantla petitioned for a law to prohibit vanilla harvesting before 7 January, meant to prevent the sale of stolen beans and ensure that only ripe beans were collected.[72] However, repeated edicts to proscribe early sales of vanilla demonstrate the futility of the effort. Year after year Spanish officials would decree the times of legal harvest, to little effect. Ultimately vanilla was simply too profitable to yield to official controls. Vanilla would become an extremely valuable, if somewhat ungovernable, commodity. Much of that value would concentrate in the hands, and pockets, of the non-Indian population, who acted as curers and exporters of the harvested beans. By the time of the Humboldt expedition at the beginning of the nineteenth century, Mexico was exporting 1,000,000 vanilla beans each year, and Papantla was well on its way to becoming a center of that production.[73]

While the cultivation of vanilla was becoming an increasing source of revenue during the eighteenth century, Papantla's other potential cash crop, tobacco, was being officially proscribed. The history of tobacco in Papantla followed a very different path from that of vanilla. Tobacco, unlike vanilla, had been actively cultivated in the area around Papantla for generations, and figured largely in Totonac culture. The tobacco plant grows easily in the Papantla environment and requires very little work to render it into a consumable or saleable product. Though not a significant cash crop, because the plant was easily cultivated and readily traded, it had an important local economic value. Yet, while vanilla cultivation and sale expanded during the last half of the eighteenth century, drawing considerable Spanish commercial attention, tobacco in the eighteenth century was targeted for destruction.

Áxc'ut (Tobacco)[74]

Tobacco is a New World crop with a rich pre-Columbian heritage.[75] Tobacco consumption took numerous forms among the various cultures of the New World.[76] Pipes excavated from archeological digs in the Veracruz region show Totonac tobacco smoking at least as early as the fourteenth century. Totonacs also chewed the plant.[77] Prior to the arrival of Europeans, tobacco had been primarily employed by the native priestly class, who often used it in high concentrations to induce visions.[78] In the colonial era, Totonacs of the northern Veracruz region made offerings of tobacco to forest spirits and used tobacco to ward off snakes and spirits of the dead. In the 1960s H. R. Harvey and Isabel Kelly found that Totonacs were using tobacco as part of house dedications and harvest offerings.[79] A 1988 study of medicinal plant use by the Totonacs found that tobacco, combined with garlic and *aguardiente*, could be used to cure hydrophobia (in this case, the literal fear of water). It was also favored as a cure for tumors, eye problems, snakebites, bronchitis, and rheumatism.[80] Tobacco earned a place of high esteem in pre-Columbian society. When Europeans arrived, tobacco was routinely used as a gift from natives to the new visitors, who after initial suspicion, came to embrace tobacco as well.[81] As Europeans developed affection for and addiction to the crop, they changed the basic nature of tobacco consumption among the native population. By taking up the habit without regard to class status, Europeans increased access to tobacco for natives as well. What had once been largely restricted to native religious elites became more available to the broader populace. A recent study by Ana Moreno-Coutiño and Beatriz Coutiño Bello concluded that by 1790, there were six million tobacco consumers in New Spain.[82]

For the majority of the colonial period, tobacco was predominantly cultivated by smallholders, who grew relatively modest amounts for personal use and trade. Some wealthier planters in the area of Orizaba organized with merchants to sell shipments in larger cities, including Mexico. However, for the most part tobacco was "a democratic crop," as little investment was needed to produce a saleable product. With just a small parcel of land to cultivate the plant and a flat surface to roll the raw leaf, anyone could produce a finished cigar.[83] Hence, the profits created by tobacco were spread thin amongst many minor producers across the Gulf Coast region. Finished tobacco products fell into three different types: *puros* (cigars), *cigarros* or *papelillos* (cigarettes), and *tabaco de polvo* (finely powdered tobacco, snuff). A 1748 survey ordered by Viceroy Revillagigedo found that *puros* or *cigarros* represented the largest market in Mexico with *tabaco de polvo* claiming very little market share. No complete survey currently details the number of *cigarrerías* (tobacco stores) in New Spain, but Susan Deans-Smith's work on the monopoly reveals some interesting generalities about the native trade. Women oversaw the majority of production and trade of tobacco products, as they most often conducted the rolling of the finished products, and comprised the preponderance of shop owners. The manufacture and sale of tobacco products was mainly conducted as a family business, with very few *cigarrerías* large enough to employ non-family members. Profits were small, rarely exceeding more than a peso per day.[84] While shops were concentrated in the larger cities for obvious reasons, cultivation was spread around the country.

For most of the colonial era, tobacco production and sale was unregulated. Nor was it often produced or marketed by large-scale cartels. Beyond the rare organization of Orizaba merchants and planters, there were few real organized trade networks. Therefore, when the crown moved to monopolize tobacco in the middle of the eighteenth century (see chapter 4) there was no large-scale lobby to oppose the process. The "democracy" of the crop, in part, would leave it open to being so easily regulated because there was no cartel to oppose it.[85] It is the consequences of this regulation in 1764 and the effects of that change that form a central focus of this book. Loss of this crop would shift economic conditions and power dynamics to the degree that the Totonac of Papantla would, after 1764, turn repeatedly to collective violence. As the local effect of the

Bourbon reforms of the second half of the eighteenth century, the monopolization of tobacco would have a profound impact on Papantla. The prohibition of this crop would unsettle the economic system in the community whereby Totonac natives had been able to secure small but necessary financial resources. So too would the loss of tobacco render certain spiritual practices costlier and hence more difficult. Though tobacco was only a part of the local Totonac economy, its loss would upend the balance of colonial order in the town, leading Totonac community members to react more strongly to other incursions into their way of life.

Before investigating the unrest that broke out during the second half of the eighteenth century in Papantla, there is another group of Papantecos to consider, the Afro-Mexican population. While the Totonac represented the majority of the Papantla population, and the Spanish a very small minority, in between was a substantial black population, whose role in the community was distinct enough to merit specific attention. This group, which was centered on the corps of the free-colored militia and granted no clear legal or communal status by the two-republic system, occupied a significant third space in Papantla that in some ways formed a bridge between natives and Spaniards, while they were simultaneously excluded from each of these communities.

Los Ausentes:
The Racial Landscape
and Reflections on 1787

A Night in 1736

Dramatis Personae
Domingo López-Spanish soldier
Juan Caitano-*Pardo* soldier

Witnesses
Clemente Palacios-Militia corporal

On the night of 16 September 1736, the light of a full moon shone through the doorway of the Papantla *casas reales* (administration building) illuminating the figures of two militia soldiers.[1] Kneeling together in firing position, they aimed their muskets out at a mob of angry Totonac natives. One soldier, Domingo López, was an *español*, a man of reputed Spanish ancestry, the other, Juan Caitano, was *pardo,* part native and part African. That racial distinction was important enough to record when the two men were later interviewed as part of the investigation into the 16 September uprising; the racial gulf between the *pardo* and the *español* was real and not insubstantial. Their racial differences had meaningful social and legal implications, which could shape where each stood in society.[2] Yet, on the night in question, such distinctions likely meant little to either man. Their thoughts were almost certainly dominated by three facts—they were fighting on the same side, they were both wounded, and they were running low on ammunition.[3]

This moment is in some ways symbolic of the greater picture of ethnic distinction in eighteenth-century Papantla. Ethnicity mattered to these people; it was a fundamental aspect of how they identified themselves and others. But the ethnic category that any given individual fit into could shift in importance under different circumstances, and was in itself plastic. The titles that they wore were not clear reflections of their ethnic makeup, but rather reflections of broader notions of how they fit into a society that ineffectively attempted to build a clearly-ordered ethnic landscape. These people were given, or embraced, certain ethnic titles. But in Papantla this did not define who they were. The first part of this chapter investigates the size of the Afro-Mexican population in Papantla. It then turns to the task of evaluating to what degree this population was both distinct from, and integrated into, the other ethnic groups in the town. With data from local parish records and the testimony found in the criminal files of the national archives, this chapter represents an early step in the process of recovering the history of Papantla's black population, and their relationships with the communities of Totonacs and Spaniards.

To understand the relationships between these groups it is necessary to consider the Spanish cosmology of racial identity in the colonies. From the outset of the colonial exercise the Spanish colonizers understood themselves, through a combination of religious, cultural, and political identity, to be superior to Africans and natives. As colonization proceeded, the offspring of combinations of these groups complicated racial identity in the colony, producing individuals of new racial mixes, or *castas*. Over the sixteenth and seventeenth centuries, the Spanish developed a semi-codified racial structure that has come to be known as the *sistema de castas*. This taxonomic system theoretically identified people by the degrees of their native, African, and Spanish ancestries. Spaniards who had children with natives produced offspring that this system labeled *mestizos* (literally "hybrids"). Africans and Spaniards conceived *mulatos*, while Africans and Natives bore *pardos* or *lobos*. In its fully developed form, the *sistema de castas* could apply titles that identified multiple generations of ancestry. However, the system, which reached its apogee in the early eighteenth century, was never standardized and terminology was inconsistently employed. The terms *pardo* or *lobo* could both refer to the child of one Indian and one black parent. But the labels *pardo* and *moreno* were often used to identify free blacks, and *pardo* was at times synonymous with *mulato*. Furthermore, though in the popular *casta* painting genre people could be racially identified as far back as four generations with terms like *cambujo* and *chamizo*, such highly specified labels were rarely, if ever, used.[4] In a very real sense, the *sistema de castas* was a vision of a racially ordered world that never truly existed in the colonies, yet its foundational notion, that racial ancestry characterized individuals and their potential in society, deeply influenced the colonial identity.

In 1787, Antonio Alcedo published his *Diccionario Geográfico-Histórico de las Indias Occidentales ó América*. This work detailed a variety of information on population centers throughout North and South America. For Papantla, Alcedo recorded fifteen families of Spaniards, 535 families of "*indios Mexicanos*," and 200 *pardos*, divided into two companies of militia.[5] Two centuries later Peter Gerhard offered population figures for the same period in what has become the standard historical geography for colonial New Spain. Gerhard's numbers for Papantla were considerably higher than Alcedo's: 1,543 Indian and 215 Spanish families in 1743, and 2,269 native tributaries in 1795. Gerhard gave no specific figures, however, for Afro-Mexicans in either year, stating only that "other non-Indians (mostly mulattos) settled there and elsewhere on cattle ranches." By the 1971 publication of Gerhard's *A Guide to the Historical Geography of New Spain*, the militia had disappeared from colonial Papantla altogether, and the Afro-Mexican population was reduced to a vague group of "non-Indians."[6]

Yet, careful investigation reveals that the number of Afro-Mexicans was actually quite high. To begin with, we can look at the *pardo* militia, a defensive military body expressly composed of men of African descent. Militia numbers can be difficult to assess accurately, as complete records are lacking. Alcedo's numbers almost certainly refer to a theoretical full military compliment rather than the actual number of individuals present. In 1768, the Papantla militia filed a petition seeking the authority to select a militia captain *"de nuestra calidad"* (of our ethnicity). At the time the lieutenant and captain of the militia were both white, a result of Bourbon military reforms that sought to put *pardo* and *mulato* militia companies under white command.[7] The petition, which highlighted the militiamen's roles as tools of the kingdom, was also a complaint against the *alcalde mayor*, for subjecting the corps to undue hardship.[8] The petition included rosters for each of four companies, which give more realistic figures, as to the actual compliment of militia soldiers.

Table 2.1 Papantla Pardo Militia Rolls, January 1768

Company	First	Second	Third	Fourth	Totals	Percentage
Total roster	67	68	69	69	273	100%
Absent	37	5	46	37	125	45.7%
Sick	8	-	1	8	17	0.6%
Fit for duty	22	63	22	24	131	47.9%

AGN, Criminal 303/2/219-222v. The above numbers do not include commissioned officers (who were often Spaniards).

Militia rolls were often inflated, failing to acknowledge when individuals moved or simply became too old to serve. Here in Papantla more than fifty percent of the soldiers registered were not available for service, at least in January 1768. Although the fighting strength of the brigade was significantly below the full complement, the roster indicates a substantial *pardo* military presence. As in Alcedo's figures, the *pardo* militia well outnumbered the Spanish population of the town. Yet even these numbers fail to describe the total size of the Afro-Mexican population. To the above numbers, one must add some wives, offspring, retired militiamen, and others that swelled the Afro-Mexican population of Papantla.

Neither Alcedo nor Gerhard offers a clear picture of this broader Afro-Mexican community in the area. This fact is a reflection of the documentation, as much as a reflection of the tendency of histories to permit Afro-Mexicans to remain secondary players in colonial New Spain. Finding Mexico's African past can be challenging. Historian Matthew Restall has pointed out, "Africans wrote little and had little access to literacy and to the legal system, yet even European sources tend to be particularly blind to the black presence in the colony, or dismissive of it."[9] Afro-Mexicans were rarely part of the numerous land disputes that natives and Spaniards so frequently filed and which provide so much documentary data. Furthermore, the economy of Mexico was far less reliant on plantation slavery than such places as Brazil and the Caribbean. Consequently, the black population of Mexico has seen less scholarship on the institution of slavery than other locales. When plantation slaves do appear in the documentary record, they generally only appear as commodities of sale, and thus the nature of their lives is infrequently recorded. To a large extent, documented Afro-Mexicans were a relatively small cadre, and this fact hides the substantial presence of Afro-Mexicans within the colony. Only recently have Afro-Mexicans become part of the

Figure 2.1 *The Meeting of Cortés and Moctezuma.* Oil on canvas. 47 ¼ x 78 ¾ n.1650. Jay I. Kislak Collection at the Library of Congress, Washington, D.C.

Figure 2.2 *Juan Garrido and Hernando Cortés meeting Aztecs from Diego Durán* Historia de las Indias de Nueva España e islas de la tierra firme, *207 (1579).* Biblioteca Digital Hispánica de la Biblioteca Nacional de España

understood dialogue of the history of New Spain, and we are just beginning to understand their role as a crucial facet of the colonial process,
rather than as a semi-relevant group who were "also there."

In his 2003 book *Africans in Colonial Mexico,* Herman L. Bennett
lamented the state of the study of blacks in colonial Latin America: "Latin
Americanists have largely moved on, believing that the early African experience remains irrelevant to the grand narrative of colonial Spanish
America."[10] It is certainly true that colonial Spanish history has tradi-
tionally been constrained by notions of a simple native versus Spanish
experience, and much of the groundbreaking work of the last four decades
has been focused on recovering the native voice far more than the voice
of blacks. Since the meeting of Moctezuma II and Cortés outside of
Tenochtitlan, our historical vision of the colonial world has been
constructed and reinforced as a two-sided encounter. Paintings such as
the seventeenth-century *Meeting of Cortés and Moctezuma* (figure 2.1)
depict that encounter of Spaniards and Mexica without the black conquistador Juan Garrido or the other Africans who participated in the
conquest.[11] The Spanish perspective, so often reluctant to recognize the
contributions of non-Spaniards, overlooked black participation in the
conquest; however, blacks can sometimes be found in images produced
by natives (see figure 2.2).[12] It is as though, from the outset, blacks were
systematically pushed off the stage of Spanish American history. The epic
story of the conquest was shaped early on by histories that described the
event as a conflict between Spaniards and Indians; blacks, if they were
there at all, were not recognized as a significant part of the process.

For generations, as historians explored the colonial period, this omis-
sion was repeated over and again, fossilizing the view that the story of
colonial Mexico was the story of Indians and Spaniards. Recently,
however, important strides have been made in Afro-Mexican historiography, and in Mexican social history in general.[13] Mexicanists are now
paying greater attention to a broader view of race and ethnicity that
encompasses peoples of African origin and their multi-hued offspring.
Yet, this process is still in its early stages. Increased and careful attention
to the nexus between the institution of the colonial military and *pardo,*
mulato, and *moreno* (the near equivalent of a *negro,* and sometimes a
euphemism for it) service may offer additional clues to those scholars
tackling broader social questions that do not necessarily concentrate on
African diasporic issues.[14]

The Bodies: Papantla's Demographic Landscape

To determine the dimensions of the area populations, parish records have
proven particularly useful and illustrative. The principal dataset for this
section of the chapter includes eight years of burial records from the

Papantla parish, between 1770 and 1778.[15] These interment entries range from the extremely Spartan, listing only the date, the name of the curate present, and the fact that a body was buried, to very complete accounts that give the deceased's name, age, residence, ethnic label, cause of death, parentage, and survivors (the latter two occasionally included ethnic denotations as well). Hence, these records can provide information on many more people besides the deceased. The documents themselves have suffered very severe worm and water damage, and consequently the information available is far from complete. Nonetheless, it is possible to identify 2,345 individuals in this sample, of whom 1,707 have clearly noted racial designations (see table 2.2).

Table 2.2 Racial Breakdown of Burials in Papantla, 1700–1778

Mestizos	Indios	Pardos/ Mulattos	Españoles	N = Total Number of Burials*
4	1,473	203	23	1,707
0.02%	84.5%	11.8%	1.3%	100%**

AAP, Defunciones 1770–1925, Papantla, Veracruz, Mexico.
*This is taken from my sample of 2,345 individuals. There are other individuals in the parish registers who are not accounted for here, as document damage prohibits clear ethnic identification.
** The percentages do not add up to 100 as 4 other *castas* (2 *castizas*, 1 *coyota*, 1 *chino*) do not appear in the chart.

Officially, *pardos* constituted a population whose racial/ethnic mix was derived from African and native ancestries, whereas *mulatos* comprised a mixture of African and Spanish heritages. For the purposes of this discussion, the *pardo* and *mulato* populations have not been finely subdivided into discrete categories, since the aim here is to establish the rough boundaries of the African-based population in Papantla. The information shown above confirms the fact that the black population of Papantla substantially outnumbered that of the Spanish. Overall, the ratio of Totonac to Afro-Papantecos to Spaniards was approximately 64:9:1; put another way, 12.2 percent of Papantla's population in the 1770s was of African descent. This figure is consistent with Restall's finding of 12.4 percent for Yucatan in 1791, and is not far off the 11.7 percent estimate for the Afro-Mexican population in the colony of New Spain as a whole in 1793. Considering that these are all estimates based on limited data, we can view these percentages as fairly consistent with one another.[16]

Of course, grouping Papantla residents into only three racial categories simplifies the complex racial spectrum envisioned by the *sistema de castas* (caste system), which theoretically provided at least a dozen, and often many more, different racial groupings and routinely yielded six or seven categories in census documents.[17] The fact that of 1,707 individuals, only four were identified as *mestizo* (the offspring of natives and Spaniards, and one of the most common ethnic combinations in colonial Mexico) leads one to speculate that the curates who recorded these burials probably did not scrupulously investigate the racial/ethnic heritage of the population, or that they simply folded the more complex varieties of racial mixture into one of the other standard categories. For instance, the offspring of marriages between Spaniards and *pardos* (of which at least one was documented in Papantla) were most likely assigned *mulato* or *pardo* labels rather than a more nuanced caste grouping, such as *zambiago*. Equally, the children of male and female blacks (*pardos* and *mulatos*) who had native spouses were also crunched into one of the more familiar statuses, rather than being labeled *lobos, jarochos*, or other terms that captured the somatic complexity of miscegenation.[18] This habit of choosing from a more limited but genotypically less detailed set of titles served to simplify record keeping and, in some ways, streamline society itself—containing excessive caste ascension and horizontal mobility through limiting the effects of intermixture. But, of course, this speculation will have to remain unresolved. It can be difficult for historians to determine what forces actually operated in society itself. In regions near Papantla, for instance, free-coloreds who had white fathers were sometimes known colloquially as *mulatos blancos* (white mulattos), emphasizing that they were "superior" to ordinary *mulatos* whose fathers may have been black or of a closely related, racially mixed stock.[19] But in the eyes of the curates recording burials, this distinction may have mattered little.

In essence, while the three main racial/ethnic groupings of Papantla provide an instructive guide to the population's overall composition, it is impossible to know just how many individuals were variants of one of the three main groupings. An undetermined number of individuals were also probably passing as either Spanish or Indian to qualify for rights specifically allotted to those populations—further complicating the overall "accuracy" of the demographic count. The "Spanish" wife of the *pardo* male found in the sample could very well have been a wealthy, light-skinned *parda* or *mestiza* who successfully aspired to whiteness in order to curtail certain limitations on her social and legal status. At the same time, it is difficult to know precisely what a *pardo, mestizo*, or *español* entailed in Papantla, since the broader colonial racial/ethnic norms that were in effect elsewhere in the colony may not have applied in this town, with its small Spanish population. This plasticity may have facilitated the passing of a few more "honorary whites," or conversely, it may have hardened the color line on whiteness. Whatever the effect, as Patrick Carroll has noted, colonial clerics "did not assign [racial/ethnic] designations on the basis of genetic background. They simply matched persons against popularly accepted somatic norms."[20] So too could race and ethnicity be determined by a combination of appearance and social status within the community—what Latin American historians (following colonial sources) have commonly referred to as *calidad* (quality).[21] To an extent, race and ethnicity in Papantla were not necessarily more important in determining one's caste than political or social rights and position.[22]

Despite these complicating influences on *casta* designation, we can safely conclude that most of those who were identified as having African ancestry in Papantla probably did have at least some African heritage, and that this group constituted a large part of the community. Importantly, they were also integrated into the other racial and ethnic groups in the region. Exogamy amongst Afro-Papantecos appears to have been fairly common. Of the twenty-six Afro-Mexican marriages where racial information can be gleaned for both parties, eight (thirty percent) were exogamous. In the sample, *pardos* appear far more exogamous than mulattos, with six *pardos* taking native spouses, as opposed to just two mulattos. This may well be a function of the status offered to members of the *pardo* militia. Marriage to a militia soldier could be used to petition for exemption from tribute requirements, to which natives were subject.[23] In 1768, at least two of Papantla's militiamen were married to *mulata* slaves, thus showing a connection between the free and unfree populations. The numerous accounts of miscegenation found in the burial records of Papantla forces us to recognize an ethnic diversity in eighteenth-century Papantla. The offspring of these unions could quite rapidly become a significant portion of the racial/ethnic landscape of the town.

Curiously, while *mulatos* and *pardos* were encountered with frequency in late-eighteenth-century Papantla, there were no recorded mentions of anyone labeled as a *negro* (which suggested "pure" African ancestry). Whether this reflects the habits and biases of the curates who recorded deaths, or is evidence that nobody in the town was African-born or descended entirely from Africans, we cannot say here with certainty. What we can state is that racial "purity" was definitely something that called the attention of some colonial officials who recorded demographic information, such as those conducting the late colonial censuses.

For Papantla, however, the lack of *negros* may be credited to the overall decline of slavery in late colonial Mexico, the lack of sugar plantations in the region (which were concentrated further south), and the paucity of other large unskilled labor industries. This restricted the economic niches available to ethnic Africans, especially slaves; on the other hand, this would not have necessarily limited the activities of free *negros*, who indeed may have resided in Papantla under the guise of *mulatos* or *pardos*. As with some natives, who could change their caste status by merely speaking Spanish and adopting European-style clothing, some *negros* may have effectively been able to accomplish the transition to *pardo*-ness or *mulato*-ness through living a free lifestyle, either as a rural peasant or artisan. Another possibility accounting for the lack of *negros* is that, given the relative lack of large-scale economic enterprises that utilized slave labor, Papantla's slaves were heavily concentrated into the role of domestics. In this arena, Spaniards preferred slaves who spoke Spanish and were already acculturated. More often than not, this meant creole slaves, or free-colored servants born in Mexico or elsewhere in the colonies. Their number disproportionately included Afro-Mexicans of racially mixed heritage.

However one may explain the absence of *negros* in the interment records, there are other significant questions posed by the interment records of 1770–1778. Why are there only four *mestizos* listed in the entire group? The 1742 census of greater Mexico recorded almost exactly the same number of *mestizos* as it did of *mulatos*, each about 11.7 percent of the overall population.[24] This percentage was somewhat lower for the bishopric of Puebla, which included Papantla—approximately eight percent each. However, once again, the numbers for *mulatos* and *mestizos* were almost exactly the same, 9,557 and 9,861 respectively.[25] Therefore, we should expect the numbers of *mestizos* to roughly approximate the figure for *mulatos* and *pardos*—that is, 203. But we find no such thing. The question is then, where have these people gone? It is not very likely that Papantla simply had an exceptional racial schema. Rather, it is far more likely that the *mestizo* population was absorbed into either the Afro-Mexican or Totonac population. Somehow the *mestizo* population was being redesignated as native or Afro-Mexican.

The next logical question then is which group was the ethnic center of gravity that was pulling other ethnicities into itself? The high number of *indios* favors the conclusion that, as the curate labeled these people, possibly with the assistance of relatives, *mestizos* became *indios*. The overall population of Mexico from the 1742 census showed *indios* to compose 68.1 percent of the overall population, and in Puebla this was somewhat higher, at 73.4 percent. Yet both of these figures are significantly below the figure of 84.5 percent demonstrated in the Papantla interment records of 1770–1778.[26] By removing 203 individuals from the number of Totonacs listed in the interment records, we get a figure of 74.3 percent, which becomes consistent with the general figures for Puebla. However, this mathematical "solution" to the mystery of the disappearing *mestizo* population fails to explain either why or how these people became native. There may have been certain advantages to being labeled as *indio* rather than *mestizo*. *Indios* in Papantla had representation within the *pochguin*, and were exempted from prosecution by the Inquisition. But with these advantages in mind, one must question why the curate who labeled these individuals permitted them to move into the *indio* category.

Another case from 1736 further complicates the search for why and where the *mestizo* category was being absorbed. In the investigation of the uprising of October 1736, two men, Pedro Hernández and Nicolas Morales, identified themselves as both *mestizos* and soldiers for the *"compania de Pardos."*[27] How was it that, and why, were these men able to claim *mestizo* ethnicity and still act as soldiers on the *pardo* militia? The second question may be more easily answered than the first. Soldier status carried with it certain advantages to mitigate the obvious threat of injury and death. As of 1688, all Papantla militiamen were exempted from tribute.[28] The attraction to this exemption may be reflected in the militia rosters of Papantla for 1768, which listed so many more soldiers than were counted as present and fit for duty. Militia rolls were sometimes inflated with the names of individuals living much too far from the unit base to be of actual service. How these two men were able to claim *mestizo* ethnicity while holding *pardo* occupations is a more challenging question that will require further study. To date, these are the only two *mestizos* that I am aware of to hold this post.

Having mapped, in at least a general sense, the ethnic makeup of Papantla, the interment data can be further mined to ascertain if any obvious distinctions were drawn culturally between these groups. The above data shows that both *mulato* and *pardo* men were marrying across ethnic lines. Papantecos certainly felt a degree of freedom to cross the ethnic barriers envisioned by the *sistema de castas*. By examining the naming patterns of the residents of Papantla, we see that there is no notable difference in the naming patterns along ethnic lines (see table 2.3).

Table 2.3 Frequency of Occurrence of Male First Names [29]

	Totonac		Pardo		Mulato		Espanol	
1	Juan	76	Joseph	11	Francisco	3	Juan	2
2	Miguel	49	Juan	10	Antonio	2	Francisco	2
3	Francisco	47	Francisco	5	Pablo	2	Alonzo	1
4	Antonio	45	Manuel	5	George	1	Andres	1
5	Manuel	39	Antonio	5	Juan	1	Antonio	1
6	Joseph	38	Pedro	4	Miguel	1	Bernardo	1
7	Salvador	33	Thomas	3			Mariano	1
8	Pedro	28	Domingo	2			Placido	1
9	Andres	21	Mariano	2			Ramos	1
10	Nicolas	18	Miguel	2				
Percent *	71.7%		42.5%		100%		100%	

*Percentage of named individuals per given ethnicity.

Table 2.3 compares the most common names amongst males with distinct ethnicities as recorded by the local curate. Among males of all ethnicities, the degree of commonality is striking. Across all groups, three names—Juan, Francisco, and Antonio—are among the top five most common. The implication is that ethnic difference in Papantla was not reflected in the names given to children. In fact, if we conflate the Afro-Mexican males we find that the third, fourth, and fifth most common names align exactly with those of Totonacs, and that the six most common names are the same. The greatest difference occurs with Spaniards, among whom there are two names, Ramos and Placido, which never occur among any of the other ethnic groups (Alonzo and Bernardo both appear among the less common Totonac names). However, given the small size of the Spanish sample, one should be cautious of crediting this difference with much statistical significance. The overall impression then is that naming patterns across all ethnicities in Papantla show little sign of any ethnic division.

Table 2.4 Frequency of Occurrence of Female First Names

	Totonac		Parda		Mulata		Espanola	
1	María	128	María	18	María	2	Paula	2
2	Francisca	42	Josepha	5	Petrona	2	Casilda	1
3	Juana	39	Juana	4	Josepha	1	Gertrudis	1
4	Anna	32	Catharina	3	Anna	1	Josepha	1
5	Josepha	23	Antonia	2	Thomasa	1	Lorenza	1
6	Catharina	19	Dominga	2	Marzelina	1	Michaela	1
7	Manuela	19	Felipa	2			Rosa	1
8	Michaela	15	Francisca	2				
9	Magdalena	13	Matiana	2				
10	Antonia	12	Nicolosa	2				
Percent *	79.7%		70.0%		100%		100%	

*Percentage of named individuals per given ethnicity. AAP, Defunciones 1770–1778.

Among women in Papantla the pattern is less dramatic (see table 2.4). Josepha is the only female name that occurs as one of the five most common across all ethnicities. Furthermore, there are names represented in the *parda*, *mulata*, and Spanish groups that are unique to that group. The Afro-Mexican and Totonac groups share more commonality with one another than they do with the Spanish group. For *pardas*, *mulatas*, and Totonacs, María and Josepha are among the most common names. The prevalence of María as the most common first name for women is consistent with Rebecca Horn's study of post-Conquest naming patterns in Coyoacan in the seventeenth century.[30] As in Horn's study, the names of women in Papantla are predominantly feminized versions of masculine names and conform exclusively to Spanish tradition. No first names in the interment records reflect either pre-Columbian or African heritage. The naming patterns displayed here cannot provide conclusive evidence on the cultural commonalities among the diverse ethnicities of Papantla. But the lack of any obvious distinction in naming patterns along ethnic lines shows that in this very fundamental aspect of individual identity, there was no clear line between *pardo*, *mulato*, native, and Spaniard.

Outlining the demographic contours of Papantla's Afro-Mexican population is considerably easier than ascertaining how they lived. The parish records rarely listed occupational information, hence we can only speculate about what the bulk of the Afro-Papanteco population was doing.[31] Some were certainly slaves in Spanish households. In 1767, the militia captain of Papantla, don Placido Pérez personally owned at least three *mulato* slaves.[32] Others were farming small plots, just like much of the Totonac population. Militia soldiers, who testified in the cases discussed in this work, identified themselves as tailors, fisherman, and farmers. Lack of information on the lives of the general Afro-Papanteco population forces us to focus on the records of the militiamen. They were part-time soldiers, and their non-militia related activities can be very difficult to access, but their military lives offer us a glimpse into at least some of the decisions and issues this group of Afro-Papantecos occasionally faced. In the uprisings of 1736 and later, in 1787, the militia was called upon to defend royal authority from native insurgents. By reflecting on these uprisings, one can examine how ethnicity played a role in the social position of this group.

Afro-Papantecos in Battle

What was the position of these *pardo* and *mulato* soldiers called up to fight local unrest? Afro-Papantecos made up a significant component of the forces used to put down both the 1736 and 1787 uprisings. Afro-Papantecos who were not members of the militia are not mentioned in the records of either conflict. But the *pardo* militia was obliged to participate, being under the control of the *alcalde mayor*. In each of these events (which will be discussed in greater detail in Chapter Three and Chapter Six, respectively), we see that the soldiers of the *pardo* militia were not merely guided by notions of ethnicity, but by personal and political systems of obligation. Failure to recognize this distinction overlooks the degree to which racial and ethnic interaction was complicated by local level politics. As we shall see, uprisings in Papantla were over agricultural rights, political authority, economic need, and social position within colonial society. Ethnicity described the participants, but largely did not select them.

Since the sixteenth century, the militia's primary function was to serve as a coastal defense force to ward off foreign incursion.[33] They were not created as a domestic guard for putting down uprisings. In fact, in

Papantla, this was one task for which they were particularly ill-suited. Though exact numbers for marriages between militia soldiers and native women in 1736 are unavailable, the *alcalde mayor* claimed that many militia soldiers failed to muster to stop the native uprising because they were married to native women. In the late eighteenth century, nearly sixty-one percent of the militiamen who recorded marital information had wed *indias* (native women).[34] This clearly put some of the soldiers into a conflict of interest when it came to fighting against local indigenous unrest. Militia soldiers had a distinct advantage as marriage partners. By 1787, tribute exemption would be conferred upon all wives of militia soldiers.[35] This benefit may well have contributed to the degree of inter-marriage between militia soldiers and local Totonac women. It is a historical truism that groups of soldiers will invariably find some outlet for their sexual and emotional desires. In Papantla, native women represented the majority of available brides. For *pardo* soldiers and Totonac women it is clear that ethnic designations were little barrier to intermarriage. Militia status and tribute exemption likely enhanced the desire for native women to cross this ethnic boundary. These marriage relationships inevitably meant that much of the social world of militia soldiers would have encompassed the native community.

This integration with the Totonac population meant that at times of native unrest the militia faced a unique problem. When putting down native unrest, *pardo* militia soldiers were forced into a third space between natives and Spaniards. Social relations of the Afro-Mexicans who made up the militia largely diminished their ethnic distinction as they took wives from different ethnic categories. But they were instruments of colonial rule, and the call of military service reasserted that ethnic distinction. The militia had an official responsibility to defend the kingdom's borders from foreign enemies. Their status as militiamen provided them with a certain degree of community identity and position within colonial society.[36] If it was as soldiers that the *pardo* militiamen had an identity as part of the system of Spanish rule, many of them nevertheless drew their family identity from their relations with local Totonacs. Whereas defending the coasts from foreign raiders was a clear battle against outsiders, in fighting the natives, the militiamen were forced to tip the balance of their commitment to either the Spanish officials or their social community. They were ordered to fight against people whom they may have known or been related to. For a group that in some ways had a difficult time integrating into either native or Spanish society, they were at times bound by conflicting responsibilities to both.

The militia soldiers were not only bound by social and occupational responsibilities. They were also subject to the complications created by the fact that, although they were a regional defense force—theoretically subject to viceregal control—they could be coopted by the local *alcalde mayor.*[37] When in 1736, only fifteen or twenty militia soldiers answered the call to arms, it could well have been the result of the fact that many lived far from town and never heard the beating of the drum meant to call them to action. But with the way that news often traveled in colonial Mexican villages—explaining the consistently high native turnout at these events—it is also very possible that these men consciously decided not to come to arms.[38] When these soldiers were called to put down Totonac collective violence, they had to choose one side or the other. They could attempt to sit out the event on the claim that they were too far from the action to hear the call. But their presence or absence would have to be explained in one way or they other. Arguably, these were the only people in Papantla who, when riot erupted, absolutely had to select an side.

The militia's loyalties were spread between their occupational responsibility and their social reality. Since the era of the conquest, Spanish authorities harbored fears about Afro-Mexicans. Afro-Mexicans were perceived as a particularly dangerous group whose loyalties to the crown were open to question.[39] Centuries of valorous service went far to ingratiate the *pardo* and *mulato* militias to the crown. But some officials maintained their concerns. The *alcaldes mayores* of Papantla twice questioned the ability of the *pardo* militia to fight off native uprisings. Yet militia abilities and crown need preserved the institution until near the end of the eighteenth century. In Papantla, this relationship perhaps caused officials to put faith in the militia's occupational loyalties; yet many of the men in service to the militia had further to wrestle with their loyalties as friends, lovers, and husbands.

Conclusion

Eighteenth-century Papantla was ethnically diverse, hosting an official body of armed Afro-Mexicans in the form of the *pardo* militia, as well as Afro-Mexican wives, children, and very likely adult males not affiliated with the militia. Afro-Mexicans appear to have occupied a third space in colonial Mexican history. This space had flexible borders, through which Afro-Mexicans moved into both Totonac and Spanish realms. Their ethnic locus was plastic. Both colonial reality and subsequent historical writing have left a hole between the two studied ethnic groups, Spaniards and natives. However, sources such as interment records reveal that the Afro-Mexican presence in Papantla was significant. A study of the experience of the militia augments the meaning of these numbers by revealing what choices and responsibilities at least some of the town's Afro-Mexicans faced. Further study of militia relationships can only reveal more questions about the nature of the Afro-Mexican experience in New Spain.

In Papantla Afro-Mexicans acted as defenders of the colonies, as laborers and farmers, and were a social group that interacted and inter-married with both whites and natives. They spanned the gap between the two groups so well recognized by history, natives and Spaniards. In spanning this gap they also undermined the concept of the *sistema de castas* in colonial New Spain. Readily identifiable ethnic distinctions were simply not a reality. Clear ethnic titles were imposed on individuals, but they did not conform to the Spanish concept of a well-ordered series of hierarchical socio-ethnic rankings.[40] This is made evident by the use of so few ethnic titles in the burial records. *Pardo, mulato, indio, mestizo*, and *español* are terms that describe but a few of the possible ethnic combinations in a society composed of the descendants of three continents. People were labeled with titles of convenience, either convenient to themselves or to those who were writing these titles down. At the same time, these terms were imposed on individuals who clearly crossed the boundaries of the *sistema de castas*. *Pardos* married *españolas*. *Indias* married *mulatos*. Papantla was home to a population that ranged across an ethnic spectrum, but the town was not rigidly divided along ethnic lines between Spaniards and Totonacs. Rather it was a place where individuals and groups manipulated the concept of ethnic distinction to achieve their own ends. In Papantla, the *sistema de castas* was both an obstacle and a tool, but it neither provided the structure for local society nor the template for divisions and loyalties during periods of discontent and revolt. Eighteenth-century realities in the colonies meant that the importance of racial identity was at times superseded by such issues as whom one met and fell in love with, or perhaps who was at one's shoulder when they were wounded and running out of ammunition.

"*Cachípat, Cachípat . . .* Get him, Get him": Collective Violence and the Uprising of 1736

The Uprising of September 16, 1736

Dramatis Personae
Spanish Officials

don Mathias de Fuenmayor Fernández	Curate of Papantla, Constable of the Inquisition
don Lucas Pérez de Oropeso	Lieutenant curate of Papantla
don Antonio de Torres Colmeno	Spanish *alcalde mayor*, Papantla
don Marcos de Cuenca	Lieutenant to the Spanish *alcalde mayor*
Clemente Palacios	Corporal, Papantla *pardo* militia,
José Cayetano	Soldier, Papantla *pardo* militia
Pedro Hernández	*Mestizo* soldier, Papantla *pardo* militia

Native Officials

don Andrés Gonzalez	Totonac *cabildo gobernador*
Martín de San Martín	Totonac *cabildo alcalde primero*
Joseph Ramirez	Totonac *cabildo alcalde*
don Pedro Ximenes	*Topile* (Totonac *cabildo* officer)

Civilians

don Francisco Pérez Luixano Bustamante	Spanish resident of Papantla
Joseph Suarez	Spanish resident of Papantla
Francisco Ramos	Totonac widower
Miguel Tejada	Accused Totonac insurgent
Francisco Tejada	Accused Totonac insurgent
Catalina	Mother of Francisco and Miguel Tejada
Francisco Grado	Free *mulato*

It all began with shouting in the church. On that Sunday morning, 16 September 1736, most of the Totonac residents of Papantla had dutifully gathered in the church for weekly services. Although going to mass was mandatory, church attendance among the Totonac population had been falling off, and to the reasoning of the lieutenant curate, don Lucas Pérez de Oropeso, this was a trend that could not continue. He had decided that this Sunday morning the flock needed more than just a sermon; it had come time to set an example. Pérez de Oropeso thus announced that he was going to whip Francisco Ramos, a Totonac widower who had been particularly remiss, skipping mass and not saying the rosary.[1] The lieutenant curate felt that giving Ramos three or four lashes would be adequate to remind his flock that mass was not an optional devotion. On hearing of this plan, however, the *gobernador* of the Totonac *cabildo*, don Andrés Gonzales, responded that the padre would do no such thing. That's when the shouting started. Two Totonac brothers, Miguel and Francisco Tejada, agreeing that the lieutenant curate could not be permitted to whip Francisco, jumped to their feet, yelling "cachípat, cachípat (Totonac for "get him, get him.")!"[2] Taking up the call, Catalina, the mother of the brothers Tejada, snatched the curate's cloak, one of the symbols of his position, from his shoulders. Suddenly feeling threatened by what was happening in his church, Oropeso fled. In terror, he ran, calling for help through the church cemetery into the plaza adjacent to the *casas reales*. Several Spaniards in the *casas reales* came out to help the priest, including the lieutenant to the *alcalde mayor*, Marcos de Cuenca.[3] Many of the Totonac churchgoers had poured into the plaza and were, according to one witness, *atumultados* (in a state of tumult).[4] Cuenca went out amongst the crowd to calm them, followed soon thereafter by the *alcalde mayor* himself, don Antonio de Torres Colmeno. Together, the two men managed to pacify the crowd, who then retired to their homes.

The incident had begun and ended quite quickly and had resulted in no injuries. However, the Spanish officialdom of Papantla considered the threat to the priest a serious transgression. In many rural communities of New Spain the clergy was often the main point of contact between the populace and the colonial state. Where Spanish populations were small, like Papantla, colonial authority was dependent on the population showing respect for both ecclesiastical and political offices. In the wake of that morning's disturbance, *alcalde mayor* Torres Colmeno felt it had become necessary to reassert that authority by having *gobernador* Gonzalez and other members of the Totonac *cabildo* brought back to the *casas reales.* Torres Colmeno pointed out to the *cabildo* officials that Gonzales' public opposition to the priest's announcement and the consequent abuse of the priest were severe infractions. To punctuate this point, Torres Colmeno took away the *gobernador's baston* (a staff which served as the physical representation of the authority of the *gobernador's* office) and put it away in the *casas reales.*[5] The *alcalde mayor* then issued a warning to the other officials of the *cabildo* that they should be careful, as they too could lose their positions. He then sent the native officials back to their homes.[6] It is unclear whether Torres Colmeno was simply making a statement by this act, a punitive reminder of who was supposed to hold the real authority in Papantla, or if he planned to then follow up this act with a petition to the viceroy to sanction a new election to replace Gonzales. Later developments, however, render this question moot.

Later that Sunday night, at about 8:00 or 9:00 p.m., Clemente Palacios, a corporal of the Papantla *"pardos y mulatos"* (the free-colored militia), who had been present at the earlier confrontation, was casually walking past the *casas reales* when he noticed that a crowd had formed at the building. *Alcalde mayor* Torres Colmeno was inside, along with *gobernador* Gonzalez, officials of the Totonac *cabildo*, and a considerable number of other natives. When Palacios made his presence known, Torres Colmeno ordered the corporal to arrest the *gobernador*. But Palacios quickly realized that this would not be possible, because "the doorway to the *casas reales* was packed with more than eighty Indians."[7] There was no way that Gonzales could be taken to the jail. Instead Torres Colmeno and corporal Palacios locked Gonzales in a room within the *casas reales* and herded the rest of the Totonacs out into the street. However, it was clear that the Totonacs were highly agitated at this stage, so, as he had done that morning, Torres Colmeno walked out into the plaza in an effort to calm the mob of native men and women and convince them to return to their homes.

This time the effort failed; the crowd would not comply. Torres Colmeno realized that his office was apparently commanding no more respect than had that of the lieutenant curate earlier in the day. So he instructed corporal Palacios to go get the captain of *pardos y mulatos* and the *caja de guerra* (a drum for calling the militia to arms). Palacios followed orders, but was able to rally only about fifteen men, as the majority lived outside of town and would not have heard the call to arms.[8] Not only were their numbers few, but they were also short on ammunition and gunpowder. Only four militiamen appeared to have had guns with them.[9] Corporal Palacios went to his own home with three men to secure additional arms, and returned to find that Torres Colmeno had left the *casas reales*. Palacios and the others found him at the *pochguin*. The members of the *cabildo* had gathered for a meeting with numerous other Totonac residents. The *alcalde mayor* feared that because of his detention of *gobernador* Gonzales, the group might be planning to riot.[10] In a poorly calculated effort to break up the meeting, Torres Colmeno drew his pistol and fired it into the air to disperse the group.[11] Rather than frightening the crowd into submission, the shot inspired two members of the meeting to throw open the doors of the building, from which the occupants unleashed a barrage of stones at Torres Colmeno. The *alcalde mayor* claimed that he was hit and wounded three times as he, corporal Palacios, and the others turned and fled.[12]

The situation had deteriorated badly and, in another echo of the conflict earlier that morning, the mob chased the *alcalde mayor* and others to the plaza and the *casas reales*. The *alcalde mayor* and the militiamen locked themselves in the *casas reales* with the crowd hard at their heels. The crowd then threw burning embers at the building in the hope of setting it on fire. Numerous windows were broken and soldiers of the militia were hit by stones; as many as six people in the building were wounded. The *alcalde mayor* ordered the militiamen to fire their weapons at the crowd, but lacking sufficient ammunition and gunpowder they were only able to get off six or eight shots, none of which found their targets. Amid the conflict, the curate, don Mathias de Fuenmayor Fernández, who had been in the building since earlier in the day, was hit in the head with a stone. Conditions in the *casas reales* were becoming desperate. The *alcalde mayor* decided to seek the assistance of his captive native *gobernador*. He went to the room in which Gonzalez had been locked only to find that Gonzalès had blocked the door from the inside. The *alcalde mayor* shouted under the door that Gonzales had to come out to help calm the crowd. Gonzalez then opened the door, looked at Torres Colmeno and countered: "Look what you have caused in this town. Get out there and *you* calm them down." It was clear to Torres Colmeno, however, that by this point power of his office would no longer be sufficient to stop the crisis. The *alcalde mayor* pleaded with Gonzalez and ultimately convinced the *gobernador* that it would be impossible for him to quiet the mob alone. Torres Colmeno eventually prevailed upon the *gobernador* to accompany him out of the building to try to pacify the mob.[13] On this night in Papantla, as had been the case throughout the history of the colonial exercise, peace, if it was going to be achieved, was going to depend not on the overwhelming authority of the Spanish state, but instead on an accord between natives and Spaniards.

Resistance

From the initial arrival of Cortés in 1519, Spanish colonization was only made possible through the formation of allegiances with at least some of the native population. At every step, natives resisted Spanish dominion, and in so doing, negotiated the limits of colonial control. In the early generations of Spanish incursion into the Americas, that negotiation often took the form of dramatic violence as colonization unfolded in a series of military conflicts. After the initial stage of conquest, the negotiation of rule continued, most often through non-violent resistance to colonial demands, but at times native communities returned to violence when their tolerance for various impositions reached the breaking point.[14]

Collective violence is necessarily a chaotic process. A single mob action can include individuals with highly varied motivations and equally varied objectives. Riots are typically born without plan and have very little organization. Consequently, any incident of collective violence is a unique event, founded on intentions as individual as the actors involved. Nonetheless, it is possible to identify patterns that can help the student of unrest understand how and why riots take place. Though the uprising of 1736 was born of the particular conditions in Papantla, it also reflected commonalities that can be seen in collective violence elsewhere in the colony.

Violent resistance is normally only one facet of a much more extensive relationship between plebeians and power holders. Collective violence, particularly in long-standing societies such as the native communities of the eighteenth-century Spanish colonies, comes at the moment when the system of control and accommodation has failed. The fact that violence tends to be very well-documented has garnered it a unique position in historical study. Historians have tended to, in the words of Murdo MacLeod, spend their efforts, "looking for the lost coin under the street-light."[15] Because it is relatively easy to examine, the use of violence by the underclasses to mediate colonial rule has often been separated from other methods by which colonized people resisted authority. Yet, studies that consider riot as a sudden reactive response to some threat, disconnected from other mechanisms of resistance often fail to credit individual actors and peasant communities with sophisticated and localized perceptions of acceptable governance.[16] In such cases, peasants are misrepresented as "an inert force," reacting violently to outside pressures rather than engaging in a constant negotiation of power.[17] But, by recognizing collective violence as the final, dramatic, and most dangerous stage in a series of negotiations between peasants and authorities, it is possible to develop a much more nuanced awareness of peasant participation in the colonial relationship.

Non-Violent Resistance

Scholarship of non-violent resistance in the Spanish colonies has demonstrated that native populations of the Americas were no less politically savvy than any other group. Natives engaged with the colonial system at all stages, from the conquest onward, and were able to manipulate the colonial system to their own ends.[18] Across the colonies, native groups employed work slowdowns, sabotage, and a sophisticated use of the colonial court systems, what James Scott famously labeled the "weapons of the weak."[19] The various methods of non-violent resistance highlight the nuanced understanding of the colonial system possessed by native communities, and further show that collective violence was not necessarily the instinctive reaction of unruly mobs, unable to redress wrongs with their heads instead of their hands. Violent resistance was instead a cautiously employed tool for specific objectives of specific value. A riot can be best understood as what Steve Stern called "a short-term variant within a long-term process of resistance and accommodation to authority."[20] Instead of resting idle when not in open riot, peasants were "continuous initiators in political relations."[21]

For every uprising documented in the archives, there were numerous events in which conditions became difficult for the plebian population yet uprising was not deemed a worthwhile option. In many cases, non-violent resistance to exploitative conditions worked. Of course confrontations that were resolved without disrupting the colonial system of order generated much smaller collections of documentary evidence, and thus are easily overshadowed by outbursts of violence. But by probing the testimony generated in those moments of violence, we can find the evidence of peasant engagement that preceded such conflicts.

Ultimately, the colonies' success was a product of negotiations, both violent and non-violent, between native populations and Spanish colonizers. Though natives acquiesced to Spanish rule, at times quite grudgingly, they also influenced the nature of that rule by demonstrating to the Spaniards through work stoppage, flight, the courts, and at times by violence, that they could set limits on Spanish authority.[22] These tactics were not discrete from one another. Legal challenges and the withholding of tribute could happen simultaneously, and violence was typically preceded by other methods of seeking redress. Indeed, non-violent acts of resistance were the customary means by which natives could reconstruct the colonial relationship into something that they could ultimately live with. The Totonac of Papantla routinely petitioned the viceroy and other officials when seeking to mitigate tribute burdens, or to moderate the arbitrary application of authority by local Spanish magistrates. In 1688, the native *cabildo* of Papantla petitioned the bishop of Puebla to help alleviate the excessive demands of the *alcalde mayor*, who had been forcing the Totonac to sell their tobacco at unfair prices. In this instance, the bishop agreed that this was unfair and ordered the *alcalde mayor* to stop the practice.[23] In this regard the Papantla Totonac were quite unexceptional. Native communities across the colonies quickly learned to understand and exploit the Spanish legal system. Spanish law in the colonies was meant in part to offer natives a sanctioned means of seeking redress for injustice. The courts could act as a relief valve for the frustrations of the subordinate population. Historian Felipe Castro Gutiérrez explained that "this system of neutralizing the social tensions was bureaucratic and slow, but secure and efficient enough to maintain stability and make unnecessary the existence of a colonial army of any importance."[24] Castro Gutiérrez went so far as to suggest that even occasional violent outbursts could have acted as means of alleviating animosities that, if left unchecked, could ferment into something much greater than a local riot and become a genuine threat to the structure of power.[25]

Jovita Baber's recent investigation of Tlaxcalan legal negotiations in the immediate wake of the conquest illustrates the creation of a system of negotiated rule. Quick to adopt Spanish legal tactics and rhetoric, in 1528 Tlaxcalan elites first petitioned for and won status as free self-governing vassals of the crown, exempt from being granted as part of an *encomienda*; and then in 1535 they secured recognition as a city, giving Tlaxcala municipal authority over neighboring *pueblos*. Such negotiations expanded Tlaxcalan authority over rival communities to beyond pre-Columbian limits while simultaneously serving the crown in their effort to contain the power of Spanish *encomenderos*. Tlaxcalan leaders chose to adopt facets of colonial municipal organization in support of a campaign to expand Tlaxcalan autonomy. Such negotiations were possible because the crown depended on native elites as allies, particularly in the early colony. Baber argues that these negotiations set a precedent in the construction of Spanish colonial rule, leading the crown to encourage viceroys to recognize indigenous municipalities across the colonies, creating "a system of compromises—a system in which political institutions accommodated and often encouraged the continuity of local customs and traditions."[26]

Non-violent resistance was thus that realm wherein colonial order was formed.[27] Despite the dramatic conquests of the Mexica and Inca Empires, Spanish authority in the American territories was anything but absolute. From its inception until independence, colonial Spanish America operated on a system that adapted and moderated over time to accommodate limits on Spanish rule imposed by native populations. Though the balance of power was increasingly in the favor of the Spanish, that power had to be tempered in order maintain a more or less peaceful colonial system. The colonial system evolved "institutions and mechanisms to maintain and reproduce the social order, while providing the possibility of modifying existing social agreements," which served to preserve the overall stability of the system itself.[28] Non-violent resistance was how that system was maintained, and beyond a certain point, violent outburst was the sign that the systems of accommodation had reached their extreme limits.

While non-violent and violent resistance were connected processes in a continuum of negotiation, it is also true that there is also a distinction to be drawn between the two. When native communities turned to violent unrest, they were crossing a very clear threshold, the point at which the colonial systems of accommodation had failed to maintain stability through non-violent means. Thus, while it is a mistake to imagine that natives were an "inert force," when not rising up in riot, acts of collective violence were nonetheless a dramatic escalation of conflict. Violent resistance is illegal, risky, and public. In the words of Andean historian Sergio Serulnikov, "mass violence was outside the law, and its very emergence was bound up in the failure (and abandonment) of legal strategies."[29] The level of risk and the public nature of this type of resistance sets it apart from other forms of resistance. Violence is but one of many means of opposing authority, but direct violent uprising represents a much more serious commitment than non-violent action.

Collective Violence

William Taylor, in his 1979 *Drinking, Homicide, and Rebellion,* divided collective violence into two categories based on the intentions of the participants. These categories were *uprisings,* designed to address a perceived problem within the system of rule, and *insurrections,* which attempt to overthrow the basis of power and thus fundamentally change the system of rule.[30] Uprisings do not fundamentally challenge relationships of authority. In fact, people engaged in uprisings often argue that they are defending the extant system from injustice and abuse. Because uprisings are small in scope, they typically do not involve significant planning. Community uprisings tend to be "uncoordinated, localized, [and] raggedly bound in space and time."[31] Uprisings are also typically more spontaneous and more readily called off when success is achieved. Participants in the uprising, according to George Wada and James C. Davis, "are momentarily conjoined not because they know where they want to go but because they do not like where they have been."[32] Uprisings are thus what E.J. Hobsbawm described in the late 1950s as "reformist" movements, in which people "accept the general framework of an institution or social arrangement, but consider it capable of improvement, where abuses have crept in."[33] Insurrections, on the other hand, are designed to change the nature of power in a very basic way. The uprisings in eighteenth-century Papantla never reached this scale and were by no means revolutionary in their intentions, despite the occasional claims to that effect made by local Spanish magistrates. They followed the model of redressing a local wrong, fixing some perceived abuse of traditional power as it was understood in the community. Some historians have suggested that the unrest of the Papantla Totonac in the latter half of the eighteenth century was part of a process that would ultimately lead to their participation in the unquestionably-revolutionary struggles of independence in the next century.[34] Though it is quite possible that the increasing unrest of the eighteenth century contributed to a recognition that broader political change was possible, prior to the Hidalgo Revolt of 1810, the riots in Papantla did not seek sweeping change.

Rioters in Papantla, as was the case throughout the colonies, regularly testified after uprisings that they took no issue with the king, but instead had been acting against some local official who they felt was abusing his power. In this regard they often portrayed themselves as siding with the crown, fighting against the misuse of colonial authority. Rioters usually did not perceive themselves as acting against the social order. They normally attacked a single individual, group, or institution, not the general conditions of an iniquitous society. In 1996 Ward Stavig described the localized nature of community relationships in native Latin American communities:

> reciprocal exchanges and obligations established the cultural dynamics, and the parameters of economic and social life, that defined Indian-Spanish relations. Such relations defined the "moral economy." Also important to the moral economy were face-to-face relationships between individual Indians, or Indian communities, and the local colonial authorities who enforced the imperial system. Colonial officials who transgressed the bounds of the moral economy could cause the Indians to see their relationship as delegitimized, leaving the official, if not the system, open to attack.[35]

For natives, exposure to colonial authority was typically in the form of local religious or political leaders who, when crisis arose, became the targets of native animosity. These outbursts were attempts to regain what the peasants saw as rightfully theirs. They were trying to reestablish an older, more just order (real or imagined), not create a new one.[36] Studies of peasant societies across the globe have shown that the peasant takes to the street in defense of his or her corporate unit much more often than in opposition to the basic system of authority. Initially, corrective measures were conducted within the rules of the colonial system. Subsequent violence attempted to reestablish "proper" colonial rule. The Papantla uprisings of the eighteenth century all held to this pattern. Typical uprisings were attempts to repair a given problem and were generally conducted with small-scale objectives. These objectives could of course shift over the course of the event from one topic of complaint to another. But one finds that among the many reasons why any community in a state of unrest rose up, there was a particular straw that broke the camel's back and that this straw was often a target of the initial assault.

When in 1979, William Taylor published his landmark *Drinking, Homicide, and Rebellion in Colonial Mexican Villages*, he sought and found clear structural consistencies in uprisings in late-colonial central and southern Mexico. He wrote, "Eighteenth-century rebellions were not random or limitless in variety. They reveal quite a definite structure and sequence of development. Most village uprisings in central Mexico . . . were alike in repertory of actions, instruments, and dramatis personae."[37] Taylor found that even in the chaos of riot, these events typically adhered to predictable patterns: rioters reflected the breadth of community populations, with women turning out at least as often as men, the church building was very often central to the event, and the jail and *casas reales* were regularly targets of attack.[38] In the case of Papantla during the eighteenth century we can find commonalities in action, as uprisings conformed to certain frequent patterns, such as the attacks on the jail and official buildings, the central role of the church building, or witnesses foregrounding local concerns while swearing allegiance to the king and the fundamental structure of rule. So too do we see the importance of individual actors and their motivations, as will be made clear in Chapter Six's examination of the 1787 uprising, in which the former *alcalde mayor* and the interests of his supporters will be vital to the outbreak of unrest.

Robert Patch described Spanish colonial control as being built on a "balance of consensus and coercion," or "a colonial pact."[39] In exchange for acquiescence to tribute demands and the acceptance of Spanish authority, native communities preserved a significant degree of local autonomy; however, this balance was prone to disturbance on the local level. Spanish regional magistrates had a great deal of autonomy in their actions and tended to use their positions to extract unreasonable amounts of labor and wealth from the natives through a variety of means. When faced with excessive demands by the local magistrate, native communities would often attempt to reestablish the balance through non-violent measures of resistance. These measures failed frequently enough to make local over-exploitation one of the major causes of native revolt.

Prominent historians have cautioned against concluding that all peasant revolts ultimately originate from economic exploitation. Mexican historian Eric Van Young has lamented that studies of collective violence, even those that purport to look away from economic factors and mine the influence of culture, frequently fall back to economic considerations as the trigger for unrest: "they tend to revert to material grievances and class conflict as providing the basic energy for revolt."[40] His criticism is valid, and one to which the current work could certainly be subjected. To tease out causes for unrest that are entirely discrete from economic concerns would require a very comprehensive source base, and small-scale events such as the uprisings in Papantla do not always yield such information.

At the same time, I argue that unrest in Papantla, while inflected by cultural and historical factors, was tied to specific economic concerns. For peasants, like the Totonac of Papantla, autonomy and even cultural practice was closely tied to material wellbeing, no matter how marginal that wellbeing may have been. In New Spain, peasant unrest was most often against Spanish authorities whose role in native communities was frequently extractive. What frustrated members of these communities were commonly threats to native economic welfare. To that end, in the case of Papantla it is quite difficult to entirely separate cultural sensibilities from economic interests. Indeed, it is the premise of the current work that economic challenge in the form of the tobacco monopoly is what upset the colonial relationship in Papantla, and in turn limited the citizenry's tolerance of other misdeeds, leading to violence. An example—discussed in greater detail in Chapter Four—illustrates the difficulty of entirely separating economic interests from other more culturally inflected causes of unrest. In 1767, Totonac natives rose up in protest of what they felt was the unjustified extradition of an imprisoned local resident from Papantla to Mexico City. Witness testimony revealed that this decision to move the prisoner was seen as an illegitimate use of the *alcalde mayor's* authority. At the same time, however, witnesses who identified the extradition as the proximate cause of the conflict also went on to justify their actions on the basis of the economic exploitation exacted by the *alcalde mayor.*

The 1736 revolt in Papantla was typical of revolts in eighteenth-century Mexico. Despite the suspicions alleged by the *alcalde mayor,* the rioters did not challenge colonial rule itself, nor did they try to expand the uprising beyond Papantla. The uprising was also not unusual in being centered on official buildings like the church and the *casas reales,* in featuring the participation of both Totonac men and women, and in quickly expanding from a small incident to a fight over legitimate local rule. While in many ways the 1736 event fit the pattern of native revolts, at the same time, local factors and individual personal relationships played crucial roles in the fomentation of discontent and the transition from discontent to revolt. In short, the local and the particular were just as important as the larger pattern and structure—both in Papantla and elsewhere in New Spain. As Papantla's history illustrates, the antagonisms that underlay revolt were not far below the surface, nor did they require much in the way of a catalyst. When the curate announced that he was going to whip one of his parishioners, he touched off animosities that extended well beyond indignation about the punishment of one unobservant local native.

The Riot Continues

After the Spanish *alcalde mayor* Torres Colmeno convinced the Totonac *gobernador* Andrés Gonzales to help him appease the crowd, the two stepped forth into the street, calling for the mob to calm down. But even the combination of Spanish and native political authority was insufficient to cause the mob to relent. Torres Colmeno then called for the curate to come out to help. The task of trying to calm native mobs frequently fell to the priest in rural communities. Often he would carry the crucifix from the altar in an effort to exert spiritual authority over the crowd. Taylor noted that though the priest was often seen as the moral authority in villages, such efforts by priests to calm angry mobs were frequently disregarded by rioters.[41] In this instance however, as the wounded curate stepped out of the *casas reales* and joined the other two men, the crowed quieted.[42] The curate called out for the natives to be calm. He announced that "many are wounded. I have been wounded in the head." Despite the conflict with the lieutenant curate earlier in the day, and the weak history of Christianization in Papantla, the pleadings of the priest—or perhaps his bloodstained visage—began to have an effect. Or perhaps the crowd at that point was satisfied with having gotten their *gobernador* released from the *casas reales*. Whatever the cause, the rioters seemed to be relenting when one Totonac man snuck up behind the three officials. He had a club in his hands and was preparing to strike the curate in the back of the head when someone in the crowd yelled at him to stop. The would-be attacker lowered his weapon. The crowd then left, once again for the *pochguin*, this time taking their *gobernador* with them.[43]

However, as they marched off into the night, the rioters were not pacified. According to corporal Palacios, they held a lengthy meeting in the *pochguin*. Later, many set forth with bugle and drum for the curate's house, where they broke in the doors, abused his groom, and set free his horse. For the rest of the night, the mob continued to move through the town in threatening gangs until nearly daylight. One group appeared to stay on guard duty, encircling the *casas reales* where the defenders had chosen to sleep. However, there were no further attacks on people during the night.[44]

The following day, crowds of armed Totonacs returned to the plaza.[45] *Gobernador* Gonzalez and other officials of the *cabildo* went to the *casas reales*, this time to make their own demand. He said that the Indians were calm now, but would not remain so. If peace was to be maintained, the *alcalde mayor* would have to sign a sworn testimony that the uprising of the previous day and night had not been the fault of the *gobernador*. Seeing no option, Torres Colmeno reluctantly signed a statement exonerating the *gobernador*. The Totonac officers then left the building. It appeared that the uprising had ended. But according to several witnesses, soon after this, the Totonac residents of Papantla began to disappear.

The *alcalde mayor* testified that *gobernador* Gonzalez and other members of the *cabildo* left for Mexico City on Tuesday,18 September, leaving instructions for Totonac guards to take to the roads and ensure that no one leave to tell the story of what had happened. Torres Colmeno claimed that the guards were under orders to attack any one who left, and that on an unspecified night they were to burn "all the houses of the Spaniards and mulattos." One local resident testified that there was a growing separatist movement among the Totonac.

Over subsequent weeks, many Totonacs began to pick up and leave town, moving into the hills to lead uncontrolled lives "sin ley ni rey" (without law or king).[46] Many were taking "their women, their children, their chickens, and all of their things."[47] For four months following the uprising, the rumors flew. Such fear of the concealed—and hence, uncontrolled—actions of natives in the woods, were not unusual. Michael Ducey has described the recurrent suspicions that Europeans held of the untamed countryside, and the ungovernable actions of natives therein. In his examination of a later uprising in Papantla in 1767, he found that Spanish officials echoed those fears as rioters secluded themselves in the hillsides outside of town.[48] Spanish officials often saw the countryside as the birthplace of imagined millenarian movements. In 1736, some witnesses held that these natives were building up stockpiles of quivers, bows, and arrows, and that they came into town at night drunk, trying to woo additional community members into joining them.[49] In January 1737, as part of an inquest overseen by Torres Colmeno, a local Spaniard, Juan Muños de Cabeza testified, as did others, that the natives were being led by a mysterious Spaniard, Joseph Suarez, who hated other Spaniards and had convinced "the Indians" to follow his orders. Muños de Cabeza claimed that the Indians gave Suarez supplies, but would not sell food to other Spaniards in town. The witness concluded his testimony with the warning that "if something isn't done soon, it is certain that total perdition is coming."[50]

Total perdition did not come. Unfortunately, the documentation fails to clearly record just how the conflict was ultimately resolved. However, records from the autumn of 1738 show that *gobernador* Gonzales and other members of the *cabildo* had been jailed, and remained incarcerated two years later when the archbishop of Puebla requested an inquest be opened into the testimony gathered by *alcalde mayor* Torres Colmeno in 1736–1737. The viceroy concurred and dispatched don Francisco Muños de Cabeza (no known relation to Juan) to ascertain the veracity of witness statements. Again, we lack a clear conclusion to this investigation. It appears that the events of Sunday, 16 September through Tuesday, 18 September 1736, did take place much as described above. However, the reality of a separatist movement operating in the mountains and planning to destroy Papantla remains questionable. Torres Colmeno himself recanted parts of his own testimony, including the claim that the Totonacs in the mountains were arming for an assault. New testimony provided in the second investigation suggested that, rather than the natives blockading the town, it had been Torres Colmeno who had deployed troops across the town, and that those Totonac families that fled to the hills had done so in fright. Pedro Hernández, a *mestizo* member of the *pardo* militia, testified in September 1738 that soldiers had patrolled the streets of Papantla for fifteen days after the uprising. He did not know who had given the order, but he said that soldiers were ordered to guard all the roads leaving Papantla and attack any natives that tried to leave.[51]

With the conflicting testimonials of 1738 and the accusation by at least one witness that the *alcalde mayor* forced witnesses to sign their testimony without having that testimony read back to them, the accuracy of any particular account of the event becomes questionable. What specifically resolved this conflict and what happened in the months following the uprising is unclear. What we can see is that the event did contain certain hallmarks that would be seen again in the uprisings of the last half of Papantla's eighteenth century. Most notably, we see that the town was divided across various groups. There was conflict between the lieutenant curate and his flock. The heads of the native and Spanish *cabildos* were at odds. Free-colored soldiers, never fully part of Spanish society, were by military responsibility forced to stand against local Totonacs, calling attention to the breadth of the ethnic complexity of the town. Specific types of divisions, such as the factionalism within the Totonac population, will be discussed in the coming chapters, but for the moment it is worth pausing here to consider the following questions: How typical was the revolt of 1736, not just in Papantla, but of resistance in eighteenth-century New Spain more broadly? To what extent does the historiography of revolt help us to understand Papantla's uprisings? And does Papantla's experience contribute in turn to our understanding of the larger phenomenon of native discontent in late-colonial Mexico?

The 1736 revolt took place during a period of comparatively diminished community violence in the viceroyalty of New Spain. Some historians have suggested that by this time, peasant communities across the colonies had settled into a detente of sorts. Natives, Spaniards, expanding *mestizo* and Afro-Mexican populations, had all reached a point of relatively peaceful interaction—a *Pax Hispanica* or *Pax Colonial*. This was by no means a time of absolute amity or one devoid of violent unrest, but prior to the last half of the eighteenth century and the expansion of the Bourbon reforms, the colony had stabilized as a more or less functional system in which collective violence had come to be seen as an abnormal event.[52] Murdo MacLeod has countered that this *Pax Hispanica* is the result of historical oversight. MacLeod argues that the Spanish colonial state managed to reduce intercommunity warfare, but replaced it with frontier wars and psychologically violent repression and localized violence that obviates the notion of a colonial peace. However, whether this notion of a "pax" is accurate or not in the first half of the eighteenth century, there is no doubt that it disappeared in the second half. A generation after the 1736 uprising, collective violence became more common in Papantla and across the colonies more broadly. Prior to the Bourbon reforms of mid-century, native unrest was, if not absent, limited. Over the centuries, the colonial system had evolved an ability to, in the words of Castro Gutiérrez, "maintain stability, provide an outlet for tensions, dissolve conflicts and control episodes of violence."[53] In the decades to come, however, the system that maintained stability would break down as crown policy changes disturbed the process of accommodation that had made riot an unusual event. As we shall see in the following chapters, royal efforts to reassert political and economic domination within the colonies during the second half of the eighteenth century unintentionally damaged the relationship between local communities and the local colonial authorities. In this process, underlying discontents within native communities were exposed, with violent consequences.

FOUR

"Tobacco for Snuff or Tobacco for Smoking, It is all Vice": Bourbon Reforms and the Uprising of 1765

The Uprising of 1765

Dramatis Personae
don Manuel Chacon   Spanish *alcalde mayor*
The Papantla Totonacs

Witnesses
Francisco Ramírez   Lieutenant of militia
don Nicolas Andrade   Spanish merchant
don Martin Gamboa   Spanish merchant

On a day in late 1764 or early 1765, when exactly it is not certain, the Totonacs of Papantla dutifully brought their tobacco harvest to the plaza in the center of town.[1] They were doing so under an order from the *alcalde mayor*, don Manuel Chacon, who was acting in accordance with regulations pertaining to the establishment of a new crown monopoly on tobacco. A witness to the process, Francisco Ramírez, a *criollo* (American-born Spaniard) militia lieutenant who witnessed the event, testified that the Papantla Totonacs were very compliant with the order. "They punctually obeyed, all of them bringing their tobacco that they harvested. . . holding back very little."[2] It must have been very hard for these people, who had planted their crop that year in the full expectation that they would be able sell some for extra income or use it for traditional ritual purposes. More poignant still must have been the fact that this was supposedly the last crop of tobacco that they would ever grow. As of this moment, tobacco cultivation was no longer legal in Papantla.

Chacon collected the tobacco, as was his responsibility per the new legislation. Based on his subsequent actions, it is somewhat less clear what he was then required to do with the tobacco. Chacon chose to fulfill this duty in a decidedly unwise manner. In front of the natives who had just brought to him the fruits of their harvest, Chacon set fire to some of the tobacco. He did this, according to one incredulous witness, because he decided that the quality of the tobacco "wasn't good."[3] If the Totonac found sacrificing their crop to new crown legislation endurable, if unpleasant, that crop's deliberate destruction before their eyes was too much. Recalling the event nearly three years later, lieutenant Ramírez would point out that Chacon was a man of poor character; whether that accusation was true or not, he was apparently a man of poor judgment.[4] Shortly after the *alcalde mayor* set fire to the tobacco, according to a number of witnesses, the Totonacs set fire to the *casas reales* and the jail, and ignited part of the building where the tobacco was being stored.[5] Though the connection between the new monopoly and the subsequent native destruction seems rather apparent, witness testimony was somewhat circumspect. Some were unable to say with certainty that the new monopoly was in fact the cause of the violence. Spanish merchant and local resident Nicolas Andrade said that even though the unrest occurred at the initiation of the monopoly, he was not sure that that was necessarily why the uprising took place. Several witnesses admitted that the *casas reales* and the jail had been burned, but claimed that there had been no riot, somewhat complicating what exactly constitutes an uprising. The incendiarism may, in Andrade's opinion, have had to do with a factional dispute between the captain of militia and a group of natives over who should hold the post of *alcalde mayor*.[6] If so, the unrest may have been retribution for an effort to oust the previous *alcalde mayor* that had been spearheaded by the militia captain and merchant don Placido Pérez, a move that had been opposed by the natives in the community.[7] On the other hand, some witnesses, such as one don Pedro Joseph de León, originally of Navarre and secretary of the Holy Office of the Inquisition, suggested that it was possible that the natives had in fact acted "in opposition to the new establishment [of the monopoly]."[8] Neither position is definitive.

The documentary record about the uprisings is, sadly, quite poor. All accounts of the event come from witnesses interviewed almost three years later as the result of another uprising in 1767. The resulting paucity of records is frustrating. Important questions are left unanswered, and it is hard to know for certain just what provocations lay behind the 1765 unrest. At the same time the remembered accounts are suggestive. The testimonies we do have certainly suggest that the installation of the tobacco monopoly in some way precipitated the rioters' outburst of destruction. However, the documentation offers very few details about the event, including the number of participants, or that is was indeed an uprising at all. Some witnesses claimed that the multiple associated acts of arson did not quite rise to the level of a *tumulto*. The divergence in testimony raises one of the basic problems of studying colonial unrest, which is determining which acts of violence were or were not uprisings. MacLeod has suggested that many small-scale acts of native unrest were over-reported by local magistrates, who would depict them as major assaults on the very foundation of colonial order. The fears or the guilt of colonial officials could shape their perceptions of any act of native discord; MacLeod explains, "a local window-smashing becomes a revolt, either because of such fears or as a justification to the authorities of the severity of repression."[9] With that in mind, it seems odd that the fires of 1765 were not recorded as a revolt of some kind. One is left to wonder to what degree the fires constituted a significant rebellion or not. The fact that this event appears only anecdotally during witness testimony gathered years later supports the possibility it was not conceived of as a major uprising at the time. Conceivably, witnesses only described the early outburst as a true uprising because they were recalling it within the context of the unrest of 1767. Nonetheless, despite the records' silence on this point, the Totonac population of Papantla was clearly very angry, enough so that they took violent action against symbols of authority in the town. They certainly expressed significant disdain, however we cannot be sure over precisely what. Was the focus of their anger the *alcalde mayor*, who was accused of poor character by the militia lieutenant? Was it hostility over the monopolization of tobacco, which touched off this outburst by the Totonacs? Perhaps the fires were some sort of retribution for a factional dispute. Or was their anger possibly a symptomatic response to an even more pervasive sense of injustice? As is so often the case in events of collective unrest, the tumult was likely the result of a combination of factors. Hostility toward the local *alcalde mayor* was common in colonial Mexican villages. However, this event occurred at the very moment of the monopoly's inception and included a direct assault on the monopoly building; this demands that the historian consider the effects of this institution on the lives of the local population. While the story of the 1765 event remains obscure, placing it in the context of massive changes going on throughout the Spanish Americas at this time can offer a perspective on how local peoples reacted to shifting conditions during the reign of Charles III.

This chapter considers the tobacco monopoly within the framework of the Bourbon reforms of the eighteenth century. These reforms provide context for the social, economic, and political changes that reshaped both Spanish colonial rule and native responses to it. One of the most significant economic reforms of this period was the creation of the tobacco monopoly. This single change would come to affect the Totonac of Papantla more fundamentally than any other reform, causing financial hardship, creating a new source of conflict between the natives and Spanish authority, and—I argue—helping to spark a series of uprisings over the next two decades. The goal of this chapter is to bridge the gap between crown policy and local experience by explaining how this series of colony-wide initiatives changed the sociopolitical order in Papantla. To understand the influence of the reform policy in Papantla, we step back to consider the state of the Spanish empire at the inception of Bourbon rule, and then focus on the reforms themselves.

The Ailing Empire

In 1700, the French Bourbon, Duke Philip of Anjou, ascended to the throne of Spain, marking the end of two centuries of Hapsburg rule. However, the title he claimed only provided him a very tenuous grip on a deteriorating empire. The Spain of 1700 was a far cry from the Spain of the sixteenth century, which had been rich on American silver and was far and away the predominant imperial power in the Atlantic World. Rather, Spain at the start of the eighteenth century was suffering economic depression and political division at home, and economic disassociation and political weakness in its far-flung colonies. Profligate Hapsburg spending on foreign wars and foreign goods had cost Spain the majority of colonial gold and silver.[10] During two centuries of Spanish administration, the Hapsburg crown had incautiously spent much of the seemingly endless wealth to be extracted from the Americas and failed to foster internal development of manufacture in the peninsula. Spain let most of its American capital be funneled off to foreign merchants, rather than investing it in Spain itself. By the waning years of Hapsburg control, Cádiz had become, in the words of David Brading, "a mere entrepôt for the exchange of American bullion for European merchandise."[11] Early on, Spain's extraordinary expenditure and lack of domestic investment had been sustainable, as its colonies were still producing large quantities of silver. However, by the end of the seventeenth century, its colonies had long since stopped filling this need. The great South American silver mine at Potosí had started to fall off as early as 1592. Mines in New Spain began to peter out soon after.[12] Loose oversight of both production and taxation of silver further reduced the volume flowing back to Spain.

Over the course of the seventeenth century, export revenues decreased while import expenses climbed.[13] With unpredictable currency values, Spanish businessmen refrained from experimental initiatives. Consequently, Spanish investment in industry, agriculture, and commerce declined. Dependency on continental rather than peninsular goods became a self-reinforcing cycle. Spanish cities lost the ability to pay for infrastructure maintenance. Land went uncultivated, and workers were forced into vagrancy in search of subsistence wages. Population decline came on the heels of economic failure as young men emigrated in search of greater prosperity. The traditional view of this period as one of unmitigated disaster for Spain is well represented by Trevor Davies's 1965 portrayal of Spanish decline as almost apocalyptic. According Davies, the need to increase the available labor pool in Spain was so severe that the crown went as far as limiting book publication on the idea that reading was a distraction from work.[14] While more recent scholars have argued that the traditional view of late Hapsburg Spain as an economic disaster is overstated, Spain in the time of Charles II was indisputably under terrific economic strain.[15]

Overseas in the American colonies, other European powers such as the Dutch and the English had been eating away at Spain's hegemony in the Americas.[16] During the seventeenth century the British rendered permanent their settlements in North America, while also intruding into the Caribbean. At the same time, the Dutch not only established settlements on the Windward Islands, but also launched successful raids into Brazil while that colony was under the authority of a Portuguese-Spanish union. By the end of the century, the French had pushed into the northern Gulf of Mexico, establishing trading settlements in what would become New Orleans, and formalized possession of the western end of Hispañola, creating the colony of Saint Domingue. Spain had lost control over its exclusive trading monopoly with its American colonies. J. H. Elliott pointed out that by the middle of the seventeenth century, the "Caribbean was internationalized and turned into a base from which illicit trade could be conducted on a large scale with mainland America."[17] An obvious challenge to the monopolistic ambitions of Spanish economic interests, illegal trade had become so rampant as to constitute a "parallel economy," in the Caribbean. Spain's inability to meet the import needs of the colonies reached such severity that illegal trade with the American colonies was at once despised and simultaneously quietly condoned by Spanish officials and a crown forced to turn a blind eye. Stanley and Barbara Stein have suggested that this contraband trade was both an unpleasant necessity and a veiled opportunity. Contraband trade endured because it could fulfill colonial needs left unmet by Spain, while its illegality preserved the high prices sought by Spanish merchants.[18] By the close of Hapsburg dominion, New Spain, Peru, and Chile had become nearly autonomous in the production of grains.[19] Much of the demand for other goods, such as wine, finished woodcrafts, and oil, was being fulfilled locally within the colonies. Those needs that the colonies could not fulfill themselves were gladly tended to by other Atlantic nations. The colonies were producing little for the mother country and needing less from it.[20]

Concurrent with these economic incursions from outside the colonies, the crown's political authority had weakened as well. Over the previous two and half centuries, Iberia had exerted poor control over colonial administration. Spain had focused far more attention on extracting wealth from the Americas than it had on ensuring that the colonies were effectively governed. So long as the colonies produced money, royal interest fell off dramatically beyond the port of Cádiz, where American bullion was unloaded. This colonial neglect was in some ways built into the administrative system. The crown had sold official postings in the American colonies. Viceroys were limited to five-years terms to discourage them from developing overly strong ties to the colonial elite. This policy had the side effect of limiting their ability to achieve very much administratively and often encouraged viceroys to devote considerable effort to efficiently profiting from their posting, at times to the cost of the home country. Viceroys famously shrugged off royal commands with the phrase "obedezco pero no cumplo" (I obey but do not comply). Colonial corruption became commonplace, and as such cost the metropolis potential revenue. The result was, by the beginning of the eighteenth century, a colony in which administrators at all levels often paid far more attention to their own financial gain than to the crown's coffers and policy. In the words of Felipe Castro Gutiérrez, "the most notable aspect of the state apparatus in New Spain was, prior to the decade of the 1760s, was its virtual non-existence."[21] During the seventeenth century local *criollo* oligarchies capitalized on crown weakness, neglect, and ham-fisted efforts to maintain economic authority, by expanding "still further their domination of life in their communities by acquiring through purchase, blackmail or encroachment extensive areas of land."[22] This growing *criollo* power was in some ways a fulfillment of exactly the fears that earlier Spanish kings felt toward the original *encomenderos*, in which a weak metropolis might fail to control the power of an American elite increasingly disconnected from Spain. By the end of the Hapsburg reign, the colonies had drifted far from the imperial metropolis.

When the enfeebled Charles II died in 1700, both the Frenchman Philip and the Austrian Archduke Charles were potential successors to the throne of Spain. France backed Philip's right to the throne, while Charles's claim was supported by Britain, The Netherlands, and Portugal, all of which feared the possibility of a united France and Spain dominating Western Europe. The result was a bitter war from 1702 until 1714. To defend his claim to the throne, Philip needed far more resources than the anemic Spain could provide. He was dependent upon French arms and French advisors. Along with French military support, Philip would bring important French ideas about bureaucratic administration and absolutist rule.[23] With French aid, he succeeded in winning European recognition of his claim to the throne. However, this success came at a high cost, as Spain had become a more austere empire, losing nearly all of its European holdings. Minorca, Gibraltar, Sicily, Naples, Sardinia, the Low Countries, and

Milan were all lost, or doled out in the treaties of Utrecht (1713) and Rastatt (1714). Philip had to renounce any claim to the throne of France for himself or his heirs. Spain, once Europe's most powerful empire, had fallen to the point that its lone remaining ally on the continent held enormous responsibility for the survival of the Spanish state.[24] The house of Bourbon had secured control of Spain, but it was militarily weak, badly administered, and poorly funded. The effort to recover the "world empire" would take place over the course of a century and eventually bring to the Americas the most substantial legal changes of the colonial era.

The Bourbon Reforms

Philip, now Philip V of Spain, began a process of remaking the Spanish Empire, influenced significantly by absolutist ideas and governmental tactics gaining popularity across Europe, and notably those employed in France.[25] To consolidate authority on the peninsula, Philip curtailed much of the Spanish nobility's power. He introduced the French intendancy system to the peninsula in 1711, initiating greater crown oversight over local officials. Philip stripped the aristocracy of Aragon and Valencia of the *fueros* (privileges that exempted groups from certain types of taxation or trial by the civil judiciary), beginning a policy of centralizing power on the throne that would unfold over the century.[26] The crown prioritized increasing revenue and streamlined domestic taxation. Philip's administration reduced customs barriers between the kingdoms comprising Spain, fiercely combatted the problem of counterfeit currency, and reformed coinage.[27] With these reforms, and others, such as enhanced oversight of accounts and the introduction of new taxes on property and income, Philip V's initial efforts met with certain success.[28] By 1715, Philip's Spain had halved the expenditures and tripled the revenue of Charles II's Spain. Yet the upsurge in Spanish economic efficiency was by no means consistent, and it was far from total.

Though Philip's efforts would remain largely contained to the Iberian Peninsula, he did initiate some administrative reform in the colonies. The colonies had grown economically and geographically into entities far too large for administrative systems that had been set up centuries earlier in the immediate wake of the conquest. Lima, for example, had administrative responsibility for a territory that stretched 4,000 miles from north to south, with major cities accessed via the Caribbean, the Pacific, and Atlantic oceans. To improve administrative control, Philip separated the northern part of the continent into the viceroyalty of New Granada in 1717, which survived for five years and was then reestablished in 1739. However, beyond this administrative change, and small initial efforts at financial reform in the colonies, Philip restricted his reorganization agenda to Spain. Only in 1759, with the ascension of Philip's third son, Charles, would Spanish royal control of the overseas empire be thoroughly addressed through comprehensive policies designed to increase the defense, value, and obedience of a dominion that had become far too independent.

Charles III's policies of reform in the colonies touched all points of contact between the crown and its dominion. The reforms were varied, unfolding over the course of three decades of his reign, and were woven together by the principles of enlightened despotism. The reformed empire was intended to bring "good governance," enhanced revenue production, military security, modernization, and greater connection between the crown and its subjects.[29] Among the means Charles used to bring the colonies back under close crown control were administrative extensions of Philip's policies. Charles created an additional South American viceroyalty in 1779 with the creation of Rio de la Plata. Charles also transported the intendancy system to the colonies.[30] Charles ultimately appointed twelve regional intendants in New Spain in 1786, who themselves supervised yet another new category of local administrators, the subdelegates.[31] In 1787 Papantla became a subdelegation of the intendancy of Veracruz.[32]

To enhance royal dominance over the administration of the colonies, Charles also set his eye on the Church. The reforms to the Church in Spain and its American holdings fit well with the Bourbon regalist philosophy. The crowns of both Portugal and Spain had held exceptional authority over the Church within their realms since the end of the fifteenth century, and had been granted the power to appoint bishops and to oversee the Church's finances. For the Spanish colonial project, political administration and church administration were inextricably bound together in what Joseph Barnadas has described as "the great politico-ecclesiastical machine of America."[33] From the inception of the colony, the Church had gone hand in hand with, and at times as a surrogate for, the state. As Enrique Florescano and Isabel Sánchez put it, "in the small towns and the outlying areas the church was the maximum authority; judges, defenders, intermediaries, educators, state and church representatives."[34] For many indigenous colonial subjects, the Church was their only interaction with the colonial state. Thus the Church was a vital facet of colonial administration in the New World. Yet, while the Church was an arm of colonial rule, by the eighteenth century it had developed, in the eyes of reformers, into a challenge to regal authority. The Church had become an institution whose powers extended beyond the merely spiritual to the point that they intruded into the governing purview of the monarchy. Over the centuries of colonial rule, the Church had grown as an institution, its power and wealth expanding dramatically. As the recipient of hundreds of years of bequests, the Church had developed into the largest banker in the colonies by the eighteenth century, and a great landholder as well. According to Clara García Ayluardo, it eventually came to enjoy "such rights, privileges, jurisdiction, and fiscal system that it had the character of a political body."[35] As part of its policy of reform on the peninsula, the crown opted to deploy that power for its own ends. The crown, according to Andrea Smidt, "worked at cementing its political authority over Spanish clergy in order to do its bidding on multiple fronts as quasi-agents of the state."[36] Yet these agents had to be carefully controlled. To eighteenth-century reformers, there was room for only one supreme political body in the Spanish Empire.

On the spiritual front, eighteenth-century reformers were also concerned about the way popular devotion had developed among its subjects. *Cofradías* (lay organizations of devotion), and popular festivals had moved devotion out of the church. While strong Catholicism was of course good in the eyes of the crown, the degree to which this devotion had manifested into a competing demand for colonial resources had become problematic.[37] Devout organizations put on lavish celebrations to patron saints. Religious brotherhoods, through demands for dues in celebration of one saint or another, were siphoning money from productive realms into non-productive acts of lay worship. This was an era of baroque piety, in which elaborate and ornate displays of faith dominated much of colonial devotion, and stood in stark contrast to the objectives of Bourbon reformers who sought to end unnecessary, and to their eyes unseemly, expressions of devotion that often left community members unable to fulfill tribute demands. Reformers sought "a religion that was less exuberant, disordered, and heterodox."[38]

Even before his ascension to the throne, while still king of Naples, Charles had recognized the necessity of ecclesiastical reform. He sought to purge the clergy of those members not performing the necessary duties of conferring the sacraments and advancing the faith. In keeping with Bourbon notions of modernization of urban environments, Charles had cemeteries moved from church grounds to unpopulated areas outside of town centers. This had two positive effects in the eyes of reformers: It reduced the sacred nature of church grounds, diminishing their status as holy sites in and of themselves, and refocusing their role as the locus of the teaching and practice of doctrine. It also furthered Bourbon public health initiatives by reducing the risks then associated with the proximity of corpses. In such ways were Bourbon religious policies connected to a broader enlightenment ideal of modernization, which connected public welfare with good governance.[39]

Within the Church, Charles confronted a specific challenge posed by the regular orders. Royal authority over the Church in the New World was always much stronger over the secular clergy than the orders, and hence the crown had favored the secular church throughout the colonial era. The regular orders, on the other hand, had become semi-autonomous instruments of local rule, and represented a conflict with Bourbon plans for more centralized control of the empire.[40] The regular church comprised the monastic orders, groups of priests who had sworn additional vows to follow the *regula* (rules) of their founders. Franciscans, Dominicans, Augustinians, and Jesuits (after 1540) adhered to vows of poverty, celibacy, and obedience. As such, these monastic orders were well-suited to evangelization missions in the difficult environments of the early colony. As the colonies expanded, the missionary orders frequently led the way, building missions on the unconquered frontiers. The secular clergy, who had taken no additional vows and lived decidedly less ascetic lives, more frequently occupied the urban centers of the colony, and were typically more receptive to the will of the Spanish monarchs. Charles particularly disliked the Jesuits, which, of the various orders in the Americas, felt least constrained by the royal chain of command, seeing themselves beholden to the Pope rather than Madrid.[41] Since their initial entry into New Spain in 1572, the Jesuits had taken on the role of educators, and were particularly powerful in colonial universities. This tied them closely to wealthy *criollos* who held all but the most powerful positions in colonial society.[42] Additionally, by the eighteenth century, the Jesuits had amassed extensive property holdings in the New World, which, if seized, could provide considerable resources to facilitate the process of reform. In 1767, following a trend initiated in France and Portugal, Charles expelled the Jesuit order from all Spanish territories. Soon thereafter, Charles outlawed the "Jesuit Doctrine." The overwhelming majority of the 678 Jesuits who were expelled from the colonies were themselves *criollos*. Consequently, not only had Charles rid himself of an entirely too autonomous institution within the colonies whose material resources could help advance his reform agenda, he had also whittled away some of the cadre of powerful American-born Spaniards whose allegiance to the crown was always somewhat suspect. Ultimately, these policies successfully brought the Church further under the authority of the crown.[43]

If Charles III saw challenges to royal authority within the colonies, the external threats to the empire were no less serious. When Charles took the throne following the death of his half-brother Ferdinand VI, he was immediately confronted with the military vulnerability of Spain's American holdings. For the previous two centuries, the colonies had been largely immune to significant predation from other European powers. Before the eighteenth century, occasional attacks on Spanish shipping or ports, while costly in the short term, never reached a level that justified significant change to Spain's policy of defending the colonies with a few heavily-armed fortresses and virtually no navy.[44] "By the mid-eighteenth century, however," notes Christon Archer, "the rise of Britain to a position of overall maritime superiority altered the situation. The fortresses of Spanish America were open to siege and possible capture." This possibility was made manifest in Spain's disastrous experience at the end of the Seven Years War (1756–1763).[45] The loss of Havana to 15,000 British troops in the summer of 1762, and the loss of Manila that fall, proved that leaving the colonies dependent on troops deployed from Spain could no longer assure their defense. The capture of Havana, though not wholly unforeseen, sent shockwaves across the ocean and through Madrid. With the loss of the capital of the Caribbean, Veracruz—the conduit for all New Spanish wealth—lay in the direct path of potential British ambitions. So vital was Havana to the empire that Charles III opted to cede Florida to the British to secure the city's return through the 1763 Treaty of Paris. Reinforcement of the recovered port city and expanded defenses for the colonies more broadly began at once.[46] Spain then embarked on a general reconsideration of its military disposition in the colonies. Peninsular regiments were deployed to New Spain as seed forces for a new colonial defense force. Inspector General Juan de Villalba proposed that a new "regiment of the Americas" be raised in Cádiz and filled out by Mexicans.[47] The colonial free-colored militia companies, which had been in service since the seventeenth century, were to be subject to far greater oversight than they had been in the previous decades. Veteran regular army soldiers would now supervise militia training and operation.[48] Naval construction was ramped up, and in little more than a decade following the loss of Havana, Spain added more than fifty fighting vessels to its fleet.[49]

All of these reform efforts, which expanded royal power in the colonies, were tied to and dependent on enhancement of the profitability of Spain's overseas holdings. From the beginning, the Bourbons employed new tactics to increase revenue from the colonies. Limited efforts began as early as the first decades of the eighteenth century, with the licensing of *aguardiente* producers and the restructure of the mercury industry in Peru. However, as with so much else, it was in the era of Charles III that significant change was undertaken in earnest. Charles needed to confront the problems engendered by centuries of poor record keeping, inefficient taxation, tax evasion, foreign incursion through contraband trade, and the simple commercial inadequacy of Spanish transatlantic shipping. Part of this policy was liberalization of trade between Spain and the colonies, allowing numerous Spanish ports to join Cádiz and Seville in their previously exclusive trade with the Americas. These new policies also eased trade restrictions between the colonies themselves. In time, the number of colonial ports open to trade with Spain would increase as well in an effort to reduce the high volume of contraband, which had flourished under restrictive Spanish trade policy.[50] Later, in 1789, the crown further eased trade by abolishing the *flota*, or fleet system, which for two centuries had sacrificed efficient commerce in exchange for security.[51] To address inefficiencies in silver production, Charles cut the cost of mercury and gunpowder, both of which were critical to that industry. The crown additionally lowered taxes on silver in an effort to discourage miners from underreporting production.[52] In 1776 tax collection was taken out of the hands of private individuals and put under the direct administration of state bureaucrats.[53]

Yet, the Bourbon reforms were not driven exclusively by financial interests. Susan Deans-Smith pointed out that, "eighteenth-century Spanish absolutism was about more than raising revenues and armies, however crucial those needs were . . . it combined what has been termed 'welfare' as well as 'warfare' objectives which resulted in increasing attempts to expand the role of the state in people's lives. These were policies influenced by Spain's selective response to the influence of enlightenment thought."[54] In the last half of the eighteenth century, enlightenment ideals were wed to financial control and social order. "Commerce," argued economic historian Ricardo Salvatore, "was conceived . . . as a revitalizing force, and instrument of imperial enhancement."[55] The reform of trade was a tool to achieve both profitability and modernity. In certain areas of commerce, the state would step back to increase the commercial participation of their subjects. This policy would, in theory, bring many subjects, including natives, into modern commercial participation. Trade "was conceived as an instrument of civilization and assimilation."[56] "The Bourbon reformers kept the 'economic' indistinguishable from the 'political' and the 'moral'—defending monarchical power, spreading the Catholic faith, and controlling overseas colonies all belonged to the same field of inquiry, colonial policy."[57] Economic reform was part of a holistic plan to remake the relationship between the crown's subjects and their sovereign.[58]

If freer markets meant modernity in some areas of colonial commerce, its inverse, monopolization was found to be more valuable in others. Entirely *laissez-faire* economics was never a goal of the crown. Rather, where liberalized trade policy could serve the economic development of the colonies in a way that profited the crown, it was embraced; at the same time, the crown was quite comfortable with more restrictive trade when that served the crown's interests. Bourbon reformers felt that certain industries, if put under direct crown authority, could generate greater wealth. In keeping with this idea, numerous colonial industries were monopolized under Bourbon rule. Gunpowder and mercury were monopolized on the basis of their strategic value, while "non-essential" products like tobacco, playing cards, and *aguardiente* were also monopolized and put under the administration of salaried officials.[59] These latter industries were recognized as having enormous profit potential while having no essential benefit to the citizenry, and as such could be justifiably reconfigured as sources of revenue for the state.

Monopolizing tobacco in New Spain was by no means a novel idea. As early as the seventeenth century, monopolization of tobacco was considered as a possible means to cover the increasing costs of governing the colonies.[60] Tobacco monopolies were successfully established in Cuba (1717), Peru (1752), and Chile (1753).[61] In 1721, Viceroy Casafuerte assembled a group to study the potential of monopolizing tobacco in New Spain, but determined at that time that it would be too costly.[62] In 1743, don Francisco Sánchez de Sierra Zagle of Mexico City reported to the viceroy that tobacco was perfect for monopolization, pointing out the great popularity of smoking, and its potential for profit.[63] A survey of the value of the tobacco trade in Mexico five years later found that *puros* (cigars) and *cigarros* (cigarettes), as opposed to *de polvo* (or loose tobacco), sales alone constituted 12,348,000 pesos.[64] Furthermore, Sierra Zagle emphasized in his case for monopolization that tobacco "is not necessary to nourish one, nor preserve life, and is [therefore] a material which is apt for monopolization." He argued that monopolization could in fact be healthful for smokers, as at that point vendors were augmenting lower grade tobacco by "using various ingredients and materials that are very damaging and prejudicial to health." Sometimes producers added wine, lime, chile water, and other materials "that cause notable ravages to the health of those that use them." Beyond the fact that unregulated tobacco was potentially unhealthy, a monopoly on tobacco was morally defensible on the grounds that people could chose to buy tobacco or not; thus, the monopoly would represent a voluntary tax "whose introduction would cause no harm, but instead bring public benefit."[65] In a rather zealous spirit of economic reform, Sierra Zagle actually went so far as to endorse monopolizing "all things that are superfluous and unnecessary for the maintenance of life."[66] A further advantage of monopolizing tobacco would be that it would likely face little challenge as it was generally grown on a small scale. As Susan Deans-Smith points out, tobacco was not a crop that made anyone a fortune. Sale was predominantly conducted by individuals, small shopkeepers, and families.[67] Thus there was no cartel of large producers to oppose government monopolization. It would, however, be another twenty-one years before the royal monopoly came to New Spain.

The creation of the tobacco monopoly (also known as the *estanco* or *renta*) in New Spain finally took place on 13 August 1764. It ultimately would become perhaps the most successful financial reform in the entire colony.[68] When fully in place, it was a system of economic licensing, sales, and taxation that produced more money for the crown than any source besides gold and silver.[69] Initially the new monopoly oversaw and taxed all tobacco sales, and would permit cultivation on a quota basis by licensed growers. Later, the monopoly would expand to control all production of manufactured tobacco goods as well. To facilitate close oversight of cultivation and to maximize efficiency, the monopoly restricted the areas in which growing licenses would be sold. Cultivation of tobacco was permitted only in the areas of Xalapa, Orizaba, and Cordoba. Sale of finished goods was allowed only in licensed *estanquillos* (shops). Production of finished cigars, cigarettes, and other tobacco products was confined to monopoly facilities; these goods were then sold in monopoly-licensed facilities. This system, when fully instituted, put tobacco under the control of the state from seedling to finished product. Tobacco manufactories were located in cities, where they served as employment opportunities for the urban poor, particularly women. Deans-Smith noted that tobacco manufactories provided a civilizing effect in the opinion of reformers by helping ensure that women were employed in "appropriate work," where they were engaged in delicate artisanry, as opposed to men, who contemporaries felt were better placed outdoors in more laborious occupations.[70] The monopoly was both an economic scheme and a manifestation of absolutist rule and enlightenment philosophy, meant to bring modern commerce and good governance to backward people.[71]

Although the monopoly served its function by creating substantial revenues for the crown, and by forging a much more intense relationship between planters, manufactory workers, and the state, it did not fulfill Sierra Zagle's promise to cause "no harm." From its inception in 1764 and for decades thereafter, it would be the cause of recurrent conflict in New Spain. These difficulties should have come as no surprise, for in 1743, don Juan de Rodezno strongly rebuked the severity of Sierra Zagle's original proposal to monopolize tobacco, arguing that for many the production of cigars and cigarettes at home was their only means of making enough money to survive. Should the monopoly be put in place without great care, it would "in reality be the monopolization of the work and industry of these craftspeople."[72] It would thus cause great disruption to the public good. Indeed, an eight-member panel convened in Mexico City to review Rodezno's denunciation of the proposed monopoly was quite sympathetic to the conditions of the poor, and decided that monopolizing tobacco would ultimately enrich a few at the cost of the poor. Rolling cigarettes and cigars, the panel concluded, was often a vital source of work for poor women and widows, and monopolizing that industry would close off a necessary means of survival. So too would all those who grew the crop be "gravely burdened."[73] Two decades later, when the monopoly was put in place in New Spain, the occupational needs of poor women, at least in the large urban areas, appears to have been considered, as the manufactories would employ women primarily. Yet the grave burdens would remain. In 1767, Sebastian Calvo de la Puerta, minister of the Royal Junta of Tobacco, noted in a proposal to improve the enforcement and profitability of the monopoly, sent to the viceroy, don Carlos Francisco de Croix: "It is certain that bunches of tobacco are the vice and passion of the natives of this kingdom."[74]

The prohibition of production in all areas outside the zones ordained by the crown alienated those who were excluded from the tobacco business. While it was highly profitable, the monopoly failed to reach a capacity sufficient to meet demand, causing frustration among consumers.[75] By centralizing production, the monopoly imposed upon itself logistical challenges that it could not always meet. The shipment of raw tobacco and paper for cigarettes to manufacturing facilities was subject to all of the vagaries and difficulties of eighteenth-century transportation. Paper for cigarettes was not manufactured in New Spain, and thus had to be imported and then transshipped overland from Veracruz.[76] Poor roads and weather hampered delivery of both raw and finished material, and even the mules needed for transportation were subject to occasional scarcity. The renta was frequently unable to assure consistent supplies.[77] Consumers faced increased costs and inconsistent and often poor quality product, all of which fostered a resentment of the monopoly.[78] That same resentment appeared among those who had previously grown tobacco and they protested "against the tobacco monopoly with its prohibition against free cultivation."[79]

Immediately upon its creation, it was clear to crown officials that the monopoly might face resistance from growers. Early on, the crown enacted strong legislation against any contraband sales or cultivation. A 9 October, 1765, order by Viceroy don Juachín Montserrat published the seriousness with which the crown intended deal with violators, stating,

> All noncompliant: illegal sellers of any class, state, or quality, as well as those who cultivate tobacco plants on their lands, shall be severely punished in the manner of defrauders and will give cause to the King to use his supreme authority, and his Judges are ordered to confiscate the associated lands . . . [80]

To ensure that these rules would be observed, Montserrat gave the monopoly great authority over both enforcement and prosecution. In December of that same year Montserrat issued judge don Jacinto Martínez de Concha orders granting him, his lieutenants, and his deputies specific authority for "the apprehension of delinquents" who contravened tobacco laws.[81] Martínez de Concha and his delegates were to be considered as having all the authority of any other judge or justice of the kingdom and were not to be obstructed "for any pretext, [in] the execution of their charge." They were to be "granted all aid and support that they need[ed] to this end, under pain of the viceroy's discretion."[82] However, repeated publication of the punishments that awaited offenders demonstrates that the monopoly found the problem of illegal production to be unrelenting. Contraband production, despite aggressive efforts to curb it, continued nonetheless.

In 1768, Viceroy don Carlos Francisco de Croix laid out thirty-seven rules to govern the prosecution of tobacco fraud. The proclamation stressed that cases were to be dealt with rapidly, preferably from denunciation to sentencing in no more than one month. The accused should have all of their properties frozen for the duration of the case. In the case of conviction, the *contrabandista* was to be ordered to pay double the amount of the contraband tobacco they were convicted of producing, distributing, or selling. In addition, they had to pay for the cost of the trial. Prices were set at 2.25 *reales* per pound for leaf tobacco, six *reales* per pound of snuff, and half a real for each individual cigar or cigarette. Beyond that, any lands related to the violation could be confiscated. If the violator were not able to produce the value of the fine, they were to face corporal punishment.[83] In a 1770 addendum to these regulations, Indians were exempted from pecuniary fines on the assumption that they could only rarely pay, but instead were to uniformly face corporal punishment— a concession of dubious mercy. The level of penalty also increased with the severity of the infraction.[84] The 1768 *bando* stipulated that in cases of recidivism, punishments should be increased. If the *contrabandista* resisted apprehension with arms they were to be given 200 lashes, and four years in the *presidio* (military fort). If the resistance caused damages or injury, the death penalty could be imposed.[85] The monopoly administrators clearly understood that violation of the monopoly legislation was a significant vulnerability and hence chose to show that they were ready to deal harshly with anyone who threatened the monopoly's success.

To enforce these regulations, the crown established an independent policing body, the *resguardo de tabaco* (tobacco guard) in 1768, tasked with seeking out and destroying illegal tobacco plots.[86] Tobacco patrols would make expeditions into the countryside, hunting contraband tobacco plots. They would note the owner of the plot, their marital status, and spouse's name. At each find they would list the number of plants found and record that the plants were destroyed. Frequently the *resguardo* would use captured contrabandists to turn over evidence of other frauds; prisoners would sometimes be kept in custody until they revealed the location of another plot, and only then be set free. Otherwise they were often turned over to the local *alcalde mayor* or the *gobernador* of the jurisdiction for punishment. In this respect, the *resguardo* was less an investigative and punitive body than a stopgap against intrusions into the legal tobacco market. Despite the highly specific nature of punishments laid out by the monopoly, the *resguardo* often imposed penalties disproportionate to the offense, including the seizure of personal possessions unrelated to the offense. Sometimes the penalties were considerably more severe.[87] The *resguardo* became a common focus of criticism. According to Deans-Smith, "it was without a doubt an institution that provoked controversy, fear, and hatred, particularly among Indian communities and small farmers that scratched out a subsistence living by selling tobacco."[88]

For the Totonac of Papantla, this resentment was born of the fact that Papantla fell outside the zones of legal cultivation, and that that method of scratching out a living was no longer permitted. At a stroke, a traditional means of subsistence commerce had been criminalized. Since time immemorial, the Papantla Totonac had used tobacco both to supply personal need and as a means to augment income through sale. Tobacco was a family-grown crop not unlike other staples. It had been incorporated into the domestic economies of families and was thus as important to family survival, in some ways, as maize. It was a source of income that was used to purchase household necessities and foods that supplemented a generally protein-poor diet. This crop had long been necessary to Totonac survival, not to mention tradition. Yet the Spanish began early on to consider the value of usurping this area of production. As early as the beginning of the seventeenth century, the region around Papantla was identified as a source of commercial exploitation in the region.[89] In 1688, at the behest of the Papantla curate, the *alcalde mayor* of Papantla and his lieutenant were severely rebuked and fined for trying to force the natives into a tobacco *repartimiento* (forced sale and purchase of goods). The curate noted that for the natives of Papantla, cultivating tobacco was essential to "sustain them, and their women and children." [90] In 1709, another *alcalde mayor* in Papantla apparently tried again to enforce a *repartimiento* on tobacco, threatening the natives with whippings and imprisonment if they did not sell him their harvests.[91] Having apparently begun to harvest his own tobacco, in 1712 Papantla's then *alcalde mayor* Don Vicente Adel, was charged with forcing the natives to transport his tobacco without compensation.[92] For the natives of the Papantla region, whether spiritual, financial, or possibly addictive, dependence on the crop was a reality. Prohibition of tobacco's cultivation was thus a double burden. When cultivation was outlawed, tobacco then needed to be purchased. The Totonac lost a means of augmenting their income and had to expend part of their dwindling earnings to purchase it from the monopoly. Consequently in Papantla contraband was rampant from the outset. In October 1776, Viceroy don Juan de Gálvez authorized the creation of a *resguardo* troop specifically for Papantla and environs.[93] José Enrique Covarrubias contends that as prices involved in cultivating tobacco increased during the last half of the eighteenth century and remuneration from the government stayed the same, it became impossible to avoid the dual problems of inattentive farming by monopoly-sanctioned growers, which led to decreased tobacco quality, and increasing contraband production.[94]

Georgina Moreno Coello argues that contraband cultivation endured in the jurisdiction of Papantla in part as a result of official complicity. Certainly clandestine tobacco plots never ceased to be a continuous feature of the Papantla landscape. Yet enforcement of the monopoly was, of necessity, poor. In need of tribute payments, *alcaldes mayores* frequently turned a blind eye to contraband tobacco production lest their tributaries be unable to pay. Moreno Coello has detailed the complicity of Spanish magistrates in Papantla's contraband cultivation. When the *resguardo* would turn over a prisoner to the *alcalde mayor*, he would often release the prisoner after extracting a bribe, disregarding the punitive measures demanded and repeatedly published by the crown. In 1777, the *resguardo* accused the *alcalde mayor* don Manuel Cornejo of Papantla of openly protecting contraband tobacco growers.[95] Later, in 1799, similar complaints would be lodged against the *subdelegado* (whose office had replaced that of the *alcalde mayor*).[96] This negligence not only ignored statutory responsibilities, but also flew in the face of the new Bourbon tax policy that stressed a renewed vigor for tribute collection.[97] In addition, the poorly organized nature of the *resguardo* contributed to the animosity felt by the populace toward the monopoly.[98] In one case in July 1776, various members of the infantry and dragoons of Mexico were themselves charged with tobacco contraband.[99] This inadequacy of the tobacco monopoly enforcement also heightened the distaste for the monopoly and *resguardo*. Because years could pass between the local rounds of the *resguardo*, the natives could not budget for what was a randomly manifest risk.[100] It was possible to successfully pass a season without being caught by the *resguardo*. Hence natives of Papantla continued to invest time and money into the production of tobacco. In 1783, the *justicias* of nearby Huachinango and Teziutlan complained to the *justicia* of Papantla that the tobacco guard frequently had to return through the area to burn illegal tobacco plants. This occurred despite the fact that the prohibition of cultivation had been repeatedly published with descriptions of penalties for transgression.[101] On an excursion between 14 February and 6 March 1791, the *resguardo* stationed at Zacatlan de Manzana, just west of the Papantla jurisdiction, found and destroyed 22,639 plants.[102] During a two-month expedition later in 1791, the Papantla *resguardo* found and destroyed another 47,679 illegal plants in thirty-three separate raids.[103] Moreno Coello suggests that in 1791 only 30 percent of violators were arrested.[104] In 1797, *resguardo* troops took canoes up the Tecolutla River and raided tobacco farms run by one Juan Señor, his son Antonio, and other Totonacs.[105] Clearly contraband never ceased for the Totonac, who found exclusion from tobacco production an impossible regulation to comply with. The Papantla Totonac maintained their dependence on the crop after monopolization, but they did so under the shadow of possible destruction of an entire season's work.

Conclusion

For the natives of Papantla, the creation of the tobacco monopoly signified the development of a new point of conflict with the colonial authorities. In late 1764 or early 1765, when the tobacco monopoly conducted its first operation in Papantla, natives turned to arson. This event marked the beginning of a friction between Papantla natives and the local rule that never ended. As Alejandra Palacios Sanchez has pointed out, this reform "coincided with a sharp increase in Totonac social protest."[106] The Papantla Totonac never admitted direct opposition to this policy, even going so far as to say the fires that natives started at the creation of the monopoly were not in opposition to this new institution. At the same time, an enduring sense of injustice at the prohibition of tobacco cultivation persisted in this community. Felipe Castro Gutierrez has contended that the Bourbon reforms in their various manifestations imposed new tensions that pre-existing systems of negotiation could no longer accommodate.[107] Similarly, Michael Ducey identified a cluster of uprisings in communities around the Huasteca that occurred in correlation with the imposition of new Bourbon reforms.[108]

Contraband cultivation continued in Papantla, and many Totonac became criminals simply by maintaining traditional agricultural practice. For the Totonac of Papantla, the tobacco monopoly was simply an unjust constraint on their economic and cultural traditions, and in this context clandestine violation of the monopoly was morally justified. As Moreno Coello has pointed out, the very persistence of contraband cultivation in Papantla suggests that the natives felt that transgressing this rule was "just and legitimate."[109] This persistent violation also demonstrates the importance of this crop in local native survival.[110] The monopoly was a success for the crown. It produced enormous revenues for the *real hacienda* (royal treasury). But this crown perspective obscures the fact that in the case of tobacco, increased crown revenue represented decreased income for poor small-scale producers. As the crown responded to grave concerns about finances and control of its colonies it created systems that served to aid in administrative and financial efficiency for the crown. Yet it did so at the cost of local stability. The initial outburst of 1765 was the only time that the Totonacs of Papantla actually destroyed the tobacco warehouse. But with the increased financial strain imposed by the presence of the monopoly, the Papantla Totonac would lose their tolerance for local threats to their autonomy and economic viability. Decades later they would still be directing anger toward the tobacco monopoly, and so too would they continuously violate the prohibition against growing tobacco. According to Moreno Coello, "clandestine cultivation of tobacco should be seen as a form of active resistance that could easily transform into violent reaction."[111]

The uprising of 1765 was not exclusively caused by the creation of the monopoly. Witnesses suggest that other conditions of strain, such as political dispute over the leadership of the town were involved in the unrest of 1765. Furthermore, as will be detailed in the following chapter, Totonac animosity toward exploitation by the *alcalde mayor* was a persistent cause of tension in this community. However, the first act of the monopoly as executed by the *alcalde mayor* don Manuel Chacon was the proximate cause of this outburst, no matter what additional animosities motivated the rioters. More importantly, this initial outburst marked the beginning of a shift in the posture of the Totonac of Papantla vis-à-vis local rule. We have seen that following 1765, the monopoly was a persistent source of frustration for the residents of this town. That frustration, the threat of prosecution, and the financial difficulty generated by the monopoly would lead the Totonac of Papantla to become much more ready to deploy violence as a tool over the course the next twenty-two years. The monopoly had changed the parameters of how power would be contested in this community.

CHAPTER

FIVE

"Kill That Dog of an *Alcalde Mayor*": *Repartimientos* and Uprising in 1767

Two years after the unrest discussed in the Chapter Four, violence again broke out in Papantla. Three times in 1767 the Totonac community rose up in riot, with the last uprising occurring in October. In this chapter we will consider the October uprising, and see that while the trigger for the event appears quite clear—the extradition of a Totonac prisoner from Papantla to Mexico City—a more complex discontent fueled the upheaval that resulted. By 1767, the Papantla Totonac had become frustrated with conditions in the town. They felt badly treated by the *alcalde mayor*, who had prohibited trade with outside communities, making himself the exclusive customer and vendor for various goods. This practice, by which local officials monopolized trade with the natives, was quite common throughout Spanish America during the entire colonial era; known as the *repartimiento de mercancías*, it had been practiced in Papantla for generations. But in 1767, it appears that the *repartimiento* had become something that the Papantla Totonac could no longer bear. Totonac testimony reads as though witnesses considered official questioning as an opportunity to get long-standing frustrations with the *alcalde mayor*, don Alonzo de la Barga, off their chests. Of course, since the testimony was recorded after a significant violation of the law, the Totonac may have felt the need to paint the *alcalde mayor* as an unjust man to avoid appearing unjust themselves. Yet the number of witnesses who complained of repeated economic exploitation by de la Barga lends credence to the notion that the *alcalde mayor* had for some time been pushing the Totonac into conditions they found intolerable, and that the extradition of Nicolas Olmos was simply the last straw that justified an outburst of pent-up anger. This conflict was triggered by a violation of the Papantla Totonac's sense of just administration on the part of the *alcalde mayor*. At the same time, Papantla's changing economic conditions in the wake of the tobacco monopoly's creation contributed to the discontent that would lead the local populace to violence.

The October Revolt of 1767

Dramatis Personae

don Alonzo de la Barga	Spanish *alcalde mayor* of Papantla
Joseph Juárez	Totonac insurgent
don Miguel Márquez	Curate of Papantla
Nicolas Olmos (alias Capa)	Totonac prisoner
don Placido Pérez	Captain of Papantla militia
don Francisco Ramírez	Spaniard, Lieutenant of Papantla militia
María Sánchez	Totonac insurgent

Witnesses

don Nicolas Andrade	Spanish merchant
don Domingo Blas Bazaras	Judge of the Real Audiencia of Manila
don Martin Gamboa	Spaniard, of Navarra
Gaspar García	Totonac, ladino, drummer for the Papantla militia
Lazaro Gonzales	Information unknown
don Thomas Mendez	Totonac *gobernador*
Nicolas Nava	Totonac, former *gobernador*
don Andrés Antonio Patiño	Spanish resident of Papantla
Nicolas Sánchez	Totonac resident of Papantla
Manuel Santiago	Totonac resident of Papantla
Miguel Santos	Totonac resident of Papantla
don Domingo JuanUgarte	Spanish lieutenant *alcalde mayor*
Antonio Uribe	Interpreter and witness

At 5:00 a.m. on 17 October 1767, an hour and a half before dawn, four mulatto soldiers of the Papantla militia went to the local jail bearing sealed documents destined for the *real audiencia* (superior court) in Mexico City.[1] At the jail, they collected their other package for the audiencia, a Totonac resident of Papantla named Nicolas de Olmos, alias "Capa." Olmos had been arrested two weeks before for repeatedly inciting riots in Papantla—two earlier that same year.[2] The *alcalde mayor* of Papantla, don Alonso de la Barga, had decided the previous day to remand Olmos to the superior court in the capital because the Papantla jail was

constructed simply of cane and hay and was thus insecure; it had been burned twice that year during the riots attributed to Olmos.[3] It is also likely that the *alcalde mayor* felt that Olmos's continued presence in the town constituted a persistent threat of additional unrest. De la Barga could hardly have been unaware that many natives in the town held animosity toward him. As Totonac resident Gaspar García would later testify about de la Barga, "Everyone is disgusted with him for the various things he has done."[4] De la Barga's fear of unrest would turn out to be well-founded.

In the predawn light of that Saturday morning, the militia soldiers prepared Olmos for travel, placing him in leg shackles and handcuffs. They then led him out of the building. As Olmos was led outside he began to cry out, alerting the Totonac community that he was being moved. Without pausing, the guard force promptly started out on their journey to the capital. As the guards hurried Olmos out of town toward the distant capital, church bell began to ring behind them;[5] native women had begun throwing rocks at the bell to sound the alarm.[6] Totonac voices could be heard yelling, "Come! Come! Join together!"[7]

With the church bells fading behind them, the militia troop headed west. However, they had not gotten far before natives began catching up with them. Natives from all districts of the town began to form up, following the small company. Within half an hour, a great number of Totonac men and women had overtaken with party, bent on stopping the extradition of the prisoner. The mob harassed the troops, and attempted to surround Olmos, as the militia resolutely tried to continue their mission.[8] The militia and their charge ultimately made it as far as the Rancho Rincón, a hacienda several miles from town on the road to Puebla, when the advancing mob became so threatening that the guards were forced to seek shelter within the hacienda's confines.[9] Whatever shelter the hacienda could afford, it was not enough to hold off the mob, and there they wrested Olmos from his captors. With Olmos in tow, they headed back to town, where they removed his shackles, and then set out in search of the *alcalde mayor*.

Upon hearing of the mob's return, *alcalde mayor* de la Barga fled, in the words of one witness, with "the courage of children," to the house of the militia captain, don Placido Pérez, adjacent to Papantla's central plaza.[10] The militia captain was not at home. He and "the major part of the [town's] Spaniards and other gente de razón," had been out of town for the week at the fisheries on the Tecolutla River.[11] Fortunately for de la Barga, Pérez's lieutenant, don Francisco Ramírez, was residing in the compound. Lieutenant Ramírez came to de la Barga's aid, lifting the *alcalde mayor* into Pérez's residence through the kitchen window. But this was of little consolation to de la Barga. According to the *alcalde mayor*, all that remained to defend him and the town were lieutenant Ramírez and six old Spaniards.[12] The native pursuers had a suspicion about where the *alcalde mayor* had sought shelter and headed toward the militia captain's compound. According to the *alcalde mayor*, they were bearing bows and arrows, machetes, and numerous firearms.[13] The Totonac mob was calling out to "kill him, kill that dog of an *alcalde mayor*."[14] The mob next tried to enter the Pérez compound, but found it locked.[15] Frustrated, they threw stones and burning embers at the four buildings that made up compound, and managed to ignite at least two cane-built structures, which subsequently burned to the ground. Fearing that the natives might storm the house, one of Captain Pérez's servants, an unnamed Totonac woman, helped hide the *alcalde mayor* in the kitchen, inside a reed sack (*bolsa de petate*).[16] Testimony by a number of witnesses claimed that the crowd sought the *alcalde mayor* solely to learn why he was sending Olmos away to Mexico. Some had heard that the *alcalde mayor's* intention was to sell the prisoner in Mexico City.[17] The *alcalde mayor*, however, insisted that the mob wanted nothing less than his life. It is worth noting that the testimony about this event falls into two categories, which are mutually exclusive. The testimony of the *alcalde mayor* paints the actions of the rioters as unrestrainedly malevolent, while at each crucial moment of the uprising, other witnesses claim much more benign behavior on the part of the rioters. Of particular significance is the fact that two of those witnesses who supported de la Barga's testimony were a current and former *gobernador* of the *cabildo*, each of whom included very specific indictments of other powerful members of the Totonac community. Thus, the testimony of what happened in October 1767 becomes as much evidence of a division within the community as it is any kind of factual accounting of the uprising.

When the insurgents failed to find the *alcalde mayor*, they turned their attentions instead to the jail, which they emptied of all of the remaining prisoners. According to the *alcalde mayor*, who was still hiding in don Placido Pérez's kitchen, at this point a certain Totonac, Joseph Juárez, took the *bara y baston* (legal symbols of judicial authority) from the *casas reales* and paraded through town claiming,

> I am the king and I am he who gives the orders, and governs. No one has to fear, but do what I say, because I will kill those who don't. I have this staff, and with this I govern.[18]

The native *gobernador*, don Thomas Mendez corroborated the *alcalde's* claim, as did Nicolas Nava, described as "indio principal," and who had been *gobernador* twice before. These two witnesses' testimony agrees so completely as to suggest collusion.[19] The claim that Juarez proclaimed himself king is strongly contradicted by several other witnesses, including Totonac resident Manuel Santiago, who claimed that native leaders Juan García and Joseph Simbron simply collected the instruments of office and placed them protectively in the *casas reales*.

Santiago added that he never saw Juárez touch the *bara y baston*.[20] *Alcalde mayor* de la Barga, on the other hand, saw calculated malice, contending that not only did Juárez usurp authority, but also that he then went on to break open sealed court documents, including some pertaining to Olmos's case.[21]

At dusk that day, de la Barga claimed that about a thousand Totonac led by Joseph Juárez and others gathered in the plaza mayor.[22] Accounts by other witnesses vary as to the size and actions of the crowd, especially between testimonials made by Totonac witnesses and that of the *alcalde mayor* himself, but the fact that the crowd was large, and included both native men and women is attested by several reports. Additionally, at least three native witnesses reiterated the charge that the insurgents who gathered that evening were bearing flintlock muskets.[23] On this evening, the natives again turned their attention to the Pérez compound. They placed sentries around don Placido Pérez's houses and corrals. As per the testimony of the *alcalde mayor*, they had resolved to recommence their attack, massing outside the compound armed with rocks, bows and arrows, and machetes. They insisted that de la Barga be brought out to them. The occupants of the compound refused to turn over the *alcalde mayor*, but eventually the crowd managed to break through the fencing of the Pérez compound and searched the interior for the *alcalde mayor*. Fortunately for the besieged de la Barga, still concealed in his reed sack, the search proved fruitless.[24]

At about 8:00 p.m. that night, other Spanish officials of the town found the local curate, don Miguel Márquez, in the church, located on the corner of the plaza adjacent to the Pérez compound, and led him out into the plaza bearing a crucifix. The officials hoped that the power of the curate's position could calm the mob's rage just as it had done during the 1736 uprising. Here again the accounts of the uprising differ considerably between witnesses. In the *alcalde mayor's* version of the event, the natives took no heed of the curate, and performed none of the rituals of respect due the priest or the crucifix. Rather, they turned to Márquez and, without doffing their hats or kneeling before the cross, they said, "We are here on business. Take the priest and that cross back into the church."[25] Without further concern for the holy man or holy objects, they resumed their search of the town for the *alcalde mayor* and anyone who opposed them. They then stationed sentries throughout the town, prohibiting anyone from leaving. Both the town officials and the mob were aware that there was no organized group available to defend the town. They knew that the as yet unmustered militia was insufficiently armed, lacking gunpowder. Thus the insurgents freely controlled Papantla. Reporting the event to the viceroy, the *alcalde mayor* noted that, "Miraculously, I survived. But I did get a wound on my leg from a thrown rock" (at what point in the conflict he received this injury is not made clear). His plight continued through the night and into the following morning. At dawn the following day, Sunday, October 18, the town bells rang again. De la Barga claimed that this was a signal to the rioters to regroup and continue their atrocities.[26]

The testimony of several witnesses paints a very different picture of the events of the evening of Saturday October 17 and morning of Sunday October 18. Many native witnesses claimed that when the curate came out of the church bearing the crucifix, the natives responded with respect and obedience. According to the testimony of Totonac Manuel Santiago, who testified through a translator, at the sight of the curate in the door of the church, all of the natives took off their hats and knelt before the sacred symbol, demonstrating the proper obeisance to these representations of the Church. They then retired to their homes, only returning to the plaza for church services at the sound of the ringing bells on Sunday morning.[27] It is quite possible that while some participants saw the appearance of the priest as cause to retire for the evening, others remained in the plaza. However events actually unfolded over the night of the seventeenth to the eighteenth, the next morning finally brought relief for the embattled *alcalde mayor*.

On that Sunday morning, captain don Placido Pérez returned with his cadre from the fisheries on the Tecolutla River. With this group he was able to call together the mulatto militia, who had otherwise been spread around the area in their homes and fields. "Thanks to God," claimed the *alcalde mayor*, "I was able to remain hidden in the house of Captain don Placido until the major part of the troop could form up."[28] With the muster of the militia troop, the major demonstration of this uprising came to an end. However, de la Barga claimed that strong control of the town by Spanish authorities was not established for another week. Thus, de la Barga remained in the house of Pérez until the following Sunday, when the *bara y baston* were finally recovered.[29]

The Aftermath of the October 1767 Revolt

On October 25, a week after the uprising, *alcalde mayor* de la Barga had the militia troops form up under the royal standard and quartered them in the *casa real*. Being a Sunday, most if not all the natives of the area could be expected to crowd into the plaza for required church services. The frightened *alcalde mayor* considered that any gathering of the natives in town constituted a threat with potential for further unrest. Whether as a result of de la Barga's show of force, or because the populace was satisfied, no further conflict arose that Sunday. However, all was not calm. Even after restoring order to the town, the *alcalde mayor* found that the leaders of the native *cabildo* were too afraid of possible native backlash to show public support for the Spanish officialdom. De La Barga claimed that this trepidation resulted from blanket death threats made by insurgents during the uprising against anyone who showed support for the *alcalde mayor*. A week after the event, de la Barga still feared that the militia force was insufficient to stop the rebels from additional scheming.

The *alcalde mayor* wrote to the viceroy that no force in any of the surrounding towns was up to adequate fighting strength. The local militia was poor, short on weapons, and, more pointedly, the majority were related through marriage to the Totonac residents they were supposed to oppose. Opposing this ill-equipped force was, according to the *alcalde mayor*, a native force that allegedly held no less than 150 guns and had access to gunpowder.[30] De la Barga asked the viceroy to place a force of twenty-five veterans in Papantla, at least until such time as all the rebels could be punished. Without a much stronger veteran force in the town, claimed de la Barga, "these insolent Indians will prevent us from administering justice. They will kill us all, and even the priest will not be saved."[31] To clarify that additional troops would be in the viceroy's interest as well as his own, de la Barga made sure to note that, "I can see that your sovereignty was violated."[32] It is not clear if the veteran force was in fact deployed to Papantla, but within six weeks order was restored to the degree that a full inquest could begin, and on 29 October 1767 a criminal investigation commenced, with *alcalde mayor* de la Barga giving the first testimony. That investigation would reveal the breadth of discontentment that pervaded much of the local Totonac populace.

The *Repartimientos* in Papantla

No matter the contradictions in witness testimony, the proximate cause of the October 1767 uprising was clearly the extradition of Nicolas Olmos. Having established this fact, investigation of the conditions within Papantla prior to the uprising helps to explain how the level of Totonac discontent reached the point that an event such as the extradition could trigger violence in the population. Unlike the obvious economic threat presented by the creation of the tobacco monopoly, the extradition of Olmos does not readily appear as a threat to the economic viability of the Totonac. I argue that the extradition of Olmos was an insult to the Papantla Totonac sense of just rule, but it was merely the latest among a series perceived abuses by the *alcalde mayor*, particularly his use of the *repartimiento*. Though exploitative *alcaldes mayores* were nothing new in Papantla in 1767, what constituted tolerable exploitation, and hence just rule in Papantla, had shifted in the wake of the introduction of the tobacco monopoly. Both of the uprisings that Olmos was credited with inciting earlier in the year were fueled by Totonac concerns about the *alcalde mayor's* monopolization of commerce in the town. By apparently removing a mouthpiece for opposition to his edicts, he was tipping what had become a fine balance between tolerable and intolerable exploitation of the Papantla Totonac. A Spanish resident of Papantla, don Andrés Antonio Patiño, noted in his testimony about the uprising that in recent years the natives had become more insolent, repeatedly burning the *casas reales* and the jail.[33] Taking Olmos away to the distant capital was more than simply an unjustified punishment for a demonstrator who had been articulating Totonac disapproval of the *alcalde mayor's* behavior. Like the residents of native communities across the colonies, the Totonac of Papantla had never wanted for reasons to be frustrated with local Spanish magistrates, but in the new Bourbon, post-tobacco-era Papantla, this most recent challenge to their ability to voice opposition exceeded local endurance. After 1765, the Papantla Totonac were suffering a new commercial restriction imposed by the crown. This restriction altered the calculus of acceptable economic exploitation by the local Spanish magistrate, and hence restructured the local moral economy and changed how rule in the community would be negotiated. Prior to the 1760s, the *repartimiento* had been a constant burden, but an endurable one. However, when the monopoly removed an important means of generating income, the routine burden imposed by the *repartimiento* became proportionally more severe. The level of discontent within the community grew. The monopoly was a crown institution, yet the Totonac could no more attack the crown than they could conquer Spain itself. In addition, the crown held a perceived legitimacy. Crown-caused problems were beyond redress, but local issues were, quite literally, within a stone's throw of the angry local population.

Much of that anger centered on Totonac distaste for the *repartimiento*. Native witnesses to the 1767 event repeatedly complained about aggressive *repartimiento* exploitation by de la Barga, which had come to challenge the traditional norms of life in Papantla and put a strain on the household economies of the Totonac. The population of Papantla had long been subject to the common risks of any colonial agricultural town: crop failure, hunger, epidemics, poor markets, and the excessive demands of Spanish officials.[34] Throughout the colonial era, Spanish officials profited from their positions in the New World colonies through both legal and extralegal institutions, and common among those was the *repartimiento*. In the broadest sense, the term *repartimiento* refers to mechanisms of exploiting native populations for labor or direct commercial gain. The first and most common form of the *repartimiento* was the labor draft, in which natives were required to give poorly-compensated labor to local Spanish officials. This system had initially been part of the *encomienda* grants given to the conquistadors as part of their compensation packages for expanding the empire. *Encomenderos* were granted control of the tribute, both material and physical, of native communities within their *encomienda*. The delivery of native laborers was orchestrated through the native *cabildo*, and that labor was to be used for public works projects, such as the construction of aqueducts, churches, monasteries, roads, or government buildings. Native labor was also essential to mining operations and agricultural production. In theory these labors were beneficial to either the wellbeing of individual natives or to the empire as a whole. It was not slavery, as it was both paid and temporary. Yet it was obligatory, and the pay was decidedly poor. Additionally, at no time was the system free of abuse. *Encomenderos* quickly chose to consider the construction of their own estates as projects of public interest, justifying the use of *repartimiento* labor for aims not specifically sanctioned by the crown. So too did lesser officials, such as *alcaldes mayores*, come to avail themselves of this opportunity to force community members to serve their own personal economic aims. *Alcaldes mayores* would frequently employ the *repartimiento* to force community members to transport their own commercial goods to neighboring communities or distant markets. Such demands were not only badly undercompensated, but for the Totonac of Papantla, as in many other communities, the *alcalde mayor's* commerce interfered with their own. Eighteenth-century accounts from Papantla cite frequent complaints by natives about commercial restrictions by various *alcaldes mayores*.[35] During the period between 1709 and 1787, the Totonac *cabildo* of Papantla lodged no less than eight formal complaints against *alcaldes mayores* for imposition of *repartimientos*. These included the forced sale of vanilla, tobacco, fruit, and the rental of mules. In 1688, Papantla residents sent several protests to the bishop in Puebla seeking relief from *repartimiento* demands made by the *alcalde mayor* and his lieutenant.[36] The *alcalde mayor* had been compelling the Totonac to sell their produce to him at unfair prices. The church authorities sided with the petitioners. They specifically noted that the *repartimiento* on tobacco was damaging to the native community, as the natives "cultivate [tobacco] in their *milpas* in order to sustain their women and children, and to pay their tribute, because they lack other fruits with which to do it," and added that, "nor should the *alcalde mayor* or his lieutenants conduct other similar extortions against the natives."[37] The bishopric of Puebla recognized the potential damage inherent in the *repartimiento* and the tendency of alcaldes to employ tactics akin to "extortion" in their efforts to turn a profit.

The *repartimiento de mercancías* was a system by which a Spanish magistrate (typically the *alcalde mayor*) would force natives to sell the fruits of their production to him. He would also often prohibit the sale of goods to anyone other than himself. The magistrate would pay for this produce in advance at prices substantially discounted from prevailing rates. The magistrate could then resell these goods outside the community at a substantial profit.[38] This system most commonly involved prepayment by the *alcalde mayor* for the later purchase of a given type of produce. In this respect, the *repartimiento* was a loan that provided ready cash to native producers well in advance of the harvest. However, the *alcalde mayor's* profit derived from the below market cost at which he purchased the crop, thus limiting the value of production for the native grower. Furthermore, the *alcalde mayor* frequently demanded, rather than offered, participation.

The corollary to forced sale of native goods was the forced purchase of goods by the natives from Spanish officials, again at prices set by the officials. These practices, regularly combined and obviously exploitative, were the means by which Spanish officials could recoup the costs of the purchase of their office, to say nothing of making a considerable profit.[39] Such exploitation was in clear violation of the intention of *repartimiento* laws created in the wake of the conquest, which had been meant to ensure the availability of native labor to build the essential infrastructure of colonization. Such penurious exploitation of the natives drew fire from those who felt a responsibility to defend them from ambitious colonizers. The ill effects of over-exploitation of native communities had been plainly shown in the first generations of conquest, and the New Laws of 1542 were a clear demonstration that the crown found it essential to interpose laws between the native population and rapacious conquistadors. Historian Ernest Sánchez Santiró described the system as "located on the fringes of legality, in that the crown issued numerous edicts (1551, 1563, 1578, 1584) prohibiting *alcaldes mayores* from participating in the *repartimientos*."[40] And Charles Gibson noted that "the *repartimiento* system of the late sixteenth century was everywhere one of compulsion and abuse, and it received continuous criticism from the clergy."[41] Indeed the crown itself was ambivalent about the *repartimientos*. At no time did it crack down on this form of native exploitation to the degree that legislation actually curtailed its usage in any meaningful way. To the extent that *repartimiento* exploitation did decrease in New Spain by the eighteenth century, it appears to have been as much the result of native population recovery and their engagement in voluntary wage labor as it was the consequence of legal prohibition.[42] The crown was clearly sympathetic to the argument that the *repartimientos*, for better or worse, served the colonial economy. In 1731, *repartimientos* were legalized in Yucatan. Supporters argued that *repartimientos* were the only way to get natives to enter into the colonial economy. Without coercion, they argued, natives were content to simply remain poor, and would not work.[43] Still others argued that the credit offered by upfront payment for *repartimiento* demands was essential for natives to fulfill their other economic responsibilities such as tribute payments.[44] The *repartimiento* was a constant cause for administrative reflection. It was routinely judged to be either meritorious or predatory, but it appears that it was never clearly established as one or the other.

In fact, the *repartimientos* always existed in a liminal space between official sanction and prohibition. On the one hand, they ensured that the labor needs of Spanish colonization could be met, especially in the wake of tremendous native population loss of the fifteenth and early sixteenth centuries; particularly, from the metropolitan perspective, the forced labor demands of the *repartimiento* were essential to keeping silver mines productive. Yet, these needs had to be balanced against strong native antipathy and recurrent Spanish abuse. Concerned about this ongoing abuse, the Crown restricted the *repartimiento* in 1601 in all areas except in mining.[45] In 1609, the use of *repartimiento* labor for domestic service was outlawed, and in 1634 it was officially abolished altogether.[46] Despite the legislative elimination of the *repartimiento*, the practice survived. The 1681 *Recopilación de Leyes de los Reinos de las Indias*, reiterated the fact that natives were expressly free to conduct their own trade at their discretion and could not be compelled into involuntary commerce or service.[47] Though the crown repeatedly banned the *repartimientos*, such prohibitions unfortunately proved absolutely ineffective in curtailing the process, and hence native antagonism toward the practice survived as well. In 1780, the *repartimientos* were banned in the kingdom of Peru in an attempt to curtail the violence breaking out amongst natives in that region.[48] In Papantla, as elsewhere across the colonies, native communities protested the *repartimiento*. Normally this took place without violence, but rather through legal avenues. The Papantla Totonac would either tolerate the process, or employ the Spanish legal system to attempt to gain outside intervention, typically from the viceroy. Whether or not this strategy worked in any given case, it certainly did not stop later *alcaldes mayores* from repeating the process. The strain created by this system of unfair commerce was essentially endemic to the colonial system. The power to deploy native efforts for personal gain was simply too attractive for many Spanish officials to pass up.

While many historians have tended to focus on the abuses meted out through the *repartimiento* system, others, such as Jeremy Baskes, have suggested that the *repartimientos* deserve a fundamental reexamination. As one of the most significant and ubiquitous economic practices in the Spanish colonies, it is critical to understand how the *repartimientos* operated and to what extent native participation was voluntary. Baskes argued that the *repartimiento* was in fact a system that was openly accepted by, and beneficial to, poorer natives. He claimed that natives in Oaxaca actively negotiated the conditions of the *repartimiento*, and "fought for better terms, evaded repayment of debts, and generally attempted to manipulate the *repartimiento* to their advantage (at least given their much weaker economic position *vis-à-vis* the *alcalde mayor*)."[49] Baskes saw *repartimiento* loans as an opportunity for poor natives in need of cash. In the cochineal economy of Oaxaca, natives could turn to the *alcalde mayor* for a *repartimiento* loan when in need, with only the promise of future cochineal produce as collateral. This, according to Baskes, gave natives access to ready cash, or in some cases agricultural necessities such as seed, in exchange for a reduced sale price on their goods. Similarly, Arij Ouweneel argued that native participation in the *repartimiento* was voluntary in the central Valley of Mexico.[50] Yet, while it is true that such a system could make credit available for some of those in direst need, the unequal relationship between creditor and debtor here is most analogous to that of sharecropping. *Alcaldes mayores* had the power to charge high interest for their loans and undervalue the crops they received as payment.

It may be that used as officially outlined the *repartimiento* could offer financial benefits to the natives who used that upfront payment to cover tribute and other obligations, particularly in the lean times that often occurred during planting season. But the system was so rife with abuse and so frequently exceeded in terms of legal limitations that it was in reality, if not in theory, detrimental to native economic wellbeing. Complaints by natives reveal the *repartimientos* to be an enduring source of frustration, rather than gratitude. Early in the eighteenth century, the bishop of Yucatan blamed abuses of the *repartimiento* as the cause for native flight from *reducciones*.[51] In the eighteenth century, colonial officials took pains to regulate the *repartimiento*, legalizing it in 1731, but setting strict limits on the amount of goods that could be contracted. It would be abolished again in the 1780s.[52] Unquestionably, among the Totonac of Papantla the *repartimiento* was onerous. For Papantla, the *repartimientos* frequently cut off access to neighboring markets, limiting their capacity to secure goods or to maintain subsistence income. These limitations were not in themselves enough to initiate revolt, but instead were addressed through the legal mechanisms of negotiation made available by the colonial system. Legal complaints demonstrate the degree to which natives disliked the *repartimiento*, but at the same time, it is the very existence of these legal actions that indicate that the Totonac felt this problem could be addressed without violence, at least prior to the latter half of the eighteenth century.

Repartimiento exploitation did not necessarily create the type of subsistence crisis that could easily explain an uprising. However, it did constitute some threat to native wellbeing. Economic strain limited native access to important household items such as cloths and tools, which were often purchased rather than made. Furthermore, the self-interested exploitation of the natives by the *alcalde mayor* appeared to natives as simply unfair. Although normally the *repartimiento* functioned in Papantla without significant conflict, at times greedy officials would demand too much, provoking a violent response. Ronald Spores (in contrast to Baskes) found that in all of the uprisings that he studied throughout Oaxaca, along with tribute demands and abuse by the *alcalde mayor*, *repartimientos* were cited as the "proximate cause," reinforcing the argument that the *repartimiento* was coercive.[53] During the October 1767 uprising in Papantla, witnesses did not cite the *repartimientos* as the proximate cause, but their testimony made it clear that the *repartimientos* were a prominent feature of the landscape of discontent. Spanish witnesses also noted native frustrations with the *repartimientos* as well.

Lieutenant *alcalde mayor* don Juan Domingo Ugarte testified that de la Barga had prohibited any trade by the natives. Ugarte further noted that he had heard complaints from several residents, including one member of the militia, about the fact that de la Barga would take all the produce of the area and resell it. Though he did not know all the details of de la Barga's commerce, Ugarte knew that de la Barga and other leading Spanish residents bought wax from the natives at one real per forty-pound bundle and resold them in Mexico for between six and seven pesos per *arroba* (11.5 kilos), a nearly 8,800 percent profit.[54]

When questioned about the uprising, Lazaro Gonzales, a Spanish-speaking Totonac resident of Papantla, stated that "the *alcalde mayor* of this jurisdiction, don Alonzo de la Barga, does not permit the Indians to conduct commerce in any manner in their own territory, nor are they permitted to leave to any other place to participate in the *feria* [large market gatherings held in Xalapa] buying or bartering goods, nor can they take the fruit that they produce."[55] González went on to accuse the *alcalde mayor* of stealing all the fruit in the area and creating a monopoly for himself. The witness said that he did not know where these things were being sold, but claimed that certainly some of it was going to Puebla and Mexico, especially the *chitle*.[56] A Spaniard, don Martín Gamboa, testified that he had heard these same complaints made about the *alcalde mayor*, that de la Barga had shut down virtually all native commerce in the town.[57] Totonac witness Manuel Santiago corroborated the claim that de la Barga had essentially monopolized the local fruit trade:[58]

> Last year the *alcalde* made them cut down all of the fruit trees that they have and which they use to help and maintain themselves, . . . the *alcalde* had published a decree threatening with prison and penalty anyone who did not obey . . . The viceroy did not help, because [the witness] knows that when some of the natives went to Mexico City intending to seek recourse, they were whipped when they returned.[59]

Apparently, de la Barga dealt with threats to his commercial monopoly severely. At the same time, Santiago's testimony, consciously or unconsciously, placed de la Barga in opposition to the paternal role that the Totonac placed on the viceroy in their testimony. Recurrent in this case and others, Totonac witnesses would swear fealty to the viceroy and the king as a preamble to an accusation against the *alcalde mayor*. In this way, they conformed to the pattern that native uprisings typically avoided making any claim to challenge the nature of authority, but were instead comfortable impugning a particular official. As we have seen with the tobacco uprising of 1764/65, native insurgents wanted to draw a clear distinction between colonial authority and local authority. A Totonac witness, Miguel Sánchez, remarked that the Papantla Totonac were loyal subjects:

He [Sánchez] knows that all of the natives, like himself, are loyal vassals of the King whom they obey, as they are to the viceroy, and that they are content, but they are not as such with the current *alcalde* who obstructs too much, and whips them when they do not pay him or the curate what they should, and for other things.[60]

Through this method of swearing allegiance to the king within their witness testimony, natives structured their case around the idea that the local official was unsuited to be a representative of crown authority. The insurgents had challenged the *alcalde mayor*, in this case because he was being unjust *vis-à-vis* the extradition of Olmos. At no time was there any claim by natives that they were challenging the status quo of being ruled by a Spanish colonial official. Instead, they portrayed the *alcalde mayor* as misusing the authority granted him by the crown. Nor did they claim that economics drove their actions. Rather they made it clear that they felt that de la Barga was an unjust leader, and used the example of his *repartimiento* demands as further evidence of the miscarriage of his office. Yet, even if Sánchez was highlighting concerns about the *repartimiento* as a sophisticated rhetorical decision, that choice speaks to the fact that Totonac witnesses understood that such a claim could attract the sympathy of the viceroy, or even the king.

The testimony of the Totonac drummer for the militia company, Gaspar García, provides an excellent example of the way in which Totonac witnesses would construct their testimony to highlight the difference between royal and local authority:

The witness is very content and is loyal to the King, as he is to the viceroy who he considers like the king, to whom he [the witness] is like a child who has [the viceroy] for a father, and he has no complaints except with the *alcalde mayor* because he is a strongman and no one can compete with him.[61]

The frequency of such claims of affection for the crown and viceroy are so common as to be formulaic. Yet the veracity of the sentiment is less significant here than is the obvious fact that the Totonacs of Papantla were aware of the importance of this distinction, and could manipulate the interrogation process to represent themselves as loyal subjects despite their attack on a local official. In this way, they freed themselves to indict the *alcalde mayor* without insulting the system that had given him his office. From this posture García, like many other witnesses, felt comfortable elucidating the depredations of the *alcalde mayor* and his use of the *repartimiento*.

They are very disgusted with the *alcalde mayor* for various things that he has done, that begin with him cutting all of the fruit trees of the town, for which he put out a decree threatening prison and punishment, which he would do to any Indian with so much as a chirmoya stick or tree next to his house.[62]

It is because the Totonac were able to separate the *alcalde mayor* from colonial rule itself that historians can find such testimony, which so openly demonstrates the degree of economic strain that the *repartimiento* placed on the Papantla Totonac community.[63]

Conclusion

The accounts of de la Barga's enforcement of the *repartimientos* and his creation of a near monopoly on commerce in Papantla certainly explain the antagonism that the natives directed at the *alcalde mayor*. De la Barga's choice to send Nicolas Olmos to Mexico City tapped into this resentment and pushed Totonac anger past the breaking point. Yet, as mentioned above, *repartimientos* and economic exploitation were nothing new in Papantla. It is possible that the revolt was spurred by the fact that de la Barga was an abusive *alcalde mayor*—perhaps crueler than any Papantla had previously seen. However, the October 1767 uprising was also part of an increasing pattern of collective violence in Papantla that was initiated at the creation of the tobacco monopoly. By 1767, the Papantla Totonac had begun to shift their perspective of what constituted acceptable behavior by the *alcalde mayor*. Prior to the latter half of the eighteenth century, the natives of Papantla rarely rioted over the *repartimiento*, or at all. Rather, the Totonac either tolerated the *repartimientos* or sought redress through legal avenues. But the 1764 creation of the tobacco monopoly changed the economic conditions of life for the local population.

Although the estimates of the number of participants in the 1767 uprising disagree, the various witnesses support the conclusion that hundreds were involved. This number represents a significant percentage of the Totonac population of the time. Don Domingo Blas Bazaras, *oidor* (judge) of the *audiencia* of Manila, claimed to have personally counted 3,134 people living in Papantla in 1767.[64] Yet we can also be sure that numerous Totonacs were not involved in this event. When examining uprisings in colonial towns it is important to avoid overgeneralizing the position of the native population. Native communities were no less prone to factional division than any other group, including Spaniards. When the fighting started in Papantla on the six occasions that it did, the participants were divided. They were not organized solely along ethnic lines. They were peasants responding to the rallying cries of their leaders. When colonial authorities imposed sentences on Olmos and thirty-one *maguines* ("leader" in Totonac) for their roles in the uprising, they were careful to describe those men as misusing their posts as officials of the *república de indios*, a tactic not entirely unlike the language used by Totonac witnesses. Each of them was banned from future elections. All were sentenced to three years of hard labor without any pay in public service to Papantla. Their first duty was to clear the hills and forests for one league in all directions from the town, "which are filled with disgusting insects, and the dens of wild beasts, and are a refuge for insolent Indians."[65] After this task was completed, they were to be at the disposal of the *alcalde mayor* or the *gobernador* of the local *cabildo*. Giving the *gobernador* authority over the punishment of these men speaks clearly to the fact that it was not merely ethnicity that governed this conflict. When life in Papantla became more economically difficult as a result of the tobacco monopoly, elite Totonacs and Spaniards alike began to fight for control of diminishing community fresources. The following chapter explores the factional divisions underlying the uprising of August 1787, and how elite ambitions were able to drive the actions of broads segments of the community.

A Fractured Pochguin: Local Factionalism and the Uprising of 1787

The criminal conduct of this *alcalde mayor* has horrified the fiscal (an attorney who represents the king ex officio), he knows of similar excesses that threaten the destruction of the necessary state of order in Papantla.[1]

Court proceeding in case against Manuel Cornejo
and Esteban Bernia. 8 April, 1787

My esteemed lord: in an act of uprising, that happened of the twenty third of this month in this cabecera, the alcalde mayor and commandant of arms don José María Morcillo . . . was gravely injured for mediating between two opposing bands of Indians.[2]

Letter of Juan Macip to Viceroy Flores. 28 August, 1787

The Uprising of August, 1787

Dramatis Personae
Spaniards

don Ildefonso Arias de Saavedra Regiment	Lieutenant Colonel Zamora
don Esteban Bernia	Brother-in-law of don Manuel Cornejo
don Joseph de Castro	Witness
José Ignacio Chaves	First sergeant, Company 2, Papantla militia
don Manuel Cornejo	*Alcalde mayor*, Papantla, 1777–April 1787

A version of this chapter was previously published in *Ethnohistory* 54:8 (2011).

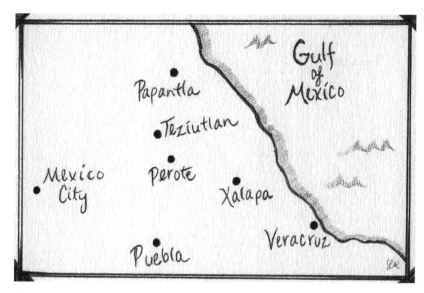

Figure 6.1 L. B. Ames, East Central Mexico, 2016. Ink on Paper. 4 x 7, author's personal collection.

don Juan Macip	Inspector for the tobacco monopoly
don Ignacio Martínez	Interim chief magistrate, Papantla, November/1787–? (Captain of Infantry, Zamora Regiment)
don Joseph María Morcillo	*Alcalde mayor*, Papantla, spring 1787–November 1787 (Captain, Zamora Regiment)
don Raphael Padrés	Commander Teziutlan militia
don Manuel Pérez Fort	Curate of Papantla
Juan de los Rios Monterde	Priest from Guanajuato
don Esteban Tizon	Subdelegate of Veracruz to Papantla, 1790
don Bernardo Troncoso	Governor of Veracruz
don Juan Fernández Villamil	Captain, Papantla militia
Totonacs	
Antonio de la Cruz Galvador	Rioter
Manuel García	Mail courier
Ignacio García	*Escribano* of the cabildo, 1787
José Martín	*Alcalde primero* of the cabildo, 1787

Totonacs (continued)

Miguel Morales	Rioter
don Andres Olarte	*Gobernador* of the cabildo, before 1787
Juan Olmedo	*Gobernador* of the cabildo, 1787
Bartolomé Pérez	Rioter
Miguel Pérez	Rioter
Rafaela	Widow

Afro-Mexicans

Simona Morales	*Mulata*, alleged mistress of José Ignacio Chaves
Isabel Risueño	*Mulata*, alleged mistress of José Ignacio Chaves

On 23 August 1787, "*dos bandos de indios opuestos*" (two opposing groups of Totonac natives) gathered outside the tobacco monopoly building in Papantla.[3] The crowd had come in anger. If they really were two distinct groups, at this point they acted as one, as local *maguines* (Totonac for leaders) incited them to violence. "Speaking out against the tobacco guards," who were two men and one old foreman, the Totonac mob shouted and threw rocks, sending the tobacco guards fleeing for their lives. The crowd bombarded the building with stones, damaging the doors. They were on the verge of destroying the building when one Totonac, Miguel Pérez, alias "Cuate," stepped in and invoked royal authority, claiming that the building was "the house of the king," and thus should not be further damaged. Pérez's protest worked; the agitators apparently did not feel that they were in conflict with the king of Spain. The insurgents left the tobacco building, instead turning their ire on the tobacco guards and other "*vecinos españoles.*"[4] Both Spaniards and Totonacs fled before the advancing mob. Many were wounded as they made for the perceived safety of the church in the center of town.[5]

The event that started at the tobacco building would turn out to be one of the most violent incidents of unrest in Papantla's colonial history. Many residents were injured in the fight. For most of the next week, Spanish residents and their native and Afro-Mexican allies would be pinned down in and around the church in the center of town. It would be more than two weeks before any reasonable semblance of order could be restored. Before the conflict was over, hundreds of troops would be dispatched to Papantla, and the senior Spanish official would be replaced for his inability to control the populace. The uprising of 1787, like all incidents of unrest, developed from a number of causes. The events of the uprising itself can demonstrate only some of the animosities that were being acted out. Yet the claim by Juan Macip, an inspector for the tobacco monopoly, that the mob at the tobacco building was actually two opposing groups, offers a clue to the causes of this event. What would appear to some Spaniards as a native riot against just rule in general, and Spanish residents in particular, was in fact part of an ongoing contest for power. This uprising was a manifestation of numerous fractures running through this community, fractures that pitted not only Totonac against Spaniard, but also Spaniard against Spaniard and Totonac against Totonac. Analysis of this riot demonstrates the degree to which colonial authority in towns like Papantla could be fragmented, and illustrates the ability of powerful natives to deploy popular discontent for political ends.

Papantla had been deeply divided for some time, with embedded hostilities among much of the population. The Totonac leadership of Papantla was divided by split allegiances, some supporting the former *alcalde mayor* don Manuel Cornejo, and others deeply opposed to the influence he apparently continued to wield even after his departure from office. This division was not limited to the native population. In subsequent investigations into the uprising, many Spaniards would come forth to criticize the actions and character of Cornejo. But Cornejo had Spanish supporters as well. Militia Sergeant José Ignacio Chaves was closely tied to the former *alcalde mayor*, and apparently acting as a proxy for Cornejo. Consequently, he too would be vilified by many local community members. Yet the 1787 conflict also bore the evidence of even longer-term discontent within this community. The geographical starting point of this riot—the tobacco building—was itself a focus of great disdain among the Totonac population of Papantla, which this chapter discusses in detail below. The events of 1787 would be a confluence of long-standing and more recent discontent that would ultimately draw in members of all parts of the Papantla community.

The Riot Continues

When the crowd that had gathered at the tobacco monopoly building reached town, they set upon the *alcalde mayor*, José María Morcillo, who, according to his own account and that of Juan Macip, fought very bravely on that first day of the fighting. For his efforts he received six severe wounds to the face.[6] Miguel Morales, a Totonac, also stood against the mob. In the accounting of Lieutenant Colonel don Ildefonso Arias de Saavedra, Morales "defended the royal authority at much risk to his own life."[7] Totonacs were fighting on both sides of this conflict, as rioters and as defenders of order. Forced to protect themselves from the riotous insurgents, those townspeople who had not retreated to the fortifications of the local church barricaded themselves in their homes. As soon as word of the riot reached Teziutlan, roughly seventy-five kilometers to the south, that town dispatched Captain don Raphael Padrés and fifty-one militia troops to aid the Papantla militia, but they would not arrive for almost a week. For the six days following the uprising at the monopoly building, the Spanish residents of Papantla, their native allies, and the local free-colored militia force were unable to regain control of the town. During the intervening days the jail was damaged, and the *casa real* was fired.[8] On 29 August, don Juan Fernández Villamil, the captain of the local free-colored militia, dispatched word to Padrés and his force, still en route, that the "insolence of the Indians continues," and implored Padrés to advance with all possible speed.[9] According to Villamil's frightening account, the rioters were "intending to burn the church to get at those taking refuge there."[10]

When Padrés' force arrived in Papantla on 30 August, the insurgent Totonacs fled for the hills, leaving native loyalists in the town. According to Padrés, the rebels did not concede at this point, but rather used their retreat in the forest to plan continued attacks. On entering the town, Padrés found local residents (Spaniards, Totonacs, and free-colored residents) still holed up in the church and in a fortified position in the cemetery adjacent to it. Although Padrés claimed that the arrival of his troops invigorated the beleaguered local militia force, the scene he found was one of terrible distress. The natives had "imprisoned and castigated the *vecinos* [local residents] of this town."[11] Many of those gathered in the church were wounded, and at least two of them were suffering from life-threatening injuries. Padrés provided the services of his field hospital to the wounded, and dispatched some of his troops to support Spaniards who were fortified in other parts of the town. He also had his guards secure the cemetery, "with the corresponding respect" due the task.[12] Despite the mixture of defenders in the church, to Padrés this clash was apparently a simple conflict pitting natives against Spaniards. Padrés described the Totonac insurgents as "rising up against justice, the tobacco monopoly, and the Spanish residents of the town."[13]

On this same day, 30 August, an additional fifty-two militiamen mobilized from the town of Perote, almost 100 kilometers to the south, to support Papantla, where they would arrive one week later.[14] Villamil secured an alternate road to the town, cutting off one of the insurgents' means of attack. Yet the *tumultarios* (rioters) did not surrender, continuing their harassment of the town from the security of the hills. In his first report from the field to the viceroy, on 1 September, Padrés argued that a more respectable force had to be moved into the town to restrain the "barbarous Indians."[15] But reinforcements would have to wait. It had been only the day before that Veracruz had received its first word of the uprising. Regular forces deployed from that city would face a slow journey up the coast as they sailed into a north wind.[16] Thus it was in the hands of the militias of Papantla, Perote, and Teziutlan to ensure the security of the town for the next ten days.

By the time 171 regulars of the Zamora Regiment out of Veracruz under the command of Arias de Saavedra arrived on 9 September, the on-site forces appear to have gained reasonable control of the situation.[17] There are no specific accounts of attacks between 30 August and 9 September. On 11 September, nineteen days after the start of the uprising, by which point 278 troops of regulars and militia had been deployed to Papantla, Padrés was able to begin making arrests.[18] He took fifty-one Totonac natives into custody.[19] But this day also proved that the situation was still tenuous. On that same afternoon, four mounted rioters set upon the native mail courier for Papantla, Manuel García, as he carried the mail through the woods outside town. García reported that his attackers were armed with muskets and violently stole the mailbag from him.[20] This incident provoked great consternation amongst Spanish officials in both Papantla and Veracruz, for not only did this indicate continued unrest in the hills outside of town, but they were also deeply upset about the loss of both the bronze shield mounted on the mail container and the militarily sensitive information contained in the correspondence.[21] Yet despite these concerns, the commander of the Zamora regiment ordered the local militia units to stand down and return to their homes.[22] No further acts of violence were recorded in association with the August uprising.[23]

Division and Unrest in Papantla

In the case of the Papantla uprising of 1787, violence was the end product of an ongoing contest for control over political authority, drawing on long-standing popular frustration, and preceded by numerous petitions and other legal efforts. As with most uprisings in colonial Mexican villages, the causes of the August 1787 uprising are buried within the centuries of unequal relations between natives and Spaniards in the colony. As was often the case during unrest in native communities, certain Spanish officials, such as Padrés, were quick to assume that native violence constituted an ethnically-oriented assault on Spanish rule. Yet such assumptions gloss over both the complexity of political factionalism within native communities and the ties often forged between native elites and Spanish officials. Native society was divided by class in much the same way that Spanish society was, and economic self-interest commonly superseded community interest. Describing the conditions around Guadalajara during the second half of the eighteenth century, Van Young pointed out that "wealth distribution within Indian pueblos became more skewed in the direction of some individuals, among them the village notables and those Indians linked with the superordinate white society. The increased economic chafing in individual pueblo communities produced intragroup tensions and a potential conflict that ill accorded with the cosmological assumptions of underlying group identity."[24] Such hierarchical division was not confined to Van Young's area of study. In Raymond Buve's examination of patronage systems in central Mexico, including the Huasteca, he found that "Pueblo society had never been egalitarian, but it became gradually less so as village elites became more wealthy and connected to the elites of Spaniards and creoles."[25] These divisions, wherein native elites allied themselves with powerful non-Spaniards, gives the lie to the idea of native unity, and highlights the ability of natives to embrace the sort of self-interest too often ascribed as the exclusive prevue of Spaniards. Consequently, political division within native communities was as common as in the politically powerful, super-ordinate Spanish society. In Papantla this intragroup tension was manifest by the "*dos bandos*" present at the tobacco building. Michael Ducey identified a similar tension in the earlier 1767 uprising. In investigations of that uprising conducted by the *alcalde mayor*, Ducey noted, the *alcalde mayor* "insisted that the Papantecos were insolent rebels against all royal authority, while the witnesses interviewed by [an outside investigator] emphasized the tradition of factionalism within the pueblo."[26] The tradition of factionalism was clearly still present in the 1787 event. Investigations into the uprising reveal that the specific fractures that would lead to the violence of 1787 had begun to form seven years earlier with the appointment of *alcalde mayor* Cornejo, and began to come to a head ten months before the uprising itself. When rioting actually broke out, it was not merely a sudden outburst by angry natives against Spaniards and Spanish rule in general. Rather, this event was the culmination of many months of maneuvers by different groups drawn from native and Spanish constituencies seeking to shape authority within Papantla.

In November 1786, a group of leaders of the Totonac community had lodged a complaint with the local curate, charging that the 17 November 1786 election for the offices of the native *cabildo* had been illegitimate.[27] The *vocales* claimed that the *alcalde mayor*, Cornejo, had used the power of his office to intimidate certain local Totonac electors and prevented them from participating in the vote.[28] Therefore, the plaintiffs claimed, the recently elected *gobernador* and other Totonac officers had been wrongfully awarded their posts. The curate supported this claim, stating that, "this election is glaringly void," and forwarded the case to the *real audiencia* in Mexico City. The curate recommended that the officers elected for the previous year maintain their posts while preparations were made to hold a new election, "without the intervention of the *alcalde mayor*" (see table 6.1).[29]

Posts within the *cabildo* were prized positions in the late colonial era.[30] Political office within the native community was a significant means of gaining economic power and position.[31] In Papantla, as in other native communities during the late eighteenth century, the native community was by no means a homogenous mass. Natives were economically strati-

Table 6.1 Partial List of Papantla's Cabildo Officers Serving in 1787

Office	Officeholder
Gobernador	Juan Olmedo
Alcalde primero	José Martín
Alcalde segundo	Manuel Santiago
Regidor	Domingo García
Escribano	Ignacio García

All of the above are described with these titles at some point in the criminal record. No record is available of the officers who served in 1786 and were supposed to have continued service in 1787 as a result of the fraudulent election. The only available data are contained in one document, which on 11 September 1787 referred to Andres Olarte, as the "Gobernador pasado" (AGN, Criminal 315/2/24). I believe that the officers listed were elected in November 1786 and served the majority of their terms in 1787. On 16 October 1787, Arias de Saavedra reported arresting *alcalde primero* José Martín and passing his commission of office to the *alcalde segundo*, Manuel Santiago. He then repeated this process between Santiago and *regidor* Domingo García. This transfer of offices would be necessary if these men were serving in 1787. In addition, Juan Olmedo, José Martín, and Ignacio García were all convicted as acting under Manuel Cornejo's control in starting the uprising of 23 August 1787. Source: This list is a reconstruction based on testimony in AGN, Criminal 315 and AGN, Criminal 539.

fied, with some possessing a degree of political and economic power and the majority living as subsistence farmers with little disposable income or time to participate in town politics. Therefore, participation in the *cabildo* was in itself a representation of status. Posts in the *cabildo* also offered more practical means of securing personal advancement.[32] Once in office as a *gobernador* or *alcalde*, these officers were charged with a variety of responsibilities, such as adjudicating minor crimes or disputes, the collection of tribute, and overseeing lawsuits brought by the native community. These responsibilities offered opportunities for commercial networking and for managing the nature of community efforts in a variety of realms. These roles could also be exploited by native officials to their own benefit through offering favors to litigants or through embezzling community funds.

Spanish officials often benefited by exerting their influence on native elections. Spanish officials could ensure the election of a favored candidate in return for added influence in the assessment of labor tribute or for control and cooperation within the native economy. Antonio Escobar Ohmstede noted that in the neighboring region of the Huasteca, disputes among native leaders often accompanied the electoral process. On various occasions factions within native community leadership challenged the legitimacy of elections on the basis of electoral tampering. Such manipulation of the *cabildo* was not uncommon.[33] Nor was such manipulation necessarily just another case of Spanish exploitation of native villagers. Van Young points out that native leaders often "worked in collusion with outsiders such as white officials, priests, and landowners. It is impossible to ascertain to what degree this kind of malfeasance on the part of Indian notables was generally recognized or protested against by the mass of village peasants, but there is some evidence to indicate that it was explicitly acknowledged and caused considerable strain within village society."[34] Such alliances were clearly in evidence during the disputed election of November 1786. Cornejo had apparently used the power of his office to influence the makeup of the native *cabildo*. This type of patronage would have netted Cornejo influence among the native officeholders. The *audiencia* was aware of the threat that this type of manipulation posed to legitimate governance and on 8 February, 1787, declared the election void and ordered that new elections be held as soon as convenient.[35]

Alienated Leadership

This first complaint lodged by the Totonac leaders appears to have triggered a cascade of accusations against Cornejo. At some point soon after the election controversy, the minister in charge of the protection of Indians wrote to the *audiencia* regarding both Cornejo and his brother-in-law, don Esteban Bernia. The letter claimed that in 1780, the first year of his tenure, Cornejo, with Bernia, had stolen 453 pesos, five *reales* from the *caja de comunidad* (community treasury), and that by 1787 the pair had stolen a total of 1,356 pesos, five *reales*—a considerable sum of money. Beyond mere theft, Cornejo was personally vilified for a variety of abuses of office, including boldly failing to carry out the orders of the viceroy, lying, committing "swindles and frauds," and creating a state of lawlessness among the Indians. Finally, the complaint implicated Cornejo in the murder of a local Indian, Juan Fernández.[36]

On 2 April, the *real audiencia* granted the request for Cornejo's removal and trial. The *real audiencia* called for the governor of Veracruz to name a replacement "possessing the qualities necessary for the responsibility of the administration of justice in the jurisdiction of Papantla," and ordered that all of Cornejo and Bernia's assets be seized.[37] Furthermore, based on the claim that Cornejo's crimes were particularly detrimental to Indians within the jurisdiction of Papantla, the *real audiencia* ordered that Cornejo and Bernia leave the jurisdiction within twenty-four hours and report to Mexico City within twelve days. Though Cornejo had been ousted for actions that harmed at least part of the native community of Papantla, later events would demonstrate that he also maintained strong allies among the Totonac.

Cornejo's dramatic downfall became still more scandalous as the charges against him mounted. His discharge was probably encouraged by a secret Inquisition investigation into his piety, which had taken place in 1782. The only account from the 1782 investigation is a denunciation of Cornejo made by a priest from Guanajuato, Juan de los Rios Monterde, who attended a burial at which Cornejo called the liturgy nonsense. Cornejo was questioned on the matter and satisfied his inquisitors. The case resulted in no further investigation and was filed away.[38] However, soon after the contested election of November 1786, the Inquisition began to reexamine Cornejo. The curate of Papantla, don Manuel Pérez Fort, denounced Cornejo, calling the *alcalde's* religious observation scandalous at best. He missed mass regularly, one time openly stating that he did so because he was up all night gambling. Cornejo would chat during the sermon and criticize its content. He manifested an aversion to priests, and once defended Freemasonry, saying that none of it was contrary to Christian law. The list of Cornejo's blasphemy went on. In late 1786 or early 1787, the viceroy commissioned Padrés to verify certain "irregularities" in Cornejo's behavior. Following a series of interviews with principal figures of the area, Padrés confirmed that Cornejo's behavior inside and outside the church showed "little or no Christianity."[39]

At this point, the Inquisition ordered a secret tribunal to assess the degree of Cornejo's depravity. Further testimony from the curate recounted a litany of offenses dating back several years. Cornejo's transgressions ranged from eating meat on prohibited days to forcing witnesses to give false testimony, to publicly having three mistresses. According to the curate, Cornejo tried to force himself on women, single and married. The curate was particularly angry with Cornejo for releasing a prisoner that the curate had put in the *casa real* for trying to take communion after the curate had banned him from the church. Cornejo released the prisoner, his own lieutenant *alcalde mayor*, and sat down to eat with him, displaying his "wish to trample the holy sacrament."[40] The portrait of Cornejo in this and other testimony at times appears almost as caricature. In an interrogation conducted in Mexico City in March 1787, a Spaniard, don Joseph de Castro said that "the accounts of his [Cornejo's] depravities in Papantla are true," and added descriptively that "he has one clouded eye."[41] Interestingly, this case served more to record Cornejo's disagreeable character and appearance than it did to contribute to his prosecution. On 28 July 1787, the curate of Papantla withdrew the gravest of his charges against Cornejo, on the grounds that it would disturb the public.[42] Events the following month would confirm that the Papantla population, or at least part of it, was already in a state of unrest. On the other hand, perhaps the curate dropped the charges because by this time Cornejo had become tied up in yet another investigation, one that was no less damning.

By July 1787, Cornejo's replacement, *alcalde mayor* don Joseph María Morcillo, had been in office for four months. Morcillo was aware that he was trying to maintain the peace in a town that was highly factionalized. Several Spaniards, including the curate, had spoken out against Cornejo. Cornejo's activities in support of his allies on the *cabildo* had so deeply exacerbated divisions among the Totonac community that some members of the native *cabildo* had sought Cornejo's removal—with success. Through legal means, this faction had been able to initiate an investigation that achieved the ouster of the highest-ranking Spanish official in town. But this of course left another group of Totonac who were angered at the loss of their patron. A third investigation, into one José Chaves, first sergeant of the second company of the Papantla militia, reveals that not only did divisions persist in this community, but Cornejo was apparently still trying to maintain some control within the town from his residence in Mexico City.

In the early summer of 1787, the new *alcalde mayor*, Morcillo, brought charges against Chaves for desertion. Chaves had apparently left his post as first sergeant without license to do so and departed Papantla. Chaves, a Spaniard, had entered military service on 1 December 1767, and on 16 November 1782 had been elevated to the rank of sergeant. In his career he had served with the Flandes Regiment and claimed to have been deployed for a time to Manila. In April 1784, Cornejo personally promoted Chaves to the post of first sergeant of Papantla's second militia company.[43] Cornejo had removed the previous sergeant, Maríano Lara, claiming that Lara was no longer fit for duty. Chaves's promotion was granted without the consent of militia Captain don Joaquín Suárez, and was "against the wishes of all of the [militia] companies."[44] Lara had been respected by his fellow soldiers and had distinguished himself in 1766 when he led a troop of "*pardos* and *mulatos*" in repelling an attack on the area by pirates.[45] Cavalry ensign don Augustín Galicias of the Papantla militia claimed that Chaves had no business being first sergeant on the grounds that he could neither read nor write, that the company doubted his claim to have served in Manila, that he had let his pasturage outside town run to ruin, and that he had had an affair with a local girl on the false promise that he would marry her.[46] This last charge was substantiated and expanded by other witnesses' testimony. Like his patron Cornejo, Chaves had several public mistresses. Two, Isabel Risueño and an unnamed widow, were identified as *mulatas*. Chaves was alleged to have fathered children with both. He was also said to have had a child with a Totonac widow named Rafaela, but she claimed that the father was not Chaves but another of Cornejo's "lackeys."[47] Chaves also apparently bedded several other women by making marriage promises that he later failed to keep. One of these, Simona Morales, also a *mulata*, was a cook whom Cornejo had introduced to Chaves.[48] He was even known to have made passes at the

Spanish daughter of Captain don Joaquín Suárez. Chaves would later claim that it had been her love for him had started the conflict—that Suárez had jailed Chaves to keep him away from his daughter—adding a personal dimension to Papantla's unrest.

It appears that neither Cornejo nor Chaves exempted any ethnic group of women from their depredations. The women who were mistreated in these circumstances were identified as native, Spanish, and *mulata*. Yet none of these women testified as witnesses in any of the documentation, despite their importance in the accusations leveled against both men. Furthermore the documentation reveals no evidence that Chaves or Cornejo faced any particular punishment for their assaults on women. If the courts or other officials would not bring suit against these men to compensate the women in some way, what options were available to mothers of Chaves's children? A century earlier, a woman in the position of Isabel Risueño might have tried to force Chaves to marry her or pay compensation. Chaves had fathered her child and in so doing had conducted an act of marriage. Had this been the seventeenth century, the unnamed daughter of Ana Mongado, another woman who was widely acknowledged to have received a marriage promise from Chaves, could have sued on those grounds.[49] As Patricia Seed noted, "in a world that relied as much on verbal contracts as on written agreements, a spoken promise was a solemn commitment. To pledge one's word was tantamount to enactment."[50] During the seventeenth century, men could be imprisoned or exiled to the Philippines for failing to fulfill a marriage promise. By the second half of the eighteenth century, however, the church had largely withdrawn from the position of enforcing marriage promises. A woman in the position of the mistresses of Chaves or Cornejo would have had to pay the costs of bringing suit and then produce compelling evidence against the defendant. In all, this was neither easy nor inexpensive. But in the case of Isabel Risueño, public testimony strongly supported the likelihood of Chaves's patrimony.[51]

Thus, there is reason to believe that these women were perhaps not merely abandoned victims in the liaisons, but likely saw little value in marrying. Chaves, liar though he may have been, did have his children baptized, and claimed in conversation to have made some effort to provide for them. But he was not legally bound to maintain this responsible behavior. With no legal contract, Chaves could cease to recognize his patrimony, and the mother would have little recourse. Ultimately, we cannot know what resolution these women wanted. We can only speculate about what choices they had. In truth, their options were few. But one must also recognize that both Cornejo and Chaves had developed terrible reputations in Papantla, and they may not have appeared to any of the mistresses as very appealing husbands. Isabel Risueño, Ana Mongado, Rafaela, and the others may very well have been exercising a choice by not appearing in suits against Cornejo or Chaves. These women could well have seen avoidance of formal bonds with such men as their wisest available option.

Cornejo and Chaves shared much more than their womanizing tendencies. Witnesses' testimony bound Chaves and Cornejo together further as it became clear that Chaves had received favors from Cornejo. Chaves had in fact worked as Cornejo's cook while in Papantla. When Chaves disappeared, many people suspected that he had gone to live with Cornejo in Mexico City. Then, in July 1787, the accusations became much more serious. Morcillo reported that "Manuel Cornejo, whose confirmed poor propensities, his proven perverse behaviors regarding the thefts from the *caja de comunidad* . . . motivated my appointment,"[52] was trying to influence the residents of Papantla, sowing sedition and encouraging unrest. *Alcalde mayor* Morcillo and don Bernardo Troncoso, the governor of Veracruz, charged Chaves with participating in a plot to undermine the rightful authority in Papantla, and on 10 August, Chaves was arrested in Cornejo's residence in Mexico City on charges of sedition.

But of course, if Chaves and Cornejo had been trying to manipulate Papantla politics, the arrest came too late to stop their effort from causing a crisis. By August 1787, Papantla had undergone significant upheaval. Then, thirteen days after Chaves's arrest in Mexico City, Papantla exploded in riot. What was happening to this town? The variety of charges leveled against the *alcalde mayor* and the breadth of witnesses that testified in each case or petition shows that hostility about the conditions in Papantla were hardly contained to "two groups of opposing Indians." The uprising of 1787 was one battle in an ongoing struggle for power in Papantla. Native leaders were divided into two separate groups, but their allegiances extended beyond the native community. Indeed, what separated these groups were their divergent associations with Spaniards and Spanish authority. Among both Cornejo's defenders and his accusers, there were Spaniards and Totonacs, soldiers and farmers, *pardos* and a priest, the powerful and the disempowered. Furthermore, while this uprising was the latest event in a political conflict over local Spanish leadership that had begun at least as early as 1786, it tapped into native animosities dating back even earlier.

Totonac Anger

The commencement of this uprising at the tobacco monopoly building is worth considering. This conflict did not begin at the *casa real*, nor with an attack on the Spanish citizenry or the *alcalde mayor*. Rather, as we have seen, it began with a riot at the tobacco monopoly warehouse. Here we see the *maguines* shrewdly deploying the anger of the local populace toward an institution that had been plaguing them for more than two decades. In a way, the hostility toward the tobacco monopoly began the riot, but leaders like Miguel Perez were able to divert that hostility toward the *alcalde mayor*. Van Young noted in his studies of eighteenth-century native riots that when internal conflict existed within native communities, such conflict could be "deflected onto substitute objects outside the group." Hostilities over various issues—in the case of Van Young's study, land shortages—could manifest as violence focused on other "proxies." For this to take place, claims Van Young, two preconditions had to exist: inequalities in the group had to be seen as unjust, and some external stress had to "significantly alter the material conditions and normative functions within which the group functions."[53] For the Totonac, the change to their material conditions had been brought about by economic constraints in the wake of the Bourbon reforms. Though more than two decades had passed between the inception of the monopoly and the riot of 1787, the occurrence of three intervening riots between those of 1765 and 1787, and the fact that the monopoly building was the starting point for this event, speaks to the fact that frustration over this change to the Papantla economy persisted. In this time of tension, the *maguines* were able to employ native animosity that had grown, in part, from the pressures of the tobacco monopoly. Natives allied to Cornejo were able to deploy native frustration to serve their own ends when it appeared that unrest, of whatever fashion, could challenge the leadership of Morcillo.

Aftermath of the Uprising of 23 August, 1787

The 11 September attack on the mail carrier García was the last violent act attributed to the uprising that began on 23 August. As summer eased into fall, Papantla appeared once again to be pacified. By 23 November, the Zamora regiment began a general demobilization.[54] Yet things in Papantla did not return to the status quo ante. That fall was a time of concern and change in Papantla. Officials in Papantla and Veracruz agreed that changes had to be made in the general military posture of the town. All mail was to be transported under the guard of two soldiers.[55] The tobacco warehouse guard was strengthened, and a security force would remain in place in Papantla at least through the spring of the following year.[56]

When Juan Olmedo, the current *gobernador* of the *cabildo*, was arrested in association with the uprising on 9 October, there was concern about electing an interim replacement. In light of the electoral violations of 1786 and the persistent division demonstrated by the August uprising, the on-site commander of the Zamora Regiment, Arias de Saavedra, opted to suspend the election and carry out the remainder of Olmedo's term with the post unfilled. Arias de Saavedra felt that "the election cannot be performed with tranquility because of the disagreement of the two opposing groups [of Totonac]."[57] The following month the elections for the *cabildo* took place at their customary time (see table 6.2). Arias de Saavedra said that they were conducted "with impartiality, tranquil calm, and uniform spirit." He went on to point out that traditional practice was maintained, "with the principal voters, as has been the custom since time immemorial."[58]

Table 6.2 Papantla's Totonac Cabildo Officers, 1787 and 1788

Office	1787	1788
Gobernador	Juan Olmedo	don Gabriel Ximenes
Alcalde primero	José Martín	Juan Olarte
Alcalde segundo	Manuel Santiago	José Morales
Regidores	Domingo García	Ermenegildo Olarte
		Julian García
		Francisco Bernavé
Escribano	Ignacio García	Pedro Pérez
Topil de la Tecpa		Francisco Pérez
Mayordomo		Juan Santiago

Source: AGN, Criminal 315/2/19, Ildefonso Arias de Saavedra certification of election results.

Further change within the Spanish governance of Papantla was also underway that fall. By the end of October, new proceedings had been started that would eventually remove Morcillo as *alcalde mayor*. In early December 1787, Morcillo left office, turning over the administration of Papantla to another military appointee. When he was removed from his post, Morcillo was charged with no offence and cited with no failure in the execution of his appointment. In fact, Arias de Saavedra praised Morcillo as a good and honorable man and cited him for his valor in the course of the August uprising. However, Morcillo was dismissed on the grounds that he lacked the confidence of the native population. The August uprising had constituted sufficient grounds to consider Morcillo unable to administer the town. He would be the last man to hold the title *alcalde mayor* in Papantla. His replacement, don Ignacio Martínez, would only be referred to in the documentation as having taken interim charge of justice in Papantla.[59] In 1787 the new Bourbon intendancy system came into place in Veracruz, and the office of *subdelegado*, subordinate to the intendant in Veracruz, replaced that of *alcalde mayor*. Morcillo's tenure as the last *alcalde mayor* of Papantla had been a mere eight months.

With the ouster of Morcillo, it appears that the uprising was actually a success for the Totonac allied with former *alcalde mayor*, Cornejo. The documentation suggests that Cornejo and Chaves's seditious efforts had gained purchase among Cornejo's allies. When the uprising began at the tobacco monopoly building, there may have been "*dos bandos de indios*" present, but it was a small segment of the Totonac leaders who were divided. The mob was angry about more general concerns stemming from such burdens as the tobacco monopoly. The results certainly favored those who opposed Morcillo. Totonac leaders had rallied the local populace with the intention of inciting a riot to undermine the sitting *alcalde mayor's* authority.[60] These leaders were exploiting a persistent discontent among the Papantla Totonac, and in so doing managed to draw a significant portion of the Totonac population into a political struggle over the Spanish leadership of the town.

The question of how the *maguines* were able to push local peasants to such dramatic action is revealing. This dispute had tapped into native anger over numerous issues in Papantla's recent past. The Totonacs of Papantla had endured the 1765 imposition of the tobacco monopoly, which forced many to lose income or engage in criminal commerce and contributed to the riot at its inception that year. They rioted in 1767, when the *alcalde mayor* tried to prohibit natives from commerce with anyone from outside the jurisdiction, and again later in 1767, when the *alcalde mayor* ordered the cutting of all of the local fruit trees on the dubious claim that they provided concealment for bandits.[61] Finally, in 1767, a third riot took place in October, when the accused architect of the two previous uprisings, Nicolas de Olmos, was ordered removed to Mexico City. In all, the Papantla Totonac had rioted on no fewer than four occasions in the twenty-two years prior to the August 1787 uprising. Though testimony from these events revealed numerous complaints about ongoing iniquities in Papantla, each event was set off by a particular prior event. What then was the trigger for the 1787 uprising? If Padrés' word is to be accepted, then the basic "barbarousness" of the natives and their disrespect for the monopoly, Spaniards, and justice, was sufficient. In fact, the documentation reveals that this passionate and bloody event was actually the calculated product of local Totonac and Spanish leaders.

The ability of local leaders to mobilize natives in uprising speaks to the nature of colonial life in this agrarian community. Uprisings typically require some kind of trigger, if not a change in the status quo that threatens to make life untenable, then something that causes enough anger to make people perceive the situation as intolerable. These causes could include conflicts over land and water rights, new legislation such as that resulting from the Bourbon reforms that challenged local economic survival strategies, or acts by Spanish leadership that threatened the local sense of justice, like the extradition of Nicolas de Olmos. In 1787, in the absence of any such catalytic event, Totonac *maguines* provoked the populace by highlighting ongoing issues. There is little evidence to indicate that the general Totonac population of Papantla was necessarily polarized by the conflicts that the electorate had with each of the *alcaldes mayores*. *Alcaldes mayores* were frequently disdained by the general populace for excesses that harmed the native community. But in this case,

Morcillo was challenged not because he was guilty of any offense to the broad Totonac population; rather, his fault was that he represented the failure of the preceding system of patronage. The leaders of the August 1787 uprising had to draw the greater population into a fight that was not necessarily based on their interest. No document explains exactly what put the mob at the tobacco monopoly building that August day, but the fact that the uprising began there and not elsewhere does permit us to speculate about the significance of the structure in this conflict. The *maguines* knew that the tobacco monopoly had been a source of great discontent to the Papantla natives for some time. This institution and the recurrent exploitation of the repartimiento were the greatest threats to Totonac economic stability in preceding decades. By gathering the Totonacs at the tobacco monopoly store, the *maguines* exploited this symbol of economic oppression to incite violence among the crowd—violence that they could use to remove Morcillo.

Interestingly, as noted above, when violence against the building itself seemed imminent, it was spared. Royal symbols were held immune from assault in Papantla and frequently elsewhere. In native eyes, even after centuries of colonial rule, the crown maintained an aura as protector of the Indians and likely appeared to possess a power too great to challenge safely. Miguel Pérez, who stopped the actual destruction of the building, was later convicted of being a leader of the uprising. He may well have known that the monopoly could anger the crowd but that an assault on a royal building would simply be asking for too much trouble. At the same time, scholars have repeatedly shown that during uprisings natives took pains to demonstrate respect for the highest levels of colonial administration, most pointedly the viceroy and the king.[62] Local officials, on the other hand, were fair game for official complaints, lawsuits, and in extreme circumstances, violence. It was the unfortunate lot of local Spanish officials to be the only viable target for native discontent with colonial rule. In these conditions, it was possible for native leaders to channel community anger to their own advantage.

Conclusion

In the end, the uprising of August 1787 was both a success and a failure. The sitting *alcalde mayor*, Morcillo, was removed from his post. Where one group of native leaders had begun a legal process that resulted in the removal of Cornejo from office, another group was able to remove his successor by demonstrating lawlessness. Although this second group could not restore Cornejo to office—Cornejo died in Mexico City prior to the conclusion of the trial—they could assure that his former enemies were not the only local group capable of effecting regime change.[63]

On 22 February 1788, fifty-two of the prisoners eventually arrested were released from jail and ordered to rebuild the jail and the *casa real* of Papantla to their pre-uprising condition. On 12 March 1789, Juan Olmedo, José Martín, Ignacio García, Antonio de la Cruz Galvador, Bartolomé Pérez, and Miguel Pérez were all convicted as leaders of the uprising. Olmedo and Martín were condemned to eight years in the presidio of the fortress of Veracruz, while García, Galvador, and Bartolomé Pérez received six years. Miguel Pérez died in jail prior to sentencing. All of the convicts were banned from ever returning to Papantla.[64]

Papantla was clearly divided in 1787. Among these divisions were native leaders in support of and opposed to the former *alcalde mayor*. The uprising of August was not a demonstration of Totonac animosity toward the Spanish or even toward Spanish rule. Ethnicity was significant in this event only in that it could be used as a tool to aid the mobilization of part of the population. Not all Totonacs held one view, nor were all Spaniards the enemy of any given Totonac group. Rather, Cornejo, a Spaniard, felt perfectly comfortable reaching across any ethnic barrier between himself and certain Totonac leaders to form alliances to their mutual benefit. Even in the scandalous realm of extramarital affairs, the investigations of 1787 revealed a town where *mulata* women shared intimacy with Spanish men, where Indian women bore the children of Spanish men, and where Spanish women were not exempt from the dishonorable conduct of their ethnic "equals."

If the natives were not politically unified, the Spaniards were no more so. José Chaves was at odds with the officer corps of the Papantla militia. The town curate clearly loathed the *alcalde mayor*. In an environment in which people of other ethnicities outnumbered Spaniards to a staggering degree, the Spaniards of Papantla certainly felt no need to circle the wagons and form a unified front against the majority other. Among the many things revealed by the events of 1787 is that in Papantla ethnicity was not the sole determining factor in the creation of allegiances, friendships, intimacies, or hatreds. Political machinations and factional interests transcended ethnic groups. In the struggle for privilege, Spaniards and natives were willing to work with one another to obtain personal rather than communal advantage. This event also demonstrates the extent to which natives were capable of manipulating the authority structure of colonial society, denying the authority of Spanish magistrates through both legal and extralegal means and, if need be, removing them from office. With such power, native leaders became practitioners, rather than simply victims, of local colonial political power.

Conclusion

Ultimately, the colonial exercise in New Spain was dependent on the colonized. Spain was able to impose its dominion on native communities, but that dominion was attenuated by continuous native resistance. As the conquest era evolved into the colonial era, Spaniards and natives developed a relationship of mutual expectations. Of course these expectations were grossly unequal and institutionally favored the interests of Spaniards over native communities. Yet a system of limits and expectations informed an accord that permitted the colonies to operate, largely free from open violence. The colonial system, consciously or organically, developed mechanisms by which conflicts between native communities and Spanish authorities could be contested and diffused, if not necessarily resolved.

The legal system permitted an official channel through which grievances could be addressed. Failing that, native peasants could curtail the authority of local Spanish magistrates by overtly or covertly ignoring regulations. While such flouting of authority could hardly be uniformly applied, under some circumstances local Spanish authorities found it in their interests to permit certain transgressions. When tobacco was monopolized, some Totonac growers receded into the surrounding *monte* and continued to cultivate the plant out of sight. Into the 1790s, *alcaldes mayores* quietly permitted this violation of Spanish regulation so that they might preserve the ability to collect tribute. Other transgressions were prosecuted by local leaders, such as in 1736, when the lieutenant curate decided to whip his absentee parishioner. In these two cases we see examples of the borders of Spanish dominion being established by resistance and retribution. It is through these means that the shape of Spanish dominion over a rural community was made. In the latter case, we have seen that these limits could extend to further rounds of contestation. In 1736, Totonac residents used the threat of violence to proclaim their rejection of the lieutenant curate's pretentions of power. Such efforts of course did not necessarily resolve the conflict to the satisfaction of all involved. Corporal punishment of natives for their failure to meet ecclesiastical responsibilities was not unusual and we can be certain that the riot of 1736 did not end the requirement for natives to attend church services. On the other hand, it very likely caused the lieutenant curate to rethink how he would enforce that rule in the future.

Most often, violence was unnecessary. Over the course of generations, colonial society had evolved into an apparatus of resistance, accommodation, and persistence, in which exploitation was balanced by sustainability. When that relationship was tipped out of balance, non-violent mechanisms meant to diffuse crisis were deployed. The enduring colonial relationship between the Totonac of Papantla and local Spanish leaders in no way suggests that the community was content. To the contrary, I argue that the Totonac of Papantla felt great dissatisfaction with local Spanish leadership and its economic exploitation; they also were divided themselves over political and economic access to power. But such displeasure could normally be mediated in the mature colony without resorting to violence. It was only in the last half of the eighteenth century, when the crown sought to fundamentally remake the rules of colonial life, that these grievances increasingly culminated in violence. With the coming of the Bourbon reforms of the mid-eighteenth century, the system of accommodation was pushed beyond its ability to absorb the demands of Spanish leaders and the expectations of the native community.

Within the native community itself, the new constraints of a post-tobacco era economy heightened the struggle for positions of power. While the tobacco monopoly did affect the native population of Papantla as a group by targeting a form of agriculture that they were particularly dependent on, that strain did not unify the Totonac into a body with unified interests. Rather, the monopoly created an economic strain for these people, which made violent resistance to a variety of other concerns all the more likely. When Totonac residents burned the *casas reales* and the jail in 1765, they did so in direct response to the prohibition of tobacco cultivation. At the same time, they were involved in a struggle over who would hold the office of *alcalde mayor*. Again, in the uprising of 1767, native leaders came down on very different sides of a power struggle over who should hold positions of leadership within the Totonac community. Regardless of what started the uprising in October of 1767, some witnesses used the criminal investigation as a chance to advance their own aims. For many that aim was to end the exploitation practiced by the *alcalde mayor*. Yet for those who defended the *alcalde mayor*, the investigation was an opportunity to undermine adversaries among the native elite. While some Totonac witnesses told a tale of orderly natives obstructing an act of injustice by the *alcalde mayor*, others, chief among them members of the native *cabildo*, decried the actions of the populace and specifically named other native individuals whom they charged with engaging in revolutionary resistance against the Spanish colonial order.

Whether the testimony of witnesses like *gobernador* don Thomas Mendez and Nicolas Nava in 1767 were accurate accounts of seditious action by certain Totonac leaders like Joseph Juárez and others, or if Mendez and Nava were using their testimony to eliminate their opposition, it is apparent that no sense of shared Totonac interest united the Papantla Totonac against local Spanish leadership. The Papantla Totonac were by no means a homogenous body that acted with a unified will.

Rather, as economic opportunities in Papantla diminished, different groups of both Totonac and Spanish elites struggled for whatever political and economic spoils remained. This town not only had a fractured *pochguin*, but a divided *república de españoles* as well. In the struggle for authority, allegiances spanned ethnic boundaries, with native elites allied to Spanish leaders in the fight over the political face of Papantla. These divisions were by no means new to the late eighteenth century, but it was in this time of Bourbon economic disruption that they were most clearly revealed in the dissolution of the *pax hispanica*.

The factionalism revealed in these uprisings was not created by the Bourbon reforms, nor was discontent with the punishments inflicted by the curate, or frustration with the predations of the *alcalde mayor*. What changed during this era was the degree to which these frustrations resulted in violence. That violence shows us something new about this period, a decreased tolerance among the native population brought about by the tobacco monopoly. It also provides a series of windows into the long-term conditions that existed in this community. This unrest was in part the manifestation of discontent that had existed for decades or longer in this community. Natives clearly felt that the *repartimientos* were an imposition on their economic freedom. The Papantla Totonac had shown frustration with the *repartimientos* at least as far back as the 1680s, and quite likely since their inception, but the increased strain of the tobacco prohibition in the area created an environment in which there was less economic leeway. This reform also highlighted Totonac difficulties with abusive local officials. As a consequence, just over two years after the imposition of the monopoly, Papantla repeatedly broke out in violence during 1767. Yet the fact that new economic strains decreased tolerance for traditional economic concerns—leading the Totonac to call out to "kill that dog of an *alcalde mayor*"—is just part of what these uprisings reveal.

In 1787, the cleft between groups of Papantla Totonac with discrete interests was made most plain. There were two opposing bands of Indians present at the tobacco monopoly building that day when the riot began. Assuredly not all of the people present were divided into those two bands. In a broad sense, the Totonac of Papantla as a group had good reason to be frustrated with the tobacco monopoly. Yet it is also true that within that crowd were members of a political faction allied with the former *alcalde mayor*. Those *maguines* who incited the riot were acting in their own interest to redress to the loss of their patron. For them this was a fight for their own privilege more than a fight for Totonac wellbeing. To deny such selfish machinations would be to oversimplify their desires and to ignore their political sophistication. It would also neglect the fact that the conflicts of the last half of the eighteenth century were not constrained to the native population. Manuel Cornejo was just one in a series of *alcaldes* who had formed alliances with Totonac leaders to amass power and wealth. When tobacco was banished from Papantla, all members of the community felt its loss. This book has focused on the reaction of the Totonac population, and their increasing use of violence, but Spanish *alcaldes* were participants in each of these conflicts, and not always as simply targets of assault. And while we have little direct articulation of the opinions of free blacks during these conflicts, we know that they were drawn into them. No part of Papanteco society was immune to the convulsions of Bourbon changes.

These violent events focused investigatory attention on the town, which created documentation of some of the concerns fears and aspirations of members of this community. These crises act as the streetlamp described by Murdo MacLeod. They shine a light on a moment in the history of this community. But the light is not focused only on a single moment of fracture in the colonial order. The light spills beyond the conflict itself, allowing us to see day-to-day experiences in this town. We see the farming and fishing that was going on. We see sexual relations unfolding among the varied members of the local populace. Even hidden in the *monte*, we see the clandestine cultivation of tobacco. As historians, we do indeed quite often seek the lost coin under the streetlamp, as that is most often where the light is. But that light captures a great deal more than the unrest it hovers above.

We get a look at what made this town unique, and why it reacted the changes of the Bourbon era the way that is did. Papantla's position as a tobacco-producing region meant that the imposition of the reforms during latter part of the eighteenth century would strike the Totonac agricultural population in a particular way. Additionally, because Papantla was a coastal town, it had a militia corps that would experience the changes of the Bourbon military reforms—reforms that left many other areas unaffected. At the same time, such towns as Papantla were undergoing changes in political administration as the intendancy system was being imposed. In some ways, Papantla was illustrative of the many other predominantly native communities that were experiencing the monopolization of locally-produced products, such as *aguardiente*. Yet for Papantecos, the shape of that reaction was created by pre-existing factors—factors that molded a very local landscape of discontent.

None of Papantla's uprisings expanded into larger revolutionary movements. Papantla's discontent developed locally and was addressed locally. This speaks to the fact that the Spanish system of colonial rule, either by intention or by default, left room for discontent to be expressed at the local level. Assaults by rioting natives were generally confined to both local targets and local issues. At the same time, natives persistently claimed their allegiance to the viceroy and the king. *Alcaldes mayores* were frequently targeted, but almost never did the assault spread to other communities or generate notions of throwing off colonial rule. In Papantla, the problem never became the system that put the *alcalde* in office. Rather the problem was the local Spanish official who was misusing the authority granted to him by that system.

Following the uprising of 1787, Papantla recorded no further rebellion until the coming of the war of independence. The office of *alcalde mayor* was replaced with that of subdelegate; this change had been intended as a measure to reduce the corruption of colonial officials. But there is little to suggest that even under this new system of oversight, colonial officials were unable to find ways to exploit their positions of power in communities like Papantla. The tobacco monopoly continued as an institution after 1787, as did contraband cultivation in Papantla. The consequences for those caught violating its edicts remained, at least for a time, quite severe. By 1791, it was clear to Viceroy Revillagigedo that the penalties outlined for infractions were in fact too severe, and needed to be moderated. In some cases contrabandists were fined triple the value of the tobacco seized. In January 1791, Revillagigedo decreased the penalties for contraband to the seizure of the illegal tobacco, payment of court costs, and no more than one month in prison for a first offence, two for a second. Interestingly, the viceroy ordered that these changes not be published, and only be issued to the judges who tried such cases, suggesting that the appearance of severe reprisals may have been more effective than their enactment.[1] Moreno Coello claims that in that same year only thirty percent of contrabandists were punished, indicating that official corruption was still rampant. Nor is there reason to believe that factional divisions between differing groups of native elites did not continue. Disputes within the native leadership of Papantla had existed since the brothers Garcia were inciting revolt in 1590, and certainly before. The continuation of the conditions that underlay the uprisings between 1765 and 1787 raises the question of why did the pattern not continue afterward. It is a very difficult question to answer.

It can be just as, if not more, difficult to explain why riots did not break out to explain why they did. The documentary record is much quieter about periods of calm than it is about times of unrest. But as we have seen, those moments of unrest that shine so brightly under the proverbial streetlamp are times when the colonial compact was being renegotiated. The riots of 1764/65, 1767, and 1787 are examples of times when other systems of accommodation broke down, when legal or illegal but non-violent means of maintaining order no longer accommodated the demands of the populace. Nonetheless, as suggested in Chapter Three, violent outbursts were a continuation of the process of negotiation, and the acts of violence were efforts to achieve those demands, to bring disputes back to the level at which they could be resolved without resorting to violence. It is possible that the uprisings discussed in this book did just that. If we can accept that non-violent resistance can serve as a means of preserving order, it follows that violent resistance can work to do the same. Felipe Castro Gutierrez argued that instead of considering frequent uprising as a sign of a crisis in social relations, "directly or indirectly, they helped to restore order, to correct the reasons for tension and reaffirm the image and respect granted to the higher authorities."[2] Thus it is possible that the series of uprisings that beset Papantla from the 1760s to the 1780s served to establish a new balance by which the colonial system could be maintained and ultimately preserved. In this way, the changes of the Bourbon reforms did not necessarily permanently upset the relationships of power in Papantla, but forced a renegotiation of that power. The system of accommodation and resistance that had served for much of the colonial era had to be adapted to the new conditions of Bourbon rule.

Of course, knowing what was to come in the early decades of the next century, it is hard to reconcile that a balance, akin to that which had preserved the colonial order during the previous centuries, had been achieved. A generation after Papantla's last colonial uprising, the entire fabric of colonial society would tear apart in an evolving war that would end Spanish rule in New Spain. Historians have scoured the latter half of the eighteenth century to find the roots of the upheaval that would lead to independence. Those roots are of course there. By the end of the eighteenth century, many powerful *criollos* had developed a sense of identity that recognized the gulf between themselves and powerful Spaniards from the peninsula. When Alexander von Humboldt traversed the Americas at the beginning of the nineteenth century, he found that many *criollos* identified themselves as "*Americanos.*" This group found inspiration in the writings of liberal thinkers and in the examples of the American and French Revolutions, which devolved power from the monarchy to a broader elite population. Leading members of the colonial church had been alienated by the constraints imposed by the reforms. Eventually, even the colony's most conservative leaders would find reason to seek independence when, over the long course of the war, the king of Spain was forced to adopt a constitution that they found far too liberal.

The Bourbon heritage of discontent among those who would become the leaders of the war of independence has been well-studied, and is today a matter of consensus. Yet what drove the participation of the plebian classes in these wars is much less certain. As this book has repeatedly shown, peasants, like those who made up the population of Papantla, rarely wanted for reasons to be frustrated with the system of rule that left them economically and politically disadvantaged and vulnerable to the predations of Spanish officials. But what we have seen in the uprisings in Papantla were conflicts that did not challenge the nature of that rule. The Papantla Totonac, like the majority of participants in late colonial uprisings, were reluctant to challenge the premise of the colonial system. Instead they focused on those efforts that could alleviate quotidian difficulties. Some have argued that participation in the uprisings of this period was part of a process whereby peasants were becoming politicized. Luis

Fernandez Díaz Sánchez has argued that it was this era of increased resistance that "incubated the ideas that would explode in the war of independence."[3] It is quite possible that as the Totonac of Papantla turned increasingly toward violence in the wake of the prohibition of tobacco they became more cognizant of the utility of violence as a tool for negotiation. Yet a generation would pass between the last of the Bourbon uprisings and the coming of independence armies to Papantla. The Totonac of Papantla had confronted change and fought their fight to reestablish acceptable norms of colonial rule. Once that effort was completed, violence was no longer necessary. The wars of independence following 1810 were a much larger-scale process, revolutionary from the outset. Hidalgo initiated his movement with the objective of radically changing society. Hence, when independence efforts spread across the colony, they were unlike what took place in the wake of the Bourbon reforms. The struggles for independence were not corrective measures to fix a broken system. They were different sorts of conflicts based on the idea that the time for negotiation was over.

Notes

Introduction

1 The native *cabildo* was the local manifestation of the *república de indios*, which was the system of native-elected leadership within colonial communities, subordinate to Spanish rule and acting as a liaison between natives and the Spanish government. See Chapter One.

2 Archivo General de la Nación de Mexico (hereafter AGN) Indios, 3/180/41v.

3 While Hernando Cortés' defeat of Tenochtitlan in 1521 and Francisco Pizarro's capture of Cuzco in 1533 are often cited as the completion of the conquest of Mesoamerica and the Andes, Spanish conquest efforts were only beginning at this stage. Further campaigns of conquest would continue for more than a century in less politically-organized parts of the Americas. The Itza Maya of Guatemala, for example, would not be conquered until 1697. For a discussion of the ongoing nature of the Spanish conquest of the Americas see Matthew Restall, "The Myth of Completion," in *The Seven Myths of the Spanish Conquest* (Oxford: Oxford University Press, 2003), 64–76.

4 Murdo Macleod, "Some Thoughts on the Pax Colonial, Colonial Violence, and Perceptions of Both," *Native Resistance and the Pax Colonial in New Spain*, ed. Susan Schroeder (Lincoln: University of Nebraska Press, 1998), 129–134.

5 See William Taylor, *Drinking, Homicide, and Rebellion in Colonial Mexican Villages* (Stanford: Stanford University Press, 1979), chapter 4; John H. Coatsworth, "Patterns of Rural Rebellion in Latin America: Mexico in Comparative Perspective," in *Riot, Rebellion and Revolution: Rural Social Conflict in Mexico*, ed. Friedrich Katz (Princeton: Princeton University Press, 1988), 30–39; Susan Schroeder, ed., *Native Resistance and the Pax Colonial in New Spain* (Lincoln and London: University of Nebraska Press, 1998); John R. Fischer, Allan J. Kuethe, and Anthony McFarlane, *Reform and Insurrection in Bourbon New Granada and Peru* (Baton Rouge: Louisiana State University Press, 1990).

In 1952, Luís González Obregón railed against the myth of the colonial *siesta* or "*modorra colonial*," arguing that riots and conspiracies were endemic throughout the colonial era, and furthermore that these movements were clear signs of a class struggle in New Spain that would ultimately culminate in the wars of independence. While González Obregón was perhaps right in dismissing the notion of a colonial slumber during which colonizer and colonized lived in harmony, his claims of class consciousness were clearly shaped by his membership among a number of Mexican scholars seeking to historicize the 1910 Revolution within a centuries-long tradition of class struggle. Luís González Obregón, *Rebeliones indígenas y precursors de la independencia Mexicana en los siglos XVI, XVII, XVIII* (Mexico City: Ediciones Fuente Cultural, 1952).

6   The last set of reforms to approach the scale of those imparted by Charles III were the New Laws of 1542. In November 1542, King Charles I issued a series of regulations designed to protect the declining native population and to curtail the growing power of conquistadors. Among their many stipulations, the New Laws ended the practice of bequeathing *encomiendas* (grants of authority over native populations). No new *encomiendas* were to be granted, and existing *encomiendas* were to escheat at the death of the current *encomendero*. The New Laws also forbade enslaving natives, and severely limited the legal means by which *encomenderos* could exploit native labor. Though ferocious opposition on the part of *encomenderos* weakened enforcement of the New Laws, the New Laws represented a fundamental shift in colonial authority from the personal leadership of conquerors to the crown.

7   Jay Kinsbruner, *Independence in Spanish America: Civil Wars Revolutions and Underdevelopment* (Albuquerque: University of New Mexico Press, 2000), 16.

8   Susan Deans-Smith, *Bureaucrats, Planters, and Workers: The Making of the Tobacco Monopoly in Bourbon Mexico* (Austin: University of Texas Press, 1992), xii.

ONE   **A Geographic and Historical Biography of a *C'achiqu'in***

1   Guy Stresser-Péan, "Ancient Sources on the Huasteca," *Handbook of Middle American Indians, Part 2, Archeology of Northern Mesoamerica*, vol. 11, ed. E.Z. Vogt (Austin: University of Texas Press, 1969), 583. See also Peter Gerhard, *A Guide to the Historical Geography of New Spain* (Norman and London: University of Oklahoma Press, 1993), 211; Michael Ducey, *A Nation of Villages: Riot and Rebellion in the Mexican Huasteca, 1750–1850* (Tucson: University of Arizona Press, 2004).

2   Antonio Escobar Ohmstede, "Los pueblos indios en las Huastecas, México, 1750–1810: formas para conservar y aumentar su territorio," in *Colonial Latin American Historical Review* 6:1 (1997), 33.

3   Henri Puig, *Végétacion de La Huasteca, Mexique: Etude Phytogéographique et Écologique* (Mexico: Mission Archeologique et Ethnologique Français au Mexique, 1976), 15.

4   Islands of Nahuatl speakers also occupy the region. H. R. Harvey and Isabel Kelly, "The Totonac," *Handbook of Middle American Indians, Part 2, Ethnology*, vol. 8, ed. E.Z. Vogt (Austin: University of Texas Press, 1969): 638–681.

5   Papantla figured centrally into Michael Ducey's 2004 study of violence in the Huasteca, *A Nation of Villages*. In *Végétation de la Huasteca*, Henri Puig considered the Tecolutla River the southern border of the Huasteca, thus adding Papantla to the northern region; Benjamin Ortiz Espejel places the northern border of Totonacapan at the Cazones River, thus placing Papantla within this region, *La cultura asediada; espacio e historia en el tropic veracruzano, el caso del Totonacapan* (Mexico City: CIESAS, 1995), 27.

6   Puig, *Végétacion de la Huasteca*, 31–34; *Papantla: cuaderno de información*

básica para la planeación municipal (Aguascalientes, Mexico: Instituto Nacional de Estadistica, Geografía e Informática, 1990), 2.

7   Emilio Kourí, *A Pueblo Divided: Business, Property, and Community in Papantla Mexico* (Stanford: Stanford University Press, 2004), 40.

8   Alan Graham ed., *Vegetation and Vegetational History of Northern Latin America* (Amsterdam: Elsevier Scientific Publishing Company, 1973), 83; Ortiz Espejel, *La Cultural Asediada*, 30.

9   Graham, *Vegetation and Vegetational History*, 116; Puig, *Végétation de la Huasteca*, 58, 69–92.

10   Isabel Kelly and Angel Palerm, *The Tajín Totonac: Part 1. History, Subsistence, Shelter and Technology* (Washington: United States Government Printing Office, 1952), 28.

11   William Saunders, "The Anthropogeography of Central Veracruz," *Revista Mexicana de Estudios Antropologicos* XIII (1952–1953), 61. Slash-and-burn agriculture has been practiced by peasant farmers for millennia in Mesoamerica along the Gulf Coast and throughout the Maya region to the south.

12   Harvey and Kelly "The Totonac," 59. Determining just how far back the cultivation of tobacco in Papantla goes can be somewhat difficult. Tobacco was certainly a crop of commercial value by the late seventeenth century. As early as 1688, Papantla Totonacs were contesting attempts to create a *repartimiento* of tobacco in the area. AGN, Indios 30/161-161v; Kourí, *A Pueblo Divided*, 62.

13   Harvey and Kelly, "The Totonac," 645.

14   Kourí, *A Pueblo Divided*, 53.

15   *Ibid.*, 47.

16   Angel Palerm, "Etnografía antigua Totonaca en el oriente de México," *Revista Mexican de Estudios Antropológicos* 13: 2 and 3 (1952–1953), 166. Antonio Alcedo, *Diccionario Geográfico-Histórico de las Indias Occidentales ó América* (Madrid: Emprenta de B. Cano, 1787), Vol. 4, 59; Juan de Carrión, *Descripción del Pueblo de Gueytlalpan* (Zacatlan, Juxupango, Matlaltan y Chila, Papantla) 30 de Mayo de 1581, ed. José García Payón (Xalapa: Universidad Veracruzana, 1965), 69.

17   Kelley and Palerm, *The Tajín Totonac*, 49; Roberto Williams García, "Etnografía prehispánica de la zona central de Veracruz," in *Revista Mexicana de Estudios Antropólogicos* 13: 2 and 3 (1952–1953), 157–162, 158; García Payón, *Descripción del Pueblo de Gueytlalpan*, 61–69; Kourí, *A Pueblo Divided*, 61.

18   Gerhard, *A Guide to the Historical Geography of New Spain*, 220.

19   Kourí, *A Pueblo Divided*, 60; See also Alfred Crosby, *The Colombian Exchange: Biological and Cultural Consequences of 1492* (Westport, CT: Greenwood Press, 1972), and Elinor Melville, *A Plague of Sheep: Environmental Consequences of the Conquest of Mexico* (Cambridge: Cambridge University Press, 1994).

20   Alcedo, *Diccionario Geográfico-Histórico*, 59.

21   March 1785 is considered the official discovery of the site. A tobacco patrol searching for contraband tobacco plots, led by don Diego Ruiz, encountered the site and the find was published in the *Gazeta de México* later that year. However, Ruiz' report on the finding of the site pointed out that the site was

known to the local Totonac Natives living in the area. Román Piña Chan and Patricia Castillo Peña, *Tajín: La Ciudad del dios Huracán* (Mexico City: Fondo de Cultura Económica, 1999), 7.

22 Rex Koontz, *Lightning Gods and Feathered Serpents: The Public Sculpture of El Tajín* (Austin: University of Texas Press, 2009), 9. People have populated the Gulf Coast in the area of the Tecolutla River since roughly 5500 BCE. Arturo Pascual Soto, *El Tajín: En Busca de Los Origenes de Una Civilización* (UNAM: Instituto de Investigaciones Estéticas/ CONACULTA: Instituto Nacional de Antropología e Historia, 2006), 31. Archeological evidence reveals clear presence of organized populations along the Gulf Coast dating as far back as 2700–1500 BCE. Certainly the famous Olmec tradition dates back to this era. In the opinion of some scholars, a clear Totonac population can be identified as early as 1500–600 BCE. Ortiz Espejel, *La Cultura Asediada*, 33; José García Payón, "Archeology of Central Veracruz," in *Handbook of Middle American Indians, Part 2, Archeology of Northern Mesoamerica*, vol. 11, ed. E.Z. Vogt (Austin: University of Texas Press, 1969): 505–542, 527. Piña Chan and Castillo Peña point to construction methods at the site that imply an Olmec tradition prior to CE 500. Piña Chan and Castillo Peña, *Tajín*, 84. This stands in contrast to García Payón who claimed occupation only began about CE 600. Jose García Payón, "Sinopsis de algunos problemas archeológicos del Totonacapan," *El México antiguo*, vol. 6: 301–332, cited in Kelly and Palerm, *The Tajín Totonac*, 14.

23 Scholars differ on the exact geographic size of El Tajín. The most recent work on the subject, Koontz's *Lightning Gods and Feathered Serpents*, claims 1,000 hectares as the city's ultimate extent, Koontz, *Lightning Gods and Feathered Serpents*, 5. Piña Chan and Castillo Peña give a figure of 355 acres. Piña Chan and Castillo Peña, *Tajín*, 15. López Austin and López Luján give a figure of 484 acres. Alfredo López Austin and Leonardo López Luján, *Mexico's Indigenous Past* (Norman: University of Oklahoma Press, 2001), 184. Michael Kampen described the archeological zone as encompassing 2,350 acres. Michael Edwin Kampen, *The Sculptures of El Tajín Veracruz, Mexico* (Gainesville: University of Florida Press, 1972), 3. While in 1992 Dailan Sainos García identified the archeological site as being one square kilometer, or roughly 250 acres, but conceded that much of the site was as yet unexplored. Dailan Sainos García, "El Tajín como patrimonio cultural de la humanidad: La puesta en valor de la zona arqueológica" *EntreVerAndo* 3 (January, 2009), 16.

24 Bernardino de Sahagún, *Historia general de las cosas de Nueva España*, Vol. III (Mexico City: Editorial Pedro Robredo, 1938); Juan de Torquemada, *Primera-[tercera] Parte De Los Veinte I Vn Libros Rituales I Monarchia Indiana: Con El Origen Y Guerras, De Los Indios Occidentales, De Sus Poblaçones Descubrimiento, Conquista, Conuersion, Y Otras Cosas Marauillosas De La Mesma Tierra: distribuyidos en tres tomos* (Madrid: N. Rodriquez Franco, 1723) (Mexico City: Editorial Porrua, 1975). The temples of the Sun and Moon are the largest structures at Teotihuacan.

25 The Toltec were envisioned by central Mexicans to be the most civilized and noble leaders in history. Thus those who could claim descent from Toltec bloodlines could claim legitimacy and prestige.

26 The terms Chichimec and Teochichimec have somewhat plastic definitions.

The Mexica used these terms to describe the nomadic and semi-nomadic peoples living to their north. Chichimec was thus used generically as a term roughly equivalent to "barbarian," but also was specifically used to identify a people living on the eastern side of Lake Texcoco.

27 Carrión, *Descripción del Pueblo de Gueytlalpan*, 60.

28 Kelly and Palerm, *The Tajín Totonac*, 20. The persistence of a significant Totonac population in the region has also drawn numerous anthropologists to study the area. Although twentieth-century anthropological studies must be employed with caution when assessing history, the work of Isabel Kelly and Angel Palerm can be helpful to the colonial historian. Their 1952 study of the Totonac revealed that certain twentieth-century Totonac traditions had survived from the pre-Columbian era and through the colonial period, such as the *voladores* ritual.

29 Myrna Santiago, "The Huasteca Rain Forest: An Environmental History," *Latin American Research Review* 46: 4 Special Issue (2011), 37–38.

30 Alejandra Palacios Sánchez, "La muerte: símbolo de vida entre los totonacas de Papantla, Veracruz" (PhD diss., Universidad Iberoamericana, 2009), 37.

31 Carrión, *Descripción del Pueblo de Gueytlalpan*, 66; Adrián Salas and María Esther Martínez, "La política del secreto en la santa inquisición y su presencia en Papantla, Veracruz (México), siglos XVII y XVIII" *Revista de antropología experimental*, 1 (2001), 197. These garrisons do not so much indicate an interest in settlement as they demonstrate the Mexica policy of garrisoning the frontiers and areas of potential resistance. Ross Hassig, *Trade, Tribute, and Transportation: The Sixteenth-Century Political Economy of the Valley of Mexico* (Norman: University of Oklahoma Press, 1985), 96.

32 Juan Zilli, *Historia Sucinta del Estado de Veracruz* (Xalapa: Universidad Veracruzana, 1943), 30; Carrión, *Descripción del Pueblo de Gueytlalpan*, 66 fn. 53.

33 Burton Kirkwood, *The History of Mexico* (Santa Barbara: ABC-CLIO, 2010), 38.

34 Palacios Sánchez, "La muerte," 37.

35 Bernal Díaz del Castillo, *Historia verdadera de la conquista de la Nueva España* Volume 1 [1632] (Paris: Libreria de Rosa, 1837), 220.

36 Kelly and Palerm, *The Tajín Totonac*, 26; William H. Prescott, *The Conquest of Mexico* (New York: The Book League of America, 1934), 76–90. Other regions that became subject to Spanish colonial rule without violent conquest include the Chontal Maya region of Acalan-Tixchel, in Yucatan; see Matthew Restall, *Maya Conquistador* (Boston: Beacon Press, 1998), 53–76.

37 Gerhard, *A Guide to the Historical Geography of New Spain*, 218.

38 Torquemada, *Monarquía Indiana*, 56.1.

39 Noble David Cook, *Born to Die: Disease and New World Conquest, 1492–1650* (Cambridge: Cambridge University Press, 1998), 135.

40 *Ibid.*, 109, 117, 136.

41 John S. Leibly, *Report to the King: Colonel Juan Camargo y Cavallero's Historical Account of New Spain, 1815* (New York: P. Lang, 1984), 68.

42 Carrión, *Descripción del Pueblo de Gueytlalpan*, 61 fn. 39.

43 Shelburne F. Cook and Woodrow Borah, *Essays in Population History: Mexico and California*, Vol. 3 (Berkeley: University of California Press, 1979), 37; Carrión, *Descripción del Pueblo de Gueytlalpan*, 61 fn. 31.

44 Cora Govers, *Performing the Community: Representation, Ritual and Reciprocity in the Totonac Highlands of Mexico* (Berlin: LIT Verlag, 2006), 48.
45 *Ibid.*
46 Luis Salas García, *Juu Papantlan: Apuntes para la historia de Papantla* (Mexico City: Gráfica Editorial Mexicana, 1979), 40–41; Carrión, *Descripción del Pueblo de Gueytlalpan*, 70. A Spanish league in the colonial era was roughly four kilometers.
47 José Rogelio Alvarez ed., *Enciclopedia de México*, México. Director Tomo XI (Encyclopædia Britannica de México, 1993), 3064; Gerhard, *A Guide to the Historical Geography of New Spain*, 219. In the late colonial era the Virgin of Conception was the focus of local devotion. Local lore held that her statue had been found in the early 1600s in a sealed crate that was supposed to contain fish, marked with a note that read "for Papantla." Alcedo, *Diccionario Geográfico-Histórico*, 60.
48 Kourí, *A Pueblo Divided*, 57.
49 Robert Ricard, *The Spiritual Conquest of Mexico: An Essay on the Apostolate and the Evangelizing Methods of the Mendicant Orders in New Spain: 1523–1572* (Berkeley: University of California Press, 1966), 274, 281.
50 Salas and Martínez, "La política del secreto, 200.
51 Carrión, *Descripción del Pueblo de Gueytlalpan*, 69.
52 Magdalena Díaz Hernández, "La intendencia de Veracruz y los repartimientos (1787–1810): A vueltas con el *salvaje* el miserable," In *Orbis incognitvs: avisos y legajos del Nuevo Mundo: homenaje al profesor Luis Navarro García*, 553–560. Universidad de Huelva, 2007, 554; Ortiz Espejel, *La Cultura Asediada*, 37; Harvey and Kelly, "The Totonac," 641. Rebecca Earle Mond offers a useful example of another such native community, which developed in a type of colonial isolation, in her study of Pasto, New Granada during the last twenty years of the eighteenth-century. Rebecca Earle Mond, "Indian Rebellion and Bourbon Reform in New Granada: Riots in Pasto, 1780–1800," *Hispanic American Historical Review* 73: 1 (Feb., 1993): 99–124.
53 Kourí, *A Pueblo Divided*, 63; Carrión, *Descripción del Pueblo de Gueytlalpan*, 70.
54 Carrión, *Descripción del Pueblo de Gueytlalpan*, 76. The term "mulata" was meant to describe the female child of a Spaniard and an African. However, this term, like all other racially based terms was applied with notable inconsistency.
55 Ducey, *A Nation of Villages*, 16; Ricard, *The Spiritual Conquest of Mexico*, 274.
56 In 1787 Papantla's jurisdiction was extensive, stretching to the coast, between the Río Cazones and the Río Tecolutla, and an even greater distance inland. Towns within Papantla's jurisdiction included Chiqualoque, Chumatlan, Coahuytlan, Coatlan, Espinal, Metlatlan, Quazintla, San Mateo, Santo Domingo, and Zozocolco. Alcedo, *Diccionario Geográfico-Histórico*, 60.
57 Population figures from the colonial period, especially from rural communities, are notoriously hard to identify with any precision. Peter Gerhard typically recorded numbers of families or tributaries in *A Guide to the Historical Geography of New Spain*. Neither of these figures (families or trib-

utaries) allows an exact account of the number of individuals in a community, and calculations for converting numbers of tributaries or families to numbers of individuals vary; five people per family is often used as a very rough estimate. For Papantla, Gerhard recorded 1,543 native and 215 Spanish families in 1743, and 2,269 native tributaries in 1795. Based on the 5:1 ratio described above, this would give populations somewhere between 8,690 and 11,345 people. Gerhard, *A Guide to the Historical Geography of New Spain*, 219, 257. See also Alcedo, *Diccionario Geográfico-Histórico de las Indias Occidentales*, vol.5, 59. Adriana Naveda Chávez-Hita and José González Sierra estimated an eighteenth-century population between 7,500 and 8,500. Adriana Naveda Chávez-Hita and José González Sierra, *Papantla* (Jalapa: Gobierno del Estado de Veracruz, Archivo General del Estado, 1990), 19. Both sets of numbers almost certainly include the population of some of the subject towns within the greater Papantla jurisdiction. When don Domingo Blaz Bazaraz, a judge from Manilla, was brought in to oversee the investigation of an uprising in Papantla in 1767, he identified 3,134 indians living in Papantla, of whom 818 were tributaries. By examining burial records for Papantla I have found that in the 1780s, 86.3 percent of the population was identified as native, while individuals labeled as *españoles*, *pardos*, *mulatos*, *mestizos*, *coyotes* and one *chino* made up the remaining 13.6 percent. Archivo Arzobispado de Papantla (hereafter AAP), Defunciones 1770–1925. Courtesy of the Church of Jesus Christ of Latter Day Saints, microfilm roll 698406.

58 See Bruce A. Castleman, *Building the King's Highway: Labor, Society, and Family on Mexico's Caminos Reales, 1757–1804* (Tucson: University of Arizona Press, 2005).

59 Kourí, *A Pueblo Divided*, 60.

60 By the 1760s there was a trade in dried fish and chicle between Guachinango and Papantla. AGI, México 1934 50–60, 63; Palacios Sánchez, "La muerte: símbolo de vida entre los totonacas de Papantla, Veracruz," 50.

61 Kourí, *A Pueblo Divided*, 56.

62 Charles Gibson, *The Aztecs Under Spanish Rule: A History of the Indians of the Valley of Mexico, 1510–1810* (Stanford: Stanford University Press, 1964), 167.

63 Ducey, *A Nation of Villages*, 11.

64 Salas and Martínez, "La política del secreto," 197; Carrión, *Descripción del Pueblo de Gueytlalpan*, 66.

65 Some sugar production did take place to the northwest of Papantla in the lowland area around Chicontepec. Archivo General de Indios de Seville (Hereafter AGI), Subdelegados 34/56/382–384. A full discussion of sugar production in colonial Veracruz is presented in Patrick Carroll, *Blacks in Colonial Veracruz: Race, Ethnicity, and Regional Development* (Austin: University of Texas Press, 1991).

66 Kourí, *A Pueblo Divided*, 7; Donovan S. Correll, "Vanilla: Its Botany, History, Cultivation and Economic Import." *Economic Botany* 7: 4 (Oct.–Dec., 1953), 291–358, 307.

67 Kourí, *A Pueblo Divided*, 32.

68 Kourí, *A Pueblo Divided*, 9; Henry Bruman, "The Culture History of Mexican Vanilla," *The Hispanic American Historical Review*, Vol. 28, No.

3 (Aug., 1948), 360–376, 370. This same process continued into the twentieth century. In Papantla today, one finds old photos on the walls of restaurants documenting this process, during which many of Papantla's cobbled streets were closed off and given over entirely to the drying pods.
69 Kourí, *A Pueblo Divided*, 20.
70 *Ibid.*, 10–15.
71 Ortiz Espejel, *La Cultura Asediada*, 30–31.
72 AGN, General de Parte 37/152/164.
73 German naturalist Alexander von Humboldt conducted an extraordinary survey of Spanish America between 1799 and 1804. In 1738 1,000 vanilla beans would sell for 45 pesos in Veracruz and 90 pesos when they reached Spain. According Alexander von Humboldt, export figures at the turn of the nineteenth century totaled roughly 1,000,000 beans annually with an annual export revenue at Veracruz of 500,000 pesos. The price had climbed to about a half peso per bean. Bruman, "The Cultural History of Mexican Vanilla," 371. Though Papantla represented only a small percentage of Mexican vanilla exports at the end of the colonial era, by 1860 it would export half of all Mexican vanilla. Kourí, *A Pueblo Divided*, 88.
74 *Áxc'ut* is Totonac for "Tobacco."
75 Prior to the conquest and after, natives throughout the Americas incorporated tobacco into religious ritual. In Mayan Guatemala it was used for medicinal purposes and by the priestly class for use in religious rites. It appears not to have been generally consumed by the common population. Jorge Luján Muñoz, "El Establecimiento de Tabaco en el Reino de Guatemala," in *Mesoamerica*, Vol. 41 (2001), 102. See also Ruben Oropeza, *Between Puffs: A History of Tobacco, Two thousand Years of Tobacco Use* (Orlando, FL: Rivercross Publishing, 2005), Chapter 2; Georgina Moreno Coello, "Alcaldes Mayores y Subdelegados frente la siembra clandestine de Tabaco: Papantla, 1765–1806" *América Latina en la Historia Económica, Revista de Investigación* 19: 3 (2012), 211.
76 To the north of the Totonac, the Huastecs employed the fairly widespread technique of tobacco enemas to produce hallucinations. Amerindians in what would become Venezuela chewed tobacco, as did other cultures. Drinking the herb also common. Francis Robicsek, *The Smoking Gods: Tobacco in Maya Art, History, and Religion* (Norman: University of Oklahoma Press. 1978), 20–23.
77 Oropeza, *Between Puffs*, 25, 50.
78 Luján Muñoz, "El Establecimiento del Estanco del Tabaco," 28.
79 Harvey and Kelly, "The Totonac," 672. Robicsek, *The Smoking Gods*, 30.
80 *Hebrolaria y etnnzoología en Papantla* (Mexico City: Dirección General de Cultural Populares, 1988), 24–25. In the case of the fear of water, one presumes that the aguardiente did as much to calm the patient's fears as any other ingredient. Modern use of tobacco as a medicine, of course, does not prove such use for tobacco during the colonial era. See also Ana Moreno-Coutiño and Beatriz Coutiño Bello, "Nicotiana Tobacum L.: Usos y Percepciones," *Ethnobiología* 10: 2 (2012), 30–32.
81 Although Columbus and his party threw out the first offering of tobacco they received, they soon developed a strong affection for this unusual plant. So new was the very idea of smoking, that the Europeans lacked the vocabulary

to describe it and referred to the process "drinking smoke." However, tobacco soon made it into common usage as Europeans took up the habit in force. Robicsek, *The Smoking Gods*, 3, 28.

82 Moreno-Coutiño and Coutiño Bello, "Nicotiana Tobacum," 33–37.

83 Deans-Smith, *Bureaucrats, Planters, and Workers*, 11; Luján Muñoz, "El Establecimiento del Estanco del Tabaco," 104. The same was also true in the Maya region in which "the cultivators of tobacco were small-scale producers, mainly poor, with limited resources, owners of small plots." Luján Muñoz, "El Establecimiento del Estanco del Tabaco," 104.

84 Deans-Smith, *Bureaucrats, Planters, and Workers*, 13.

85 *Ibid.*, 13–14.

TWO *Los Ausentes*: The Ethnic Landscape and Reflections on 1787

1 AGN, Criminal 284/5/139v.

2 See Robert Jackson, *Race, Caste, and Status: Indians in Colonial Spanish America* (Albuquerque: University of New Mexico Press, 1999), 4; Douglas Cope, *The Limits of Racial Domination: Plebian Society in Colonial Mexico City, 1660–1720* (Madison: University of Wisconsin Press, 1994), 18; Ilona Katzew, *Casta Painting: Images of Race in Eighteenth-Century Mexico* (New Haven: Yale University Press, 2004), 40.

3 AGN, Criminal 284/2/137v.

4 See Magali Carrera, *Imagining Identity in New Spain: Race, Lineage, and the Colonial Body in Portraiture and Casta Paintings* (Austin: University of Texas Press, 2003), 36–38, 44–105; and Ben Vinson III, *Bearing Arms for His Majesty: The Free Colored Militia in Colonial* Mexico (Stanford: Stanford University Press, 2001), 200.

5 Alcedo, *Diccionario Geográfico-Histórico*, 59.

6 Gerhard, *A Guide to the Historical Geography of New Spain*, 219.

7 See Chapter Four.

8 AGN, Criminal 303/2/225. In this sense the tone of the petition is similar to the Totonac indictments of the *alcalde mayor* seen in Chapter 5.

9 Matthew Restall, *The Black Middle: Africans, Mayas, and Spaniards in Colonial Yucatan* (Stanford: Stanford University Press, 2009), 2.

10 Herman Bennett, *Africans in Colonial Mexico: Absolutism, Christianity, and Afro-Creole Consciousness, 1570–1640* (Indianapolis: Indiana University Press, 2003), 11.

11 Margaret A. Jackson and Rebecca P. Brienen, eds., *Visions of Empire: Picturing the Conquest in Colonial Mexico* (Coral Gables, Fl.: University of Miami and Jay I. Kislak Foundation, 2003), plate 3, 45; Matthew Restall, "The Spanish Creation of the Conquest," in *Invasion and Transformation: Interdisciplinary Perspectives on the Conquest of Mexico*, ed. Margaret Jackson, 93–102 (Boulder: University Press of Colorado, 2007).

12 For an in depth study of the role of Africans in the conquest see Matthew Restall, "Black Conquistadors: Armed Africans in Colonial Spanish America," in *The Americas*, 57:2 (October 2000), 171–205, and Matthew Restall, "Invisible Warriors," in *Seven Myths of the Spanish Conquest*.

13 Notable recent titles in the literature on Afro-Mexico include: Patrick Carroll, *Blacks in Colonial Veracruz* (Austin: University of Texas Press, 1991); Ben

Vinson III, *Bearing Arms for his Majesty*; Restall ed., *Beyond Black and Red: African-Native Relations in Colonial Latin America* (Albuquerque: University of New Mexico Press, 2005); Restall, *The Black Middle: Africans, Mayas, and Spaniards in the Yucatan*; Laura Lewis, *Hall of Mirrors: Power, Witchcraft, and Caste in Colonial Mexico* (Durham: Duke University Press, 2003); Nicole Von Germeten, *Black Blood Brothers: Confraternities and Social Mobility for Afro-Mexicans*; Frank T. Proctor III, *Damned Notions of Liberty: Slavery, Culture, and Power in Colonial Mexico, 1640–1769* (Gainesville: University Press of Florida, 2006); Andrew B. Fisher and Matthew D. O'Hara eds., *Imperial Subjects: Race and Identity in Colonial Latin America* (Durham: Duke University Press); Jane G. Landers and Barry M. Robinson eds., *Slaves, Subjects and Subversives: Blacks in Colonial Latin America* (Albuquerque: University of New Mexico Press, 2006); Magali Carrera, *Imagining Identity in New Spain.*

14   Jake Frederick, "Pardos Enterados: Unearthing Black Papantla in the Eighteenth Century," *Journal of Colonialism and Colonial History* 5: 1 (2004): 2.

15   AAP, Defunciones 1770–1925, microfilm roll 698406. The only surviving parish records from Papantla's colonial period are interment records from September 1770 to June 1778.

16   Restall, *The Black Middle*, 12; Gonzalo Aguirre Beltrán, *La población negra de México, 1519–1810: estudio etnohistórico* (Mexico City: Fondo de Cultura Económica, 1989). I must also add here that testimony in AGN, Criminal 304 makes several references to a Portuguese man of some means who lived in Papantla in 1767. How he fit into the racial titles of the *sistema de castas* or what number of non-Spanish Europeans may have lived in Papantla, I cannot say with certainty. My impression from the documentation, however, is that the Portuguese ethnicity of this man was certainly one of the ways that he was identified within the Papantla community.

17   Magali Carrera, *Imagining Identity*, 37.

18   The social exogamy of black populations, particularly in the region of Veracruz, is a well-known phenomenon. But its specific intra-regional patterns are less studied. Whereas, on the whole, black exogamy in Veracruz tended to follow a pattern whereby *pardos* established links with Indians and *mulatos* with whites, the interment records of Papantla do not sustain this pattern. Of course, part of the reason why *mulatos* were unable to sustain tighter relationships with whites was due to the extremely small size of the population of *españoles* in residence. However, even if the white population was larger, it is difficult to determine if whites and *mulatos* would have had greater cross-racial contact in intimate familial relations. Perhaps the model of Papantla is useful in understanding other areas where fairly large populations of *indios* and blacks abounded, although in western provinces, such as Igualapa, blacks and natives in the late eighteenth century exhibited little intermarriage—despite the miniscule presence of whites. See: Ben Vinson III, "The Racial Profile of a Rural Mexican Province in the 'Costa Chica': Igualapa in 1791," *The Americas* 16: 2 (2000): 269–282; and Patrick Carroll, "Los Mexicanos Negros, El Mestizaje y los Fundamentos Olvidados de la 'Raza Cósmica:' Una Perspectiva Regional" *Historia Mexicana* 56: 3 (1995): 403–438.

19 Vinson, *Bearing Arms for His Majesty*, 202.

20 Carroll, *Blacks in Colonial Veracruz*, 113.

21 Good recent discussion on the complexities of understanding the interlocking relationship between social status and racial/ethnic status can be found in Lewis, *Hall of Mirrors*, 22–26, 33–35. See also Robert Schwaller, *Géneros de Gente in Early Colonial Mexico: Defining Racial Difference* (Norman: University of Oklahoma Press, 2016).

22 The idea that the *sistema* or *sociedad de castas* was a concrete ethnic ranking has been coming under fire in recent years. In-depth investigations of the significance of ethnicity as a barrier to social movements repeatedly find that ethnic rules were open to a great deal of manipulation. For an excellent examination of this phenomena in Mexico City see Cope, *The Limits of Racial Domination*.

23 Cynthia Milton and Ben Vinson III, "Counting Heads: Race and Non-Native Tribute Policy in Colonial Spanish America." *The Journal of Colonialism and Colonial History* 3:3 (2002), 1–18. For similar trends in Guatemala see Paul Lokken, "Marriage as Slave Emancipation in Seventeenth Century Rural Guatemala." *The Americas* 58:2 (2001): 197.

24 The ethnic breakdown for this census included only *indios, españoles, mestizos, mulatos,* and *negros*. Hence, *mulatos* and *pardos* have been grouped together. Aguirre Beltrán, *La Población Negra de México*, 221.

25 In the census of 1793, the relative numbers of both *mestizos* and *mulatos* persisted, at roughly eleven percent of the overall population.

26 By 1793 the population recorded as *indio* for New Spain was down to 61 percent.

27 AGN, Criminal 284/5/209v; AGN, Criminal 284/5/213v.

28 AGN, Criminal 303/2/223v. Furthermore, militia soldiers in certain locations and times were granted the *fuero*, which conferred legal immunities and provided for trial by the military as opposed to civil courts. However, this was far less common than tribute exemption. Vinson, *Bearing Arms for His Majesty*, 28.

29 The inspiration for presenting naming patterns in this way is drawn in part from Rebecca Horn, "Gender and Social Identity: Nahua Naming Patterns in Postconquest Central Mexico," *Indian Women of Early Mexico* eds. Susan Schroeder, Stephanie Wood, and Robert Haskett, 1-5-122 (Norman: University of Oklahoma Press, 1997).

30 Horn, "Gender and Social Identity," 108–115. Female naming patterns are also consistent with Restall's study of Spanish and Afro-Yucatecan names, *The Black Middle*, Chapter 2.

31 Between 1770 and 1775 the burial records include only two occupations, that of a deceased *alcalde mayor*, and a *parda* slave.

32 AGN, Criminal 303/2/200-251.

33 Units of free *pardos* and *morenos* were first organized in Mexico in 1550. Ben Vinson III, "Los Milicianos Pardos y la Relación Estatal Durante el Siglo XVIII en México," In *Fuerzas Militares en Iberoamérica, Siglos XVIII y XIX*. Edited by Juan Ortiz Escamilla (Mexico City: Universidad Veracruzana, El Colegio de Michoacán, El Colegio de México. 2005), 48.

34 AGN, Criminal 303/2/201.

35 AGN, Criminal 303/2/223v. This exemption was sometimes claimed by a

variety of relatives besides wives. Vinson, "Los Milicianos Pardos y la Relación Estatal," 56.

36 Vinson, *Bearing Arms for His Majesty, passim.*

37 Vinson, "Los Milicianos Pardos y la Relación Estatal," 52.

38 William Taylor suggested that entire communities would turn out for such events. Taylor, *Drinking Homicide, and Rebellion*, 116. This certainly seems to be the case. News spread quickly in small communities, and large segments of the population turned out, at least to see what was happening. However, Taylor claims that when "virtually the entire community turned out for local rebellions," they were all acting as part of the uprising. He specifically extends this claim to Papantla. This notion is not borne out by the documentary evidence.

39 Vinson, "Los Milicianos Pardos y la Relación Estatal," 48.

40 See Jake Frederick, "Without Impediment: Crossing Racial Boundaries in Colonial Mexico," *The Americas* 67: 4 (April, 2011): 495–515.

THREE *"Cachípat, Cachípat . . .* Get him, Get him": Collective Violence and the Uprising of 1736

1 A certain level of corporal punishment for failure to appear at mass was not, in and of itself, considered illegitimate provided that it was not perceived as excessive. Eric Van Young, *The Other Rebellion: Popular Violence, Ideology, and the Mexican Struggle for Independence, 1810–1821* (Stanford: Stanford University Press, 2001), 213.

2 AGN, Criminal 284/5/142r. The documentation for this case consists of 162 folios of testimony. Numerous witnesses from all sides of the event were interviewed between 16 October 1736, and 28 January 1737. Further interviews to confirm the testimony of the original investigation and to broaden the witness base were conducted between 13 September and 6 October 1738. The reader will notice that the following account draws heavily from a small sample of these sources. This is done for the sake of preserving the narrative flow of the event. The facts recounted are generally corroborated by several sources. Where testimony is disputed it is specifically noted.

3 AGN, Criminal 284/5/139.

4 AGN, Criminal 284/5/136v.

5 AGN, Criminal 284/5/139.

6 AGN, Criminal 284/5/136v.

7 AGN, Criminal 284/5/137.

8 Three months later, Torres Colmeno would claim that the turnout was in reality so low because "the rest are married to native women," suggesting that their loyalty to the *alcalde mayor* in the face of a native mob was open to question. AGN, Criminal 284/5/164v.

9 AGN, Criminal 284/5/151.

10 AGN, Criminal 284/5/139.

11 Torres Colmeno claimed that he went to the *pochguin* and tried to talk the throng into going home. They then started throwing stones at him, hitting him three times. Then one of the men that had accompanied the *alcalde mayor* fired his pistol to frighten the natives off, but the tactic failed, "a los que iban conmigo en cuyo tiempo dispare una pistola, a fin que espantarlos,

y hacer los retirar, pero no fue bastante." The discrepancy between the testimony of Torres Colmeno and Palacios is significant. I have chosen to use the testimony of Palacios because a later investigation of 1738 found that certain witness testimony from the initial 1736–1737 investigation was inaccurate. When asked to confirm his testimony, corporal Palacios reaffirmed that his own testimony had been generally accurate. AGN, Criminal 284/5/204v. Confirmation of the testimony of Clemente Palacios 13 September 1738. Pedro Torres, a free *pardo* resident of Papantla also indicated that he heard a pistol shot that night prior to the fighting. AGN, Criminal 284/5/215v. Joseph Rodriguez, a member of the militia also testified that the pistol shot came before the mob began throwing stones. AGN, Criminal 284/5/217.

12   AGN, Criminal 284/5/139v.

13   AGN, Criminal 284/5/138.

14   An excellent discussion of the ongoing process of conquest can be found in Restall's "Under the Lordship of the King," in *The Seven Myths of the Spanish Conquest.*

15   Macleod, "Some Thoughts on the Pax Colonial," 138.

16   A stark example of such a philosophy was shown in economist W.W. Rostow's "social tension chart," which correlated rebellion in nineteenth-century England with wheat prices. In this model peasant action was reduced to predictable reaction to external inputs. Though economic strain has been shown a very important cause of peasant unrest, such a model as Rostow's fails to consider cultural sensibilities as a significant cause of unrest. W. W. Rostow, *British Economy of the Nineteenth Century* (Oxford: Clarendon Press, 1948), 124.

17   Steve Stern, *Resistance, Rebellion, and Consciousness in the Andean Peasant World, Eighteenth to Twentieth Centuries* (Madison: The University of Wisconsin Press, 1987), 9.

18   An excellent recent work on the native manipulation of colonial power structures is Ethelia Ruiz Medrano and Susan Kellogg eds., *Negotiation Within Domination: New Spain's Indian Pueblos Confront the Spanish State* (Boulder: University of Colorado Press, 2010).

19   James Scott, *Weapons of the Weak: Everyday Forms of Peasant Resistance* (New Haven: Yale University Press, 1985). Steve Stern described native methods of non-violent resistance that readily adapted to and operated within the bounds of colonial society without wholly conceding autonomy as "reactive adaptation." Stern. *Resistance, Rebellion, and Consciousness.*

20   *Ibid.,* 11.

21   *Ibid.,* 8.

22   Ronald Spores wrote that when contending with Spanish colonial pressures, indigenous communities had five options: acquiescence and acceptance, employing the colonial courts, withholding tribute and labor, flight, and open resistance. Ronald Spores, "Differential Responses to Colonial Control among the Mixtecs and Zapotecs of Oaxaca," in *Native Resistance and the Pax Colonial in New Spain,* ed. Susan Schroeder (Lincoln and London: University of Nebraska Press. 1998), 46.

23   AGN, Indios 30/168/161-161v; see also Chapter Four.

24   Felipe Castro Gutiérrez, *Nueva ley y Nuevo rey: reformas borbónicas y rebelión popular en Nueva España* (Zamora, Michoacán: El Colegio de

Michoacán, 1996), 29. Eric Van Young later described village riots as "an accepted and enduring aspect of political culture during the colonial era." Van Young, *The Other Rebellion*, 501.

25 Castro Gutiérrez, *Nueva ley y nuevo rey*, 31.

26 Jovita Baber, "Empire, Indians, and the Negotiation for the Status of City in Tlaxcala, 1521–1550," in *Negotiation Within Domination: New Spain's Indian Pueblos Confront the Spanish State*, eds. Ethelia Ruiz Medrano and Susan Kellogg (Boulder, CO: University of Colorado Press, 2010), 33.

27 "Passive resistance" is often used to describe non-violent methods of resistance. I choose to avoid the term "passive resistance" as it implies a lack of active decision-making on the part of the practitioners.

28 Castro Gutiérrez, *Nueva ley y nuevo rey*, 26.

29 Sergio Serulnikov, *Subverting Colonial Authority: Challenges to Spanish Rule in Eighteenth-Century Southern Andes* (Durham: Duke University Press, 2003), 125.

30 Taylor, *Drinking Homicide and Rebellion*, 113–151.

31 Charles Tilly, "Revolutions and Collective Violence," in *Handbook of Political Science*, vol. 3., eds. Fred I. Greenstein and Nelson W. Polsby (Reading, MA: Addison-Wellesley Publishing Co, 1975), 505–506.

32 George Wada and James C. Davis "Riots and Rioters," *Western Political Quarterly* 10: 4 (1957): 864.

33 E. J. Hobsbawm, *Primitive Rebels: Studies in Archaic Forms of Social Movement in the 19th and 20th Centuries* (New York and London: W.W. Norton and Company, 1959), 10. Insurrections represent something far different than simply a larger version of local violence. An insurrection is founded on the assumption that the rules of society as they exist are intolerable and must be changed at their foundation. They are intended to reshape the mechanisms of rule or replace the highest levels of ruling authority. Insurrections are much rarer than uprisings, require more organization and planning than uprisings, and must draw adherents from outside the local sphere. Because the objectives of revolutionary movements are larger in scope, their participants come from a broader spectrum of the populace. Thus one of the defining features of a revolutionary movement is that it draws participants from across corporate boundaries, what Charles Tilly described as "association-based" connections. Association-based movements align people on the basis of guild, religion, or some sort of extra-community organization. Furthermore, because insurrections directly threaten the ruling system of authority they are normally punished with much greater severity, and thus require rebels to accept much greater risk than do members of a mob uprising. Tilly, "Revolutions and Collective Violence." See also Charles Tilly, *From Mobilization to Revolution* (Reading, MA: Addison Wesley Publishing Co, 1978), 69–90.

34 See Ducey, *A Nation of Villages*. The topic of late eighteenth-century unrest as it relates to mobilization is discussed further in Chapter Seven.

35 Ward Stavig, "Conflict, Violence and Resistance," in *The Countryside in Colonial Latin America*, ed. Luisa Schell Hoberman and Susan Migden Socolow (Albuquerque: University of New Mexico Press, 1996), 226.

36 James C. Scott, *The Moral Economy of the Peasant: Rebellion and Subsistence in Southeast Asia* (New Haven: Yale University Press, 1976), 11.

Scholars have repeatedly found that peasant rebellions around the world are infrequently oriented toward any major social change. Joel Migdal points out that the interest of the peasant rarely looks to something so abstract as the nature of political structure. Migdal views uprisings from the perspective of the individual peasant, whose most important object is always the maintenance of his or her family: "His goals are limited and orientated to the administrative solution of his family's mundane problems rather than directed to the policy level of politics." Joel Migdal, *Peasants, Politics, and Revolution: Pressures Toward Political and Social Change in the Third World* (Princeton: Princeton University Press, 1974), 22.

37 Taylor, *Drinking Homicide and Rebellion*, 115.
38 *Ibid.*, 115–119.
39 Robert Patch, *Maya Revolt and Revolution in the Eighteenth Century* (Armonk, New York: Sharpe, 2002), 23, 11.
40 Van Young, *The Other Rebellion*, 11.
41 Taylor, *Drinking, Homicide, and Rebellion*, 120.
42 AGN, Criminal 284/5/138.
43 AGN, Criminal 284/5/138.
44 AGN, Criminal 284/5/151v.
45 AGN, Criminal 284/5/163.
46 AGN, Criminal 284/5/176.
47 AGN, Criminal 284/5/179.
48 Ducey, *A Nation of Villages*, 41.
49 AGN, Criminal 284/5/177v.
50 AGN, Criminal 284/5/177.
51 AGN, Criminal 284/5/211.
52 Joel Migdal's 1974 *Peasants, Politics, and Revolution* claimed that peasant economies, prior to invasion of capitalist forces, tended to be relatively equal within the communities. The incursion of outside economic forces creates a more highly stratified community with one group being more successful than another. Access to the outside economy becomes privileged to the successful group. Self-interest in joining that outside economy creates division within the community. "This growing income gap has precipitated the historical weakening of those institutions which had been able to suppress the feelings of peasants oriented toward outside mobility. The result of this change and stratification is the destruction of community systems that had ensured redistribution within the community," Migdal, *Peasants, Politics, and Revolution*, 19. Communities also divide into political factions. The weakening of community bonds, as demonstrated in the economic example above, can lead to division within the community along political lines. In colonial Mexico local offices were held by natives rather than outside Spanish authorities. Hence the local groups would come into conflict with one another over local leadership.
53 Castro Gutiérrez, *Nuevo ley y nuevo rey*, 95.

FOUR **"Tobacco for Snuff or Tobacco for Smoking, It is all Vice": Bourbon Reforms and the Uprising of 1764**

1 No contemporary accounts give the year of the uprising. Testimony from

1767 described the event as having happened "a few years past. At the start of the monopoly." The monopoly was signed into law in August 1764, and was only publicized in December of that year. Hence it is possible that the uprising took place as early as 1764, but no less possible that it happened in early 1765. The most recent work that touches on the uprising is Georgina Moreno Coello's 2012 article, "Alcaldes mayores y subdelegados frente la siembra clandestine de Tabaco: Papantla, 1765–1806," which dates the uprising to 1765. For simplicity's sake, I will use the year 1765 in the text.

2   AGN, Criminal 308/3/76.
3   AGI, Méxcio 1934 77v.
4   *Ibid.*
5   AGN, Criminal 304/102v. AGN, Criminal 304/2/97v. This building was replaced and would be the site of the start of the 1787 uprising.
6   AGI, México 1934, 40-40v.
7   AGI, México 1934, 40; AGN, Criminal 303/4/353v; AGN, Criminal 308/3/75. See also Ducey, *A Nation of Villages*, 33.
8   AGN, Criminal 304/92v.
9   Macleod, "Some Thoughts on the Pax Colonial," 133.
10 Henry Kamen notes that "from 1640–1763, almost all of the bullion reaching the peninsula was re-exported to other European countries and to Asia." Henry Kamen, *Empire: How Spain Became a World Power, 1492–1763* (New York: Harper Collins, 2003), 449.
11 David Brading, "Bourbon Spain and its Empire," in *The Cambridge History of Latin America, Volume 1: Colonial Latin America* ed. Leslie Bethell (Cambridge: Cambridge University Press, 1984), 389.
12 Enrique Florescano and Isabel Gil Sánchez, "1750–1808: La época de las reformas borbónicas y del crecimiento económico," *Cuadernos de trabajo del departimiento de investigaciones históricas* (Mexico City: INAH, 1974): 10. The House of Hapsburg had made some effort to contend with the economy's decline. The Hapsburg crown turned to debasing copper coinage to increase revenues. Though this method was effective in the short term—the crown could purchase copper at one price and double its value through reminting—this led to a weakening of the currency and ultimately rising prices for Spanish products.
13 R. Trevor Davies, *Spain in Decline: 1621–1700* (London: Macmillan, 1965), 92–95.
14 Davies, *Spain in Decline*, 98.
15 Henry Kamen has recently argued that Spain was not in fact in a state of decline at the end of the seventeenth century, but that economic crisis was precipitated by the War of Succession, which alienated Spain's traditional allies. He writes, "Spain was no worse off in 1700 than it had been in 1600, or 1500; indeed, its economy and population were now in better shape than ever. The difference was that its success as an imperial power had depended on the collaboration, both as allies and as enemies, of the major states of the West." Kamen, *Empire*, 443. This thesis runs counter to much that has been written about the state of Spanish affairs at the fall of the house of Hapsburg, including much of Kamen's earlier work. In fact, in the same work Kamen gives an extensive accounting of Spain's poor state of affairs at the start of the War of Succession. He cites Spain's utter military incapacity, pointing out

that it lacked modern equipment, sufficient naval forces, uniforms, wages, and even gunpowder. Spanish debt was high, expenditure on warfare was high, and by the late seventeenth century, American mine production was low. By the beginning of the eighteenth century Spain had become so destitute that the crown was forced to permit trade with the British and Dutch, even though these two nations were at war with Spain. Kamen, *Empire*, 442. Kamen's claim that Spain was in no way in a state of decline is somewhat mystifying, and seems to presume that the previous two centuries lacked any kind of "golden age" as is so commonly claimed in the literature. In an earlier work, Kamen himself argued that Spain's "golden age" took place at a time when censorship was becoming commonplace, and Spain was in some ways becoming culturally entrenched, eschewing foreign ideas and expelling the Moors. Henry Kamen, *Spain, 1469–1714* (London: Longman, 1983), 190–195. Kamen claims that early on Spain began self-destructive imperial policies that sowed the seeds of its eventual decline. I agree with Kamen that, from the outset, Spain embarked on financial and even cultural policies that would have disastrous consequences over the course of the seventeenth century. However, I am inclined to agree with such scholars as R. Trevor Davies, Anthony Pagden, Enrique Florescano, and others, who see the waning years of Hapsburg rule as a time of true decline for the peninsula and the empire.

16   G.V. Scammall, "'A Very Profitable and Advantageous Trade': British Smuggling in the Iberian Americas circa 1500–1750," *Itinerario* 24: 3–4 (2000): 152.

17   J. H. Elliott, "Spain and America in the Sixteenth and Seventeenth Centuries," in *The Cambridge History of Latin America, Volume 1, Colonial Latin America*, ed. Leslie Bethell (Cambridge: Cambridge University Press, 1984), 334.

18   Stanley J. Stein and Barbara H. Stein, *Silver, Trade, and War: Spain and America in the Making of Early Modern Europe* (Baltimore: Johns Hopkins University Press, 2000), 18; Scammall, "'A Very Profitable and Advantageous Trade'," 168.

19   José Velasco Toro, "La política desamortizadora y sus efectos en la región de Papantla, Veracruz," *La palabra y el hombre* 72 (1989): 137.

20   Murdo Macleod, "Spain and America: The Atlantic Trade, 1492–1720," *The Cambridge History of Latin America, Volume 1: Colonial Latin America*. ed. Leslie Bethell (Cambridge: Cambridge University Press, 1984), 371; Scammall, "'A Very Profitable and Advantageous Trade,'" *passim*.

21   Gutiérrez, *Nueva ley y nuevo rey*, 26.

22   Elliot, "Spain and America in the Sixteenth and Seventeenth Centuries," 335.

23   While historians generally accept that the Bourbon reforms were nonetheless influenced by French conceptions of modern monarchical rule, scholars such at Alan Kuethe, Lowel Blaisdell, and Horst Pietschmann have credibly argued that those reforms were considerably shaped by Spanish, and even Italian, ministers. See Allan Kuethe and Lowell Blaisdell, "French Influence and the Origins of the Bourbon Colonial Reorganization," *Hispanic American Historical Review* 71: 1 (1991); and Horst Pietschmann, "Antecedentes españoles e hispanoamericanos de las intendencias," in *Memoria del cuarto congreso Venezolano de historia* (Caracas: Academia Nacional de la Historia, 1983); David Brading also contends that the office of intendant as

employed by Spain held much greater power than French intendants, on whom the office was modeled. David Brading, "Bourbon Spain and Its American Empire," 395.

24 The Treaty of Utrecht eliminated the threat of a unified French Spanish empire by stipulating that Philip renounce any claim by himself or his heirs to the throne of France.

25 See also Gabriel Paquette, *Enlightenment, Governance, and Reform in Spain and its Empire, 1759–1808* (New York: Palgrave, 2011), 5.

26 Carr, *Spain*, 176.

27 Earl J. Hamilton, "Money and Economic Recovery in Spain Under the First Bourbon, 1701–1746," *The Journal of Modern History* 15: 3 (1943).

28 Brading, "Bourbon Spain and its American Empire," 391; Carr, *Spain*, 177.

29 Kenneth Andrien has recently argued that the reforms enacted in the last half of the eighteenth century varied considerably across the different regions of the Americas, and that we should not think of the reforms as a coordinated series of edicts that translated the singular intentions of the crown into consistently applied policy across the vast expanse of the American colonies. Kenneth Andrien, "The Politics of Reform in Spain's Atlantic Empire during the Late Bourbon Period: The Visita of José García de León y Pizarro in Quito," *Journal of Latin American Studies* 41: 4 (2009).

30 Long since insinuated into rule on the peninsula, these intendants were bureaucrats with well-defined areas of administrative responsibility, who were well-paid and responsible directly to the crown. The intendants were first introduced to the colonies in Cuba in 1764. Allan Kuethe and Lowell Blaisdell, "French Influence and the Origins of the Bourbon Colonial Reorganization," *The Hispanic American Historical Review* 71: 1 (1991), 579.

31 Brading, "Bourbon Spain and its American Empire," 407. The viceroyalty of La Plata received eight intendants in 1782, and Peru received eight in 1784. Cuba, Chile, Caracas received a total of six intendants.

32 Gerhard, *A Guide to the Historical Geography of New Spain*, 218.

33 Joseph M. Barnadas, "The Catholic Church in America" in *The Cambridge History of Latin America, Volume 1 Colonial Latin America*, ed. Leslie Bethell (Cambridge: Cambridge University Press, 1984), 522.

34 Florescano and Sánchez, "1750–1808: La época de las reformas borbónicas y del crecimiento económico," 29.

35 Clara García Ayluardo, "Re-formar la iglesia novohispana," in *Las reformas borbónicas, 1750–1808*, ed. Clara García Ayluardo (Mexico: CIDE, 2010), 226.

36 Andrea J. Smidt, "Bourbon Regalism and the Importation of Gallicanism: The Political Path for a State Religion in Eighteenth-Century Spain," *Anuario de historia de la iglesia* 19 (2010): 26.

37 D. A. Brading, "Tridentine Catholicism and Enlightened Despotism in Bourbon Mexico," *Journal of Latin American Studies* 15: 1 (May, 1983): 5, 11–12, 16.

38 García Ayluardo, *Las reformas borbónicas*, 231.

39 Ricardo Anguita Cantero, *Ordenanza y policía urbana : Los orígenes de la reglamentación edificatoria en España, 1750–1900* (Monográfica Arte Y Arqueología; Universidad de Granada, 1997), 104–105.

40 Castro Gutiérrez, *Nueva ley y nuevo rey*, 106.
41 Barnadas, "The Catholic Church in America," 537.
42 García Ayluardo, *Las reformas borbónicas*, 237.
43 Barnadas, "The Catholic Church in America," 538.
44 Christon Archer, *The Army in Bourbon Mexico, 1760–1810* (Albuquerque: University of New Mexico Press, 1977), 1–8.
45 Archer, *The Army in Bourbon Mexico*, 3; see also Lyle N. McAlister, "The Reorganization of the Army of New Spain, 1763–1766," *The Hispanic American Historical Review* 33:1 (1953).
46 Kuethe and Blaisedale, "French Influence and the Origins of the Bourbon Colonial Reorganization," 591–592.
47 Archer, *The Army in Bourbon Mexico*, 10. See also Alan Kuethe, "The Early Reforms of Charles III in the Viceroyalty of New Granada," in *Reform and Insurrection in Bourbon New Granada and Peru*, ed. John R. Fisher, Allan Kuethe, Anthony McFarlane (Baton Rouge: Louisiana State University Press, 1990), 23–26.
48 Vinson, *Bearing Arms for His Majesty*, 37–38. Also free-colored militia units, common throughout the colony, were forced to accept white officers during the first stage of reform efforts. Papantla's free-colored militia would protest this situation, resulting in a complete failure to appoint any new officers. By 1779, Papantla had no officer-grade militiamen in their ranks. Vinson, *Bearing Arms for His Majesty*, 21.
49 Richard Harding, *Seapower and Naval Warfare, 1650–1830* (London: UCL Press, 2001), 232.
50 Stanley J. Stein and Barbara H. Stein, *Apogee of Empire: Spain and New Spain in the Age of Charles III, 1759–1789* (Baltimore: Johns Hopkins University Press, 2003), 20–22, 44–45.
51 J. H. Parry, *The Spanish Seaborne Empire* (Berkeley: University of California Press, 1990), 286.
The *flota* was a convoy system meant to protect Spanish shipping from pirates. Goods for overseas shipping were collected in major Iberian and American ports to await armed escorts. Thus goods were shipped infrequently, normally only twice a year. Limiting the number of sailings across the ocean greatly reduced the risk of foreign predation, but also severely strained commerce. See Kris Lane, *Pillaging the Empire: Piracy in the Americas, 1500–1750* (Armonk NY: M.E. Sharpe, 1998).
52 Timothy Walton, *The Spanish Treasure Fleets* (Sarasota: Pineapple Press, 1994), 176.
53 David Brading, *Miners and Merchants in Bourbon Mexico, 1763–1820* (Cambridge: Cambridge University Press, 1971), 29.
54 Deans-Smith, *Bureaucrats, Planters, and Workers*, xvi.
55 Ricardo Salvatore, "The Strength of Markets in Latin America's Sociopolitical Discourse, 1750–1850," *Latin American Perspectives* 26: 1 (1999): 25.
56 *Ibid.*, 27.
57 *Ibid.*, 35.
58 See also Díaz Hernández, "La intendencia de Veracruz y los repartimientos (1787–1810)."
59 Brading, *Miners and Merchants*, 29.

60   Clara Elena Suárez Argüello, *Camino real y larga: la arriería en la Nueva España* (Mexico: Ciesas, 1997), 115.

61   Deans-Smith, "The Money Plant: The Royal Tobacco Monopoly of New Spain, 1765–1821," in *The Economies of Mexico and Peru During the Late Colonial Period, 1760–1810*. (Berlin: Colloquium Verlag Berlin, 1989), 361.

62   José Enrique Covarrubias, *La moneda de cobre en México, 1760–1842: un problema administrativo*. (México: Universidad Nacional Autónoma de México, 2000), 179.

63   AGN, Tabaco 390/2/1.

64   Deans-Smith, *Bureaucrats, Planters, and Workers*, 9.

65   AGN, Tabaco 390/2/2, 2v, 3. Catalina Vizcarra noted in her study of the Peruvian tobacco industry, because tobacco was unnecessary to preserve health, monopolization was "consistent with the Bourbon view that in order to build a prosperous empire the crown had to promote the wellbeing of the population at large." Catalina Vizcarra, "Bourbon Intervention in the Peruvian Tobacco Industry, 1752–1813," *Journal of Latin American Studies* 39: 3 (2007): 568.

66   AGN, Tabaco 390/2/2.

67   Deans-Smith, *Bureaucrats, Planters, and Workers*, 11.

68   José González Sierra, *Monopolio de humo: elementos para la historia del tabaco en México y algunos conflictos de tabaqueros veracruzanos, 1915–1930* (Xalapa: Universidad Veracruzana, 1987), 48. See also Deans-Smith, *Bureaucrats, Planters, and Workers*, 7–15.

69   Deans-Smith, *Bureaucrats, Planters, and Workers*, 61. In 1764, the Kingdom of New Granada introduced the monopoly on a limited scale. By 1772 the tobacco monopoly in New Granada would be single largest source of revenue in the kingdom. Kuethe, "The Early Reforms of Charles III in New Granada," 30–31.

70   Deans-Smith, *Bureaucrats, Planters, and Workers*, 30. 7,000 workers labored in the Mexico City tobacco manufactory. Suárez Argüello, *Camino real y larga*, 119.

71   See Silvia Arrom, *Containing the Poor: The Mexico City Poor House, 1774–1871* (Durham: Duke University Press, 2000).

72   AGN, Tabaco 390/2/6v.

73   AGN, Tabaco 290/2/15-30v.

74   AGI, México 2256.

75   Moreno Coello, "Alcaldes mayores y subdelegados," 221.

76   Suárez Argüello, *Camino real y larga*, 120.

77   *Ibid.*

78   Castro Gutiérrez, *Nueva ley y nuevo rey*, 103.

79   Palacios Sánchez, 56.

80   AGN, México 2256; AGN, Bandos 6/18/39.

81   AGN, México 2256.

82   AGN, Bando 6/23/54.

83   AGN, Tabaco 252/2.

84   AGN, Tabaco 252/2, paragraph VIII.

85   AGN, Tabaco 252/1. The penalty of 200 lashes appears to have been the brainchild of Sierra Zagle, who suggested it in his initial evaluation of the suitability of tobacco for monopolization. Two hundred lashes was a very

considerable punishment and could very well have been fatal in and of itself. AGN, Tabaco 390/2/3.

86 AGN, Bandos 6/23/54; AGN, Mexico 1523; AGN, Criminal 714/4/11-130; Deans-Smith, *Bureaucrats, Planters, and Workers*, 24.

87 Deans-Smith cites one account of the *resguardo* killing a contrabandista. Deans-Smith, *Bureaucrats, Planters, and Workers*, 34. In fact, the royal attorney claimed in 1791 that penalties imposed on contraband tobacco growers were "excessive." His petition resulted in a Royal Order lessening penalties for tobacco contraband crimes. AGN, Tobacco 134.

88 Deans-Smith, *Bureaucrats, Planters, and Workers*, 33.

89 Díaz Hernández, "Contrabandistas tabaqueros en la region de Veracruz," 202.

90 AGN, Indios 30/168/161-161v.

91 AGN, Tierras 2899/26/353-4.

92 AGN, Indios 38/22/24-26v.

93 AGN, Reales Cedulas 109/34/1.

94 Covarrubias, *La Moneda de Cobre*, 181.

95 Moreno Coello, "Alcaldes mayores y subdelegados," 215. Official complicity was not limited to Papantla. In 1768, the director of the monopoly in Guatemala claimed that local administrators were fomenting the practice of contraband cultivation. Carlos Uriel del Carpio-Penagos, "Producción y comercio de tabaco en Centroamérica a fines del período colonial," *LiminaR. Estudios Sociales y Humanísticos* 12: 2 (2014): 200.

96 *Ibid.*, 222–223.

97 Deans-Smith: *Bureaucrats, Planters, and Workers*, xviii, 34. A similar hardship took place in New Granada where local officials lost a source of tax revenue with the prohibition of private *aguardiente* production. Earle Mond, "Indian Rebellion and Bourbon Reform in New Granada," 104.

98 Deans-Smith, *Bureaucrats, Planters, and Workers*, 49. It is worth noting that in the southern part of Veracruz, in the district of Cordoba, the tobacco monopoly contributed to the demise of slavery in that region as the sugar plantations subsided to the tobacco production, which is much less, labor intensive. Carroll, *Blacks in Colonial Veracruz*, 95.

99 AGN, Correspondencia de Varias Autoridades 30/61/131. The soldiers were absolved of any wrongdoing in November of the same year. AGN, Correspondencia de Various Autoridades 30/61/206-208v.

100 Deans-Smith, *Bureaucrats, Planters, and Workers*, 49.

101 AGN, Alcaldes Mayores 9/64/88-88v.

102 The raids yielded an average of 1,078 plants per raid. AGN, Criminal 714/4/103-109v. It is noteworthy that many of the days during this six-week mission were not spent in active search.

103 AGN, Criminal 714/4/80-92.

104 Moreno Coello, "Alcaldes mayores y subdelegados," 222.

105 AGN, Intendencias 80/10/s.n.

106 Palacios Sanchez, "La muerte: símbolo de vida entre los totonacas de Papantla, Veracruz," 55.

107 Castro Gutiérrez, *Nueva ley y nuevo rey*, 37.

108 Ducey, *A Nation of Villages*, 25.

109 Moreno Coello, "Alcaldes mayores y subdelegados," 208.
110 See also Luján Muñoz, "El establecimiento del estanco del tabaco," *passim*. Luján Muñoz notes that in Guatemala it was the poorest class of society that was affected most gravely by the monopolization of tobacco.
111 Moreno Coello, "Alcaldes mayores y subdelegados," 231.

FIVE **"Kill That Dog of an *Alcalde Mayor*": *Repartimientos* and Uprising in 1767**

1 AGN, Criminal 304/1/107. Several accounts put the number of militia soldiers at four. One claims that there were eight militia soldiers transporting Olmos. AGN, Criminal 304/1/106v.
2 AGN, Criminal 304/1/107. The testimony of Manuel Santiago, a Totonac resident of Papantla, also suggests that Olmos was jailed in part for having been rude to the curate.
3 AGN, Criminal 304/1/83v.
4 AGN, Criminal 304/1/118.
5 At this time the church bell was not housed in the church, but on the hilltop just south of the church.
6 AGI, México 1934 69.
7 AGI, México 1934 582v-583.
8 AGN, Criminal 304/1/84.
9 AGI, México 1935 44v. Testimony by the interpreter Antonio Uribe described the Rancho Rincon as being "quatro leguas," (four leagues) from town. A conflicting account, from AGI México, Microfilm 1935/58, claims that the Rancho Rincón was only three leagues from town. Given that Olmos was shackled, I am inclined to believe the credibility of the shorter distance.
10 AGN, Criminal 304/1/107.
11 AGN, Criminal 304/1/85v.
12 AGN, Criminal 304/1/107.
13 The presence of machetes is attested in AGN, Criminal 304/103v. However, the presence of firearms in this event is contradicted by several testimonials. The majority of the testimony does appear to corroborate the notion that at least some natives owned firearms. Some witnesses, both native and Spanish, claimed that these weapons appeared during the uprising. AGN, Criminal 304/1/112; AGN, Criminal 304/1/111. During the colonial era it was illegal for natives to own firearms. Testimony by the lieutenant *alcalde mayor* of Tamiagua, roughly 70 miles north of Papantla, stated that the natives had 150 flintlocks and another 50 matchlocks. AGN, Criminal 304/1/97v. Others claimed that these weapons were used by the natives for hunting only, and were not carried during the uprising. AGN, Criminal 304/115v; AGI, México 1934 54v.

The source of the weapons is unclear. One witness claimed that some of the weapons had been purchased from the militia captain, don Placido Pérez, and others claim that they were bought from a boat that came from Veracruz and Campeche. AGN, Criminal 304/117v. The native witness, Miguel Santiago, claimed that British vessels had come to the coast, but he was unsure if these vessels had sold the munitions, but he thought that it was possible. AGN, Criminal 304/109. During this time British vessels somewhat routinely sold contraband along the coast. Further testimonial implies that natives were buying gunpowder from alcalde mayor de la Barga himself. AGI, México, 1935/62v.

14 AGN, Criminal 304/1/84.

15 AGN, Criminal 304/1/107.

16 AGN, Criminal 304/1/ 84; AGI, México 1934 47v.

17 AGI, México 1934 53v, 67v.

18 "yo soy el rey y soy el que mando y govienrno; nadie tenga miedo y hagan lo que se les dize, por que sino se les mata[r] y traia en las manos dicho Baston, con el que and[] bo gobernando; . . ." AGN, Criminal 304/1/84v.

19 AGI, México 1934, 580v.-589; AGI, México 1934, 589-598v. Testimony of Nicolas Nava.

20 AGI, México 1934 47-48.

21 AGN, Criminal 304/1/84v.

22 AGN, Criminal 304/1/84v. Lieutenant to the *alcalde mayor*, don Juan Domingo Ugarte, testified that a large portion of the Indians of Papantla engaged in the uprising. AGN, Criminal 304/1/97.

23 AGN, Criminal 304/1/97v,111, 112, 117v. See also note 10.

24 AGN, Criminal 304/1/85.

25 AGN, Criminal 304/1/85.

26 *Ibid.*

27 AGN, Criminal 304/1/107, 111, 112, 116v.

28 AGN, Criminal 304/1/85v.

29 *Ibid.*

30 AGN, Criminal 304/1/87-87v.

31 AGN, Criminal 304/1/86v.

32 AGN, Criminal 304/1/85. Later, when referring to the uprising in January 1768, de la Barga said the uprising happened because of "falta de respecto que tuvieron a la real jurisdicción" (they lacked respect for the royal authority). AGN, Criminal 303/2/222v.

33 AGI, México 1934 751v.

34 Carlos Rubén Ruiz Medrano, "Rebeliones indígenas en la época colonial: el tumulto indígena de Papantla de 1767." *Mesoamerica* 32 (1996): 340.

35 AGN, Indios 30/168/161r-v; AGN, Tierras 2899/26/353; AGN, Criminal 289/5/138-219; AGN, Subdelegados 34/56/382/384; AGN, Criminal 303/346-353; AGN, Criminal 312/9/248-250; AGI, México 2256. See also Ruiz Medrano, "Rebeliones Indígenas en la Epoca Colonial."

36 During the colonial period, the diocese of Papantla was within the bishopric of Puebla.

37 "cultivan sus milpas para sustenarse yo sus mugeres e hijos que pagan los reales tributes porque no tienen otros frutos de que hacerlo . . . Alcalde mayor ni su thenientes . . . semejantes daños estorsiones por lo que referido han ocurrido antes . . ." AGN, Indios 30/168/161.

38 The *repartimiento de mercancías* could also be used to force production in certain areas, such as artisanal works or lumbering. This type of *repartimiento* predominantly occurred in areas with a significant landless native population. Margarita Menegus, "La economía indígena y su articulación al mercado en nueva españa. El repartimiento forzozo de mercancías," in *El repartimiento forzoso de mercancías en México, Perú y Filipinas.* ed.

Margarita Menegus (Mexico City: Centro de Estudios Sobre la Universidad-UNAM, 2000), 13–14.

39 Laura Machuca, "El Impacto del Repartimiento de Mercancías en la Provincia de Tehuantepec durante el Siglo XVIII: Los Pueblos de la Grana," in *El repartimiento forzoso de mercancías en méxico, peru, y filipinas*. Ed. Margarita Menegus (México City: Instituto de Investigaciones Dr. José María Luis Mora, Centro de Estudios sobre la Universidad-UNAM, 2000).

40 Ernest Sánchez Santiró, "Una modernización conservadora; el reformismo borbónico y su impacto sobre la economía, la fiscalidad y las instituciones," in *Las reformas borbónicas, 1750–1808*, ed. Clara García Ayluardo editor (Mexico City: CIDE, 2010), 308.

41 Gibson, *The Aztecs Under Spanish Rule*, 233.

42 Eric Van Young, *Hacienda and Market in Eighteenth-Century Mexico: The Rural Economy of the Guadalajara Region, 1675–1820* (Berkeley: University of California Press, 1981), 243–44.

43 Robert Patch, *Maya and Spaniard in Yucatan, 1648–1812* (Stanford: Stanford University Press, 1993), 163.

44 Patch, *Maya and Spaniard in Yucatan*, 156.

45 Gibson, *The Aztecs Under Spanish Rule*, 233.

46 Bernardo García Martínez, *Los pueblos de las Sierra: El poder y el espacio entre los indios del norte de Puebla hasta 1700* (Mexico City: El Colegio de Mexico, 1987), 251; Van Young, *Hacienda and Market in Eighteenth-Century Mexico*, 244.

47 *Recopilación de leyes de los reynos de las Indias* (1681), book 6, title 1, law 28, 191v.

48 John Fisher, *Bourbon Peru, 1750–1824* (Liverpool: Liverpool University Press, 2003), 33.

49 Jeremy Baskes, *Indians, Merchants, and Markets: A Reinterpretation of the Repartimiento and Spanish-Indian Economic Relations in Colonial Oaxaca, 1750–1821* (Stanford: Stanford University Press, 2000), 6.

50 Arij Ouweneel, "El gobernador de indios, el repartimiento de comercios y la caja de comunidad en los pueblos de indios del México central (Siglo XVIII)," in *El repartimiento forzoso de mercancías en México, Perú y Filipinas*. ed. Margarita Menegus (Mexico City: Centro de Estudios Sobre la Universidad-UNAM, 2000), 66.

51 Patch *Maya and Spaniard in Yucatan*, 56.

52 Juan Marchena Fernández, "The Social World of the Military in Peru and New Granada," in *Reform and Insurrection in Bourbon New Granada* eds. John R. Fisher, Alan Kuethe, and Anthony McFarlane (Baton Rouge: Louisiana State University, 1990), 81.

53 Spores, "Differential Responses to Colonial Control," 44.

54 AGI, México 1934, 30v.

55 "el actual alcalde de aquella Jurisdicción Don Alonso de la Barga no les permite comercian de manera alguna con los Yndios de su territorio, y assi no les dexa ni da lugar á que haciendo feria, comprando ni permitando los generos que llevan saquen de aquel País los frutos que producen." AGN, Criminal 304/98. The opening page of this testimony from Lazaro González is lost. Therefore, his background, ethnicity, and place of residence remain unclear.

56 AGN, Criminal 304/1/98v-99. *Chitle*, more commonly known as *chicle*, is the gummy resin produce by the zapote tree.

57 AGN, Criminal 304/1/102.

58 AGN, Criminal 304/1/103v.

59 Testimony that had to be given through a translator was often recorded in the third person. "habrá in año que a todos los naturales del Pueblo les hizo cortar todos los arboles frutales que tenían y les servían para ayuda de mantenerse que el declarante tenia ocho frutales, y también le los hizo cortar por el pie que para ello dicho Alcalde mayor hecho bando amenazando con prisión y con pena que todos obedecieron puntalmente callaron y no huvo alvoroto alguno que no acudieron al Señor Virrey por que saben que quando alguno de ellos ba a Mexico, y entiende que es algún recurso contra él quando buelben los prende y azota." AGN, Criminal 304/1/109v.

60 "Que sabe que todos aquellos naturales como también el declarante son fieles vasayos del Rey a quien obedecen como también al Señor Virrey que están contentos pero que no les están assi con el Alcalde Mayor actual por que los obstiga demasiado asotandolos quando a él y al Cura no pagan lo que deven y por otras qualquieras cosas . . ." AGN, Criminal 304/1/109.

61 "Que el declarante es muy contento y es fiel con el Rey como también con el Señor virrey que lo considera como él con sus hijos que lo tiene por Padre y que no tienen queja alguna sino con el Alcalde mayor por ser este un hombre tan fuerte que ninguno puede contextar con él; Que están con dicho Alcalde mayor mui disgustados por barias cosas que les ha hecho; que entró haciendo cortar como se cortan todos los arboles frutales del Pueblo para lo que hecho bando con amenaza de prisión y de pena que se execute en uno de los Yndios por que avia dejado un palo o árbol de anono junto á sus casa." AGN, Criminal 304/1/118-118v.

62 "que el declarante es muy contento y es fiel con el Rey como también con el Señor virrey que lo considera como él con sus hijos que lo tiene por Padre y que no tienen queja alguna sino con el Alcalde mayor por ser estar un hombre tan fuerte que ninguno puede contextar con él; Que están con dicho Alcalde mayor mui disgustados por barias cosas que les ha hecho; que entró haciendo cortar como se cortan todos los arboles frutales del Pueblo para lo que hecho bando con amenaza de prisión y de pena que se execute en uno de los Yndios por que avia dejado un palo o árbol de anono junto á sus casa." AGN, Criminal 304/1/118.

63 Beyond forcing Totonacs to sell their goods at low cost and monopolizing the fruit trade, de la Barga also forced the natives to transport his cargoes and threatened that anyone who did not comply would be arrested and whipped. AGN, Criminal 304/1/103v.

64 AGN, General de Parte 44/190/180.

65 AGN, General de Parte 44/190/182. Bazaras specifically prohibited the use of fire for this project because of the danger of wildfire. Bazaras also noted that these men should also be permitted to conduct the normal business required for the maintenance of their families, such as working in their *milpas*.

SIX   A Fractured Pochguin: Local Factionalism and the Uprising of 1787

1   AGN, General de Parte 67/206/82.
2   AGN, Indiferente de Guerra 414a/8/1.
3   AGN, Indiferente de Guerra 414a/8/1.
4   AGN, Indiferente de Guerra 414a/8/1-1v.
5   AGI, México 1528/817.
6   AGN, Criminal 315/2/38v; AGN, Indiferente de Guerra 414a/8/1v.
7   AGN, Criminal 315/2/16.
8   AGN, Criminal 315/2/84. The extent of the damage to either building is not clearly stated.
9   AGN, Criminal 315/2/34.
10   AGN, Criminal 315/2/34-34v.
11   AGN, Criminal 315/2/35v.
12   AGN, Criminal 315/2/34v.
13   AGN, Criminal 315/2/34.
14   AGN, Criminal 315/2/69.
15   AGN, Criminal 315/2/36.
16   AGN, Correspondencias de Varios Autoridades 40/15/66-67.
17   The Zamora Regiment was from Spain. It had a theoretical full strength of the 1,377 troops, though the actual force compliment was rarely complete. Archer, *The Army in Bourbon Mexico,* 22. The force that deployed for Papantla was a sampling of that body, which included grenadiers, fusiliers, infantry, and four swivel guns commandeered from the boats that had transported them. AGN, Criminal 315/2/78. It should be noted that in colonial New Spain, the free-colored militia forces, which were defending Papantla until regulars could arrive, were never designed as a force to defend against internal uprising. They were established in and near coastal towns to contend with foreign raiders, primarily British and French. A full examination of the free-colored militia in Papantla and elsewhere in the colony can be found in Vinson, *Bearing Arms for His Majesty,* 19–21.
18   This figure includes only off-site troops that came to aid Papantla. There were fifty-one troops from Teziutlan, fifty-two from Perote, and 171 of the Zamora regiment from Veracruz. There are no figures on the number of Papantla militiamen who mustered for the 1787 uprising. A complete muster record from 1767 lists 278 individuals. Only 133 of those men were listed as present, the rest being recorded as absent or too sick to muster. It is very unlikely that all 133 of these men would have turned out for the 1787 event. AGN, Criminal 303/2/219-221v. In any case, the Papantla force appears to have been ill-equipped for the battle. When in December 1787, Arias de Saavedra was put in charge of the militia armory, he found it to be largely unserviceable. AGN, Indiferente de Guerra 414a/51.
19   AGN, Criminal 315/2/40.
20   AGN, Criminal 315/2/41v.
21   AGN, Criminal 315/2/84v.
22   AGI, México 1532/731/5.
23   See also Ducey, *A Nation of Villages,* 43–47.
24   Eric Van Young, "Conflict and Solidarity in Indian Village Life: The Guadalajara Region in the Late Colonial Period," *The Hispanic American*

Historical Review 64: 1 (February, 1984): 55–79, 58.
25 Raymond Buve, "Political Patronage and Politics at the Village Level in Central Mexico: Continuity and Change in Patterns from the Late Colonial Period to the End of the French Intervention (1867)" *Bulletin of Latin American Research* 11: 1 (January, 1992): 1–28, 4.
26 Ducey, *A Nation of Villages*, 33.
27 AGN, Indios 69/349/269-269v.
28 AGN, General de Parte 67/206/81v-82, court proceeding in case against Cornejo and Bernia, 8 April 1787. Charles Gibson found a similar situation in a disputed 1676 election in Cuauhtitlan. Gibson, *Aztecs Under Spanish Rule*, 174. Furthermore, this influence over elections is consistent with Gibson's claim that *corregidores* and *tenientes* were instructed to prevent the election of "drunkards, rebellious or uncooperative men, persons of 'bad character,'" Gibson, 177. On elections elsewhere in colonial New Spain, see Robert Haskett, *Indigenous Rulers: An Ethnohistory of Town Government in Colonial Cuernavaca* (Albuquerque: University of New Mexico Press, 1991), Chapter 2; and Matthew Restall, *The Maya World: Yucatec Culture and Society, 1550–1850* (Stanford: Stanford University Press, 1997), Chapter 20.
29 AGN, Indios 69/349/269-269v.
30 Gibson argues that in the Valley of Mexico offices in the *república de indios* eventually came to be viewed as burdensome responsibilities imposed by the Spaniards. Gibson, *Aztecs Under Spanish Rule*, 192–193. Although I do not question Gibson's claim, the record suggests that offices in the cabildo of Papantla did represent both authority and an opportunity that was attractive to many in Papantla.
31 Ducey, "From Village Riot to Regional Rebellion: Social Protest in the Huasteca, Mexico 1760–1870," PhD Dissertation (Chicago: University of Chicago, 1992), 5.
32 See Van Young, "Conflict and Solidarity," 71.
33 Antonio Escobar Ohmstede, "Del gobierno indígena al ayuntamiento constitucional en las Huastecas hidalguense y veracruzana, 1780–1853," *Estudios Mexicanos*, 12: 1 (Winter, 1996): 1-26.9-12; See also Taylor, *Drinking, Homicide, and Rebellion*, 139.
34 Eric Van Young "Moving Toward Revolt: Agrarian Origins of the Hidalgo Rebellion in the Guadalajara Region," in *Riot, Rebellion, and Revolution: Rural Social Conflict in Mexico*, ed. Friedrich Katz. (Princeton: University of Princeton Press, 1988): 176–204, 198.
35 AGN, Indios 69/349/269v.
36 No date or other details are provided about the alleged homicide. AGN, General de Parte 67/206/81v-82.
37 *Ibid.*
38 AGN, Inquisition, 1216/9/296-317.
39 AGN, Inquisición 1216/9/302.
40 AGN, Inquisición 1216/9/305v.
41 AGN, Inquisición 1216/8/314v.
42 AGN, Inquisición 1216/8/317.
43 AGN, Criminal 539/5/171.
44 AGN, Criminal 539/5/181v, the failure to notify Suárez of the promotion is

noted in AGN, Criminal 539/5/180, testimony of Ensign Manuel Castaño.

45 AGN, Criminal 539/5/170, the testimony is extremely difficult to assess as Lara himself swore in 1784 that he was too infirm to serve any further. However, in both the Inquisition investigation against Cornejo and the criminal case against Chaves, Cornejo was accused of forcing individuals to swear false testimony. In 1787, during questioning about Cornejo and Chaves, Lara was described as healthy and robust. AGN, Criminal 539/5/175.

46 AGN, Criminal 539/5/182.

47 AGN, Criminal 539/5/178v.

48 AGN, Criminal 539/5/183v.

49 AGN, Criminal 539/5/178v.

50 Patricia Seed, *To Love, Honor, and Obey in Colonial Mexico: Conflicts Over Marriage Choice, 1574–1821* (Stanford: Stanford University Press, 1988), 99.

51 AGN, Criminal 539/5/178.

52 AGN, Criminal 539/5/161.

53 Van Young, "Conflict and Solidarity," 60. See also Van Young, "Moving toward Revolt," 199. Van Young also aptly describes the targets of such deflected hostility as "a lightning rod for peasant discontent." Eric Van Young, "Agrarian Rebellion and Defense of Community: Meaning and Collective Violence in Late Colonial and Independence Era Mexico," *Journal of Social History* 27: 2 (Winter, 1993): 245–269, 246.

54 AGN, Criminal 315/2/112.

55 AGN, Criminal 312/2/45.

56 AGN, Criminal 315/2/113. Archer notes in *Army in Bourbon Mexico* that the Papantla rebellion raised grave concerns about the capability of the local militias, who proved unable to rapidly contain this uprising and another in Acayucan (also in Veracruz) in October of the same year. In addition, the need to dispatch so many troops of the army to assist in these two uprisings raised doubts about the army's freedom and ability to defend the coasts of the region.

57 AGN, Criminal 315/2/87v.

58 AGN, Criminal 315/2/19v.

59 AGN, Criminal 315/2/55.

60 AGN, Criminal 315/2/27.

61 AGN, Criminal 304/2/102. See also Ruiz Medrano, "Rebeliones indígenas en la epoca colonial: El tumulto indígena de Papantla en 1767."

62 Carlos Rubén Ruiz Medrano has argued that native uprisings were conceived as part of a continuum of methods of resistance that included legal channels and that when natives took to the streets in violent unrest, such action did not preclude the simultaneous use of accepted legal methods of power negotiation. Carlos Rubén Ruiz Medrano, "El tumulto de abril de 1757 en Actopan. Coerción laboral y las formas de movilización y resistencia social de las comunidades indígenas," *Estudios de Historia Novohispana* 36 (2007): 101–129.

63 AGN, Criminal 539/5/206.

64 AGN, Criminal 539/5/208v.

Conclusion

1 AGN, Tabaco 134/7.

2 Castro Gutiérrez, *Nueva ley y nuevo rey*, 31–32.

3 Luis Fernando Díaz Sanchez, "Las reformas borbónicas y la formación del descontento, 1765–1808," in *Foro de Guanajuato: nuevas interpretaciones de la Independencia de México*, ed. José Luis Lara Valdés, (Guanajuato: Colegio de Historiadores de Guanajuato, 2009), 129.

Bibliography

Archives

AGN Archivo General de la Nación, Mexico City, Mexico
Alcabales
Alcaldes Mayores
Archivo Histórico de las Haciendas
Bandos
Correos
Correspondencias de Various Autoridades
Criminal
General de Parte
Indiferente de Guerra
Indios
Industria y Comercio
Inquisición
Intendencias
Ordenanzas
Reales Cédulas
Rios y Acequias
Subdelegados
Tabaco
Tierras
Tributos

AGI Archivo General de Indias, Seville, Spain
Civil
Contratación
Cuba
México
Estado
Uniformes

BNM Biblioteca Nacional de México, Mexico City, Mexico
Lafragua 399
Lafragua 844

PAA Papantla Archdiocene Archive, Papantla, Veracruz, Mexico
Defunciones 1770–1925. Courtesy Church of Jesus Christ of Latter Day Saints

Secondary Sources

Aguirre Beltrán, Gonzalo. *La población negra de México, 1519–1810: estudio etnohistórico*, Mexico City: Fondo de Cultura Económica, 1959.

Alcedo, Antonio de. *Diccionario Geografico-Histórico de las Indias Occidentales o América*. Madrid: En la Emprenta de B. Cano, 1787.

Andrien, Kenneth. "The Politics of Reform in Spain's Atlantic Empire during the Late Bourbon Period: The *Visita* of José García de León y Pizarro in Quito," *Journal of Latin American Studies* 41: 4 (2009): 637–662.

Anguita Cantero, Ricardo. *Ordenanza y policía urbana: Los orígenes de la reglamentación edificatoria en España, 1750–1900*. Monográfica Arte Y Arqueología: Universidad de Granada, 1997.

Archer, Christon. "Pardos, Indians, and the Army of New Spain: Inter-Relationships and Conflicts, 1780–1810." *Journal of Latin American Studies* 6: 2 (1974): 231–255.

———. *The Army in Bourbon Mexico*. Albuquerque: University of New Mexico Press, 1977.

Arrom, Silvia Marina. *Containing the Poor: The Mexico City Poor House, 1774–1871*. Durham: Duke University Press, 2000.

Baber, Jovita. "Empire, Indians, and the Negotiation for the Status of City in Tlaxcala, 1521–1550." In *Negotiation Within Domination: New Spain's Indian Pueblos Confront the Spanish State*, edited by Ethelia Ruiz Medrano and Susan Kellogg, 19–44. Boulder, CO: University of Colorado Press, 2010.

Barnadas, Joseph M. "The Catholic Church in America." In *The Cambridge History of Latin America, Volume 1 Colonial Latin America*, edited by Leslie Bethell, 511–540. Cambridge: Cambridge University Press, 1984.

Baskes, Jeremy. *Indians, Merchants, and Markets: A Reinterpretation of The Repartimiento and Spanish Indian Economic Relations in Colonial Oaxaca, 1750–1821*. Stanford: Stanford: University Press, 2000.

Bennett, Herman L. *Africans in Colonial Mexico: Absolutism, Christianity, and Afro-Creole Consciousness, 1570–1640*. Indianapolis: Indiana University Press, 2003.

Blaisdell, Lowell. "French Influence and the Origins of the Bourbon Colonial Reorganization." *Hispanic American Historical Review* 71: 1 (1991): 579–607.

Brading, David. *Miners and Merchants in Bourbon Mexico 1763–1810*. Cambridge: Cambridge University Press, 1971.

———. "Tridentine Catholicism and Enlightened Despotism in Bourbon Mexico." *Journal of Latin American Studies* 15: 1 (May, 1983): 1–22.

———. "Bourbon Spain and its Empire." In *The Cambridge History of Latin America, Volume 1: Colonial Latin America*, edited by Leslie Bethell, 389–440. Cambridge: Cambridge University Press, 1984.

Bruman, Henry J. "The Cultural History of Mexican Vanilla." *Hispanic American Historical Review* 28: 3 (1948): 360–376.

Buve, Raymond. "Political Patronage and Politics at the Village Level in Central Mexico: Continuity and Change in Patterns from the Late Colonial Period to the End of the French Intervention (1867)." *Bulletin of Latin American Research* 11: 1 (Jan., 1992): 1–28.

Carpio Penagos, Carlos Uriel del. "Producción y comercio de tabaco en

Centroamérica a fines del período colonial." *LiminaR. Estudios Sociales y Humanísticos* 12: 2 (2014): 195–208.

Carr, Raymond. *Spain: A History.* Oxford: Oxford University Press, 2000.

Carrera, Magali. *Imagining Identity in New Spain: Race, Lineage, and the Colonial Body in Portraiture and Casta Paintings.* Austin: University of Texas Press, 2003.

Carrión Juan de. *Descripción del pueblo de Gueytlalpan (Zacatlan, Juxupango, Matlaltan y Chila, Papantla) 30 de Mayo de 1581 (Reclación de Papantla).* Edited by José García Payón. Xalapa: Universidad Veracruzana, 1965.

Carroll, Patrick J. *Blacks in Colonial Veracruz: Race, Ethnicity, and Regional Development.* Austin: University of Texas Press, 1991.

———. "Los Mexicanos negros, el mestizaje y los fundamentos olvidados de la 'Raza Cósmica:' Una perspectiva regional." *Historia Mexicana* XLIV: 3 (1995): 403–438.

Castleman, Bruce A. *Building the King's Highway: Labor, Society, and Family on Mexico's Caminos Reales, 1757–1804.* Tucson: University of Arizona Press, 2005.

Castro Gutiérrez, Felipe. *Nueva ley y nuevo rey: reformas borbónicas y rebellion popular en Nueva España.* Zamora, Michoacán: El Colegio de Michoacán, 1996.

Coatsworth, John H. "Patterns of Rural Rebellion in Latin America: Mexico in Comparative Perspective." In *Riot, Rebellion and Revolution: Rural Social Conflict in Mexico,* edited by Friedrich Katz, 30–39. Princeton: Princeton University Press, 1988.

Cook, Noble David. *Born to Die: Disease and New World Conquest, 1492–1650.* Cambridge: Cambridge University Press, 1998.

Cook, Shelburne F. and Woodrow Borah. *Essays in Population History: Mexico and California* Vol. 3. Berkeley: University of California Press, 1979.

Cope, R. Douglas. *The Limits of Racial Domination: Plebian Society in Colonial Mexico City, 1660–1720.* Madison: University of Wisconsin Press, 1994.

Correll, Donovan S. "Vanilla: Its Botany, History, Cultivation and Economic Import." *Economic Botany* 7: 4 (1953): 291–358.

Covarrubias, José Enrique. *La moneda de cobre en México, 1760–1842: Un problema administrativo.* Mexico City: Universidad Nacional Autónoma de México, 2000.

Crosby, Alfred. *The Columbian Exchange: Biological and Cultural Consequences of 1492.* Westport, CT: Greenwood Press, 1972.

Davies, R. Trevor. *Spain in Decline, 1621–1700.* London: Macmillan and Co, 1965.

Deans-Smith, Susan. *"The Money Plant: The Royal Tobacco Monopoly of New Spain, 1765–1821."* In *The Economies of Mexico and Peru During the Late Colonial Period, 1760–1810,* edited by Nils Jacobsen and Hans-Jürgen Puhle, 361–387. Berlin: Colloquium Verlag Berlin, 1989.

———. *Bureaucrats, Planters, and Workers: The Making of the Tobacco Monopoly in Bourbon Mexico.* Austin: University of Texas Press, 1992.

Díaz del Castillo, Bernal. *Historia verdadera de la conquista de la Nueva España.* Volume 1 [1632]. Paris: Libreria de Rosa, 1837.

Díaz Hernández, Magdalena. "La intendencia de Veracruz y los repartimientos

(1787–1810): A vueltas con el *salvaje* el miserable." In *Orbis incognitvs: avisos y legajos del Nuevo Mundo: homenaje al profesor Luis Navarro García*, 553–560. Universidad de Huelva, 2007.

———. "Contrabandistas tabaqueros en la región de Veracruz (1765–1807). El sistema alternatico al estanco del Tabaco." *Chronica Nova* 34 (2008): 199–217.

Díaz Sánchez, Luis Fernando. "Las reformas borbónicas y la formación del descontento, 1765–1808." In *Foro de Guanajuato: nuevas interpretaciones de la Independencia de México*, edited by José Luis Lara Valdés, 129–148. Guanajuato: Colegio de Historiadores de Guanajuato, 2009.

Ducey, Michael. "From Village Riot to Regional Rebellion: Social Protest in the Huasteca, Mexico 1760–1870," PhD diss. Chicago: University of Chicago, 1992.

———. "Viven sin ley ni rey: Rebelliones coloniales en Papantla, 1760–1790." In *Procesos Rurales e Historia Regional (Sierra y Costa Totonacas de Veracruz)*, edited by Victoria Chenaut, 15–49. Mexico: CIESAS, 1996.

———. *A Nation of Villages: Riot and Rebellion in the Mexican Huasteca, 1750–1850*. Tucson: University of Arizona Press, 2004.

Earle Mond, Rebecca. "Indian Rebellion and Bourbon Reform in New Granada: Riots in Pasto, 1780–1800." *Hispanic American Historical Review* 73: 1 (1993): 99–124.

Elliott, J.H. "Spain and America in the Sixteenth and Seventeenth Centuries." In *The Cambridge History of Latin America, Volume 1, Colonial Latin America*, edited by Leslie Bethell, 287–340. Cambridge: Cambridge University Press, 1984.

———. *Spain and its World, 1500–1700*. New Haven: Yale University Press, 1989.

Escobar Ohmstede, Antonio. "Del gobierno indígena al Ayuntamiento constitucional en las Huastecas hidalguense y veracruzana, 1780–1853." *Estudios Mexicanos* 12: 1 (Winter 1996): 1–26.

———. "Los pueblos indios en las Huastecas, México, 1750–1810: formas para conservar y aumentar su territorio." *Colonial Latin American Historical Review* 6: 1 (1997): 31–66.

———. *De la costa a la sierra: las Huastecas, 1750–1900*. Juárez: Centro de Investigaciones y Estudios Superiores en Antropología Social, 1998.

———. "Indígenas y conflictos en el periodo colonial tardío novohispano: el caso de las Huastecas, 1750–1820." *Nuevo Mundo Mundos Nuevos* (2009).

Fisher, Andrew B. and Matthew D. O'Hara eds. *Imperial Subjects: Race and Identity in Colonial Latin America*. Durham: Duke University Press, 2009.

Fisher, John. *Commercial Relations Between Spain and Spanish America in the Era of Free Trade, 1778–1796*. Manchester: Center for Latin American Studies, 1985.

———, and Allan Kuethe and Anthony McFarlane. *Reform and Insurrection in Bourbon New Granada and Peru*. Baton Rouge: Louisiana State University Press, 1990.

———. *Bourbon Peru, 1750–1824*. Liverpool: Liverpool University Press, 2003.

Florescano, Enrique and Isabel Gil Sánchez. *1750–1808: La época de las reformas borbónicas y del crecimiento económico*. Mexico City: INAH, 1974.

Frederick, Jake. "Pardos Enterados: Unearthing Black Papantla in the Eighteenth Century." *Journal of Colonialism and Colonial History* 5: 2 (2004).

————. "Without Impediment: Crossing Racial Boundaries in Colonial Mexico." *The Americas* 67: 4 (2011): 495–515.

————. "A Fractured Pochgui: Local Factionalism in Eighteenth-Century Papantla." *Ethnohistory* 54: 8 (2011): 561–583.

García Ayluardo, Clara. ed. *Las reformas borbónicas, 1750–1808*. Mexico City: CIDE, 2010.

García Martínez, Bernardo. *Los pueblos de las sierra: el poder y el espacio entre los indios del norte de Puebla hasta 1700*. Mexico City: El Colegio de Mexico, 1987.

García Payón, José. "Archeology of Central Veracruz." In *Handbook of Middle American Indians, Part 2, Archeology of Northern Mesoamerica*, vol. 11, ed. E.Z. Vogt, 505–542. Austin: University of Texas Press, 1969.

Gerhard, Peter. *A Guide to the Historical Geography of New Spain*. Norman and London: University of Oklahoma Press, 1993.

Germeten, Nicole Von. *Black Blood Brothers: Confraternities and Social Mobility for Afro-Mexicans*. Gainesville: University Press of Florida, 2006.

Gibson, Charles. *The Aztecs Under Spanish Rule: A History of the Indians of the Valley of Mexico, 1519–1810*. Stanford: Stanford University Press, 1964.

González Obregón, Luis. *Rebeliones indígenas y precusores de la independencia mexicana en los siglos XVI, XVII, XVIII*. Mexico City: Ediciones Fuente Cultural, 1952.

González Sierra, José G. *Monopolio del humo: elementos para la historia del tabaco en México y algunos conflictos de tabaqueros veracruzanos, 1915–1930*. Xalapa, México: Universidad Veracruzana, Centro de Investigaciones Históricas, 1987.

Govers, Cora. *Performing the Community: Representation, Ritual and Reciprocity in the Totonac Highlands of Mexico*. Berlin: LIT Verlag, 2006.

Graham, Alan. ed. *Vegetation and Vegetational History of Northern Latin America*. Amsterdam: Elsevier Scientific Publishing Company, 1973.

Hamilton, Earl. "Money and Economic Recovery in Spain Under the First Bourbon, 1701–1746." *The Journal of Modern History* 15: 3 (1943): 192–206.

Hamnett, Brian R. *Roots of Insurgency: Mexican Regions, 1750–1824*. Cambridge: Cambridge University Press, 1986.

Harding, Richard. *Seapower and Naval Warfare, 1650–1830*. London: UCL Press, 2001.

Harvey, H.R. and Isabel Kelly. "The Totonac." In *Handbook of Middle American Indians, Part 2: Ethnology*, vol. 8, edited by E.Z. Vogt, 638–681. Austin: University of Texas Press, 1969.

Haskett, Robert. *Indigenous Rulers: An Ethnohistory of the Town Government of Colonial Cuernavaca*. Albuquerque: University of New Mexico Press, 1991.

Hassig, Ross. *Trade, Tribute, and Transportation: The Sixteenth-Century Political Economy of the Valley of Mexico*. Norman: University of Oklahoma Press, 1985.

Hobsbawm, E.J. *Primitive Rebels: Studies in Archaic Forms of Social Movement in the 19th and 20th Centuries*. New York and London: W.W. Norton and Company, 1959.

Horn, Rebecca. "Gender and Social Identity: Nahua Naming Patterns in Post-Conquest Central Mexico." *Indian Women of Early Mexico*, edited by Susan

Schroeder, Stephanie Wood, and Robert Haskett, 105–122. Norman: University of Oklahoma Press, 1997.

Jackson, Margaret A. and Rebecca P. Brienen eds. *Visions of Empire: Picturing the Conquest in Colonial Mexico.* Coral Gables, FL: University of Miami and J.I. Kislak Foundation, 2003.

Jackson, Robert H. *Race, Caste, and Status: Indians in Colonial Spanish America.* Albuquerque: University of New Mexico Press, 1999.

Kamen, Henry. *Spain, 1469–1714.* London: Longman, 1983.

———. *Empire: How Spain Became a World Power, 1492–1763.* New York: Harper Collins, 2003.

Kampen, Michael Edwin. *The Sculptures of El Tajín Veracruz, Mexico.* Gainesville: University of Florida Press, 1972.

Kelley, Isabel and Angel Palerm. *The Tajín Totonac: Part 1. History, Subsistence, Shelter and Technology.* Washington D.C.: United States General Printing Office, 1952.

Kinsbruner, Jay. *Independence in Spanish America: Civil Wars Revolutions and Underdevelopment.* Albuquerque: University of New Mexico Press, 2000.

Kirkwood, Burton. *The History of Mexico.* Santa Barbara: ABC-CLIO, 2010.

Koontz, Rex. *Lightning Gods and Feathered Serpents: The Public Sculpture of El Tajín.* Austin: University of Texas Press, 2009.

Kourí, Emilio. *A Pueblo Divided: Business, Property, and Community in Papantla, Mexico.* Stanford: Stanford University Press, 2004.

Kuethe, Alan. "The Early Reforms of Charles III in the Viceroyalty of New Granada." In *Reform and Insurrection in Bourbon New Granada and Peru,* edited by John R. Fisher, Allan Kuethe, Anthony McFarlane, 23–26. Baton Rouge: Louisiana State University Press, 1990.

Kuethe, Allan and Lowell Blaisdell. "French Influence and the Origins of the Bourbon Colonial Reorganization." *The Hispanic American Historical Review* 71: 1 (1991): 579–607.

Landers, Jane and Barry M. Robinson. eds. *Slaves, Subjects and Subversives: Blacks in Colonial Latin America.* Albuquerque: University of New Mexico Press, 2006.

Lane, Kris. *Pillaging the Empire: Piracy in the Americas, 1500–1750.* Armonk NY: M.E. Sharpe, 1998.

Leibly, John S. *Report to the King: Colonel Juan Camargo y Cavallero's Historical Account of New Spain, 1815.* New York: P. Lang, 1984.

Lewis, Laura A. *Hall of Mirrors: Power, Witchcraft, and Caste in Colonial Mexico.* Durham and London: Duke University Press, 2003.

Lokken, Paul. "Marriage and Slave Emancipation in Seventeenth Century Rural Guatemala" *The Americas* 58: 2 (2001): 175–200.

López Austin, Alfredo and Leobardo López Luján. *Mexico's Indigenous Past.* Translated by Bernardo R. Ortiz de Montenallano. Norman: Univesity of Oklahoma Press, 2001.

Luján Muñoz, Jorge. "El establecimiento del estanco del tabaco en el reino de Guatemala." *Mesoamerica* 22: 41 (2001): 99–136.

Machuca, Laura. "El impacto del repartimiento de mercancías en la provincia de Tehuantepec durante el siglo XVIII: Los pueblos de la grana." In *El repartimiento forzoso de Mercancías en Mexico, Peru, y Filipinas,* edited by Margarita Menegus, 120–145. México City: Instituto de Investigaciones Dr.

José María Luis Mora, Centro de Estudios Sobre la Universidad-UNAM, 2000.

MacLeod, Murdo J. "Spain and America: The Atlantic Trade, 1492–1720." In *The Cambridge History of Latin America, Volume 1: Colonial Latin America*, edited by Leslie Bethell, 341–389. Cambridge: Cambridge University Press, 1984.

———. "Some Thoughts on the Pax Colonial, Colonial Violence, and Perceptions of Both." In *Native Resistance and the Pax Colonial in New Spain*, edited by Susan Schroeder, 129–142. Lincoln: University of Nebraska Press, 1998.

Masferrer Kan, Elio Roberto. "Cambio y continuidad entre los totonacos de la Sierra Norte de Puebla." Master's thesis, Universidad Iberoamericana, 2006.

Marchena Fernández, Juan. "The Social World of the Military in Peru and New Granada." In *Reform and Insurrection in Bourbon New Granada*, edited by John R. Fisher, Alan Kuethe, and Anthony McFarlane. Baton Rouge: Louisiana State University, 1990.

McAlister, Lyle N. "The Reorganization of the Army of New Spain, 1763–1766." *The Hispanic American Historical Review* 33:1 (1953): 1–32.

Melville, Elinor. *A Plague of Sheep: Environmental Consequences of the Conquest of Mexico*. Cambridge: Cambridge University Press, 1994.

Menegus, Margarita. "La economía indígena y su articulación al mercado en nueva españa. El repartimiento forzozo de mercancías." *El repartimiento forzozo de mercancías en México, Perú y Filipinas*, edited by Margarita Menegus, 9–64. Mexico City: Centro de Estudios Sobre la Universidad-UNAM, 2000.

———. *Los Indios en la historia de México, siglos XVI al XIX: balance y perspectivas*. Mexico City: FCE, CIDE, 2006.

Migdal, Joel S. *Peasants, Politics, and Revolution: Pressures Toward Political and Social Change in the Third World*. Princeton: Princeton University Press, 1974.

Milton, Cynthia and Ben Vinson III. "Counting Heads: Race and Non-Native Tribute Policy in Colonial Spanish America." *The Journal of Colonialism and Colonial History* 3: 3 (2002): 1–18.

Mond, Rebecca Earle. "Indian Rebellion and Bourbon Reform in New Granada: Riots in Pasto, 1780–1800." *The Hispanic American Historical Review* 73: 1 (1993): 99–124.

Moreno Coello, Georgina. "Alcaldes Mayores y Subdelegados frente la siembra clandestine de Tabaco: Papantla, 1765–1806." *América Latina en la Historia Económica, Revista de Investigación* 19: 3 (2012): 206–234.

Moreno-Coutiño, Ana and Beatriz Coutiño Bello. "Nicotiana Tobacum L.: Usos y percepciones." *Ethnobiología* 10: 2 (2012): 29–39.

Naveda Chávez-Hita, Adriana and González Sierra, José G. *Papantla*. Jalapa: Gobierno del Estado de Veracruz, Archivo General del Estado, 1990.

Oropeza, Ruben. *Between Puffs: A History of Tobacco, Two Thousand Years of Tobacco Use*. Orlando, FL: Rivercross Publishing, 2005.

Ortiz Espejel, Benjamin. *La cultura asediada; espacio y historia en el tropico veracruzano, el caso del Totonacapan*. Mexico City: CIESAS, 1995.

Ouweneel, Arij. "El gobernador de indios, el repartimiento de comercios y la caja de comunidad en los pueblos de indios del México central (Siglo XVIII)." In *El repartimiento forzozo de mercancías en México, Perú y Filipinas*, edited by Margarita Menegus, 65–97. Mexico City: Centro de Estudios Sobre la Universidad-UNAM, 2000.

Palacios Sánchez, Alejandra. "La muerte: símbolo de vida entre los totonacas de Papantla, Veracruz" PhD diss., Universidad Iberoamericana, 2009.

Palerm, Angel. "Etnografía antigua totonaca en el oriente de México." *Revista Mexicana de Estudios Antropológicos* 13: 2 and 3 (1952–1953): 163–173.

Papantla: cuaderno de información básica para la planeación municipal. Aguascalientes, Mexico: Instituto Nacional de Estadistica, Geografía e Informática, 1990.

Paquette, Gabriel. *Enlightenment, Governance, and Reform in Spain and its Empire, 1759–1808.* New York: Palgrave, 2011.

Pascual Soto, Arturo. *El Tajín: En Busca de Los Origenes de Una Civilización.* Mexico City: CONACULTA: Instituto Nacional de Antropología e Historia, 2006.

Parry, J. H. *The Spanish Seaborne Empire.* Berkeley: University of California Press, 1990.

Patch, Robert. *Maya and Spaniard in Yucatan, 1648–1812.* Stanford: Stanford University Press, 1993.

———. *Maya Revolt and Revolution in the Eighteenth Century.* Armonk, New York and London: M.E. Sharpe, 2002.

Pietschmann, Horst. "Antecedentes españoles e hispanoamericanos de las intendencias." *Memoria del cuarto congreso Venezolano de historia.* Caracas: Academia Nacional de la Historia, 1983: 417–432.

Piña Chan, Román and Patricia Castillo Peña. *Tajín: La ciudad del dios huracán.* Mexico City: Fondo de Cultura Económica, 1999.

Prescott, William. *Conquest of Mexico.* New York: The Book League of America, 1934.

Puig, Henri. *Végétacion de La Huasteca, Mexique: Etude Phytogéographique et Écologique.* Mexico: Mission Archeologique et Ethnologique Français au Mexique, 1976.

Restall, Matthew. *The Maya World: Yucatec Culture and Society, 1550–1850.* Stanford: Stanford University Press, 1997.

———. *Maya Conquistador.* Boston: Beacon Press, 1998.

———. *Seven Myths of the Spanish Conquest.* Oxford: Oxford University Press, 2003.

———. "Maya Ethnogenesis." *The Journal of Latin American Anthropology* 9: 1 (2004): 64–89.

———. "The Spanish Creation of the Conquest." *Invasion and Transformation: Interdisciplinary Perspectives on the Conquest of Mexico,* edited by Margaret Jackson, 93–102. Boulder: University Press of Colorado, 2007.

———. *Beyond Black and Red: African-Native Relations in Colonial Latin America.* Albuquerque: University of New Mexico Press, 2005.

———. *The Black Middle: Africans, Mayas, and Spaniards in Colonial Yucatan.* Stanford: Stanford University Press, 2009.

Ricard, Robert. *The Spiritual Conquest of Mexico: An Essay on the Apostolate and the Evangelizing Methods of the Mendicant Orders in New Spain: 1523–1572.* Berkeley: University of California Press, 1966.

Robicsek, Francis. *The Smoking Gods: Tobacco in Maya Art, History, and Religion.* Norman: Oklahoma, 1978.

Rogelio Alvarez, José, ed. *Enciclopedia de México.* Tomo XI. México. Instituto de laEnciclopedia de México, 1993.

Rostow, W. W. *British Economy of the Nineteenth Century*. Oxford: Clarendon Press, 1948.
Ruiz Medrano, Carlos Rubén. "Rebeliones indígenas en la epoca colonial: el tumulto indígena de Papantla de 1767." *Mesoamerica* 32 (1996): 339–353.
———. "El tumulto de abril de 1757 en Actopan: Coerción laboral y las formas de movilización y resistencia social de las comunidaded indígenas." *Estudios de Historia Novohispana* 36 (2007): 101–129.
Ruiz Medrano, Ethelia and Susan Kellogg. *Negotiation Within Domination: New Spain's Indian Pueblos Confront the Spanish State*. Boulder: University of Colorado Press, 2010.
Sahagún, Bernardino de. *Historia general de las cosas de nueva españa*, Vol. III. Mexico City: Editorial Pedro Robredo, 1938.
Sainos García, Dailan. "El Tajín como patrimonio cultural de la humanidad: La puesta en valor de la zona arqueológica" *EntreVerAndo* 3 (2009): 16–17.
Salas, Adrián and María Esther Martínez. "La política del secreto en la santa inquisición y su presencia en Papantla, Veracruz (México), siglos XVII y XVIII." *Revista de antropología experimental* 1 (2001): 197–203.
Salas García, Luis. *Juu Papantlan: Apuntes para la historia de Papantla*. Mexico City: Gráfica Editorial Mexicana, 1979.
Salvatore, Ricardo D. "The Strength of Markets in Latin America's Sociopolitical Discourse, 1750–1850." *Latin American Perspectives* 26: 1 (1999): 22–43.
Sánchez Santiró, Ernest. "Una modernización conservadora; el reformismo borbónico y su impacto sobre la economía, la fiscalidad y las instituciones." *Las reformas borbónicas, 1750–1808*, edited by Clara García Ayluardo, 288–336. Mexico City: CIDE, 2010.
Santiago, Myrna. "The Huasteca Rain Forest: An Environmental History." *Latin American Research Review* 46: 4 (2011): 32–54.
Saunders, William. "The Anthropogeography of Central Veracruz." *Revista Mexicana de Estudios Antropológicos* XIII (1952–53): 27–78.
Scammall, G.V. "'A Very Profitable and Advantageous Trade': British Smuggling in the Iberian Americas Circa 1500–1750." *Itinerario* 24: 3–4 (2000): 135–172.
Schroeder, Susan ed. *Native Resistance and the Pax Colonial in New Spain*. Lincoln and London. University of Nebraska Press, 1998.
Schwaller, Robert C. *Géneros de Gente in Early Colonial Mexico: Defining Racial Difference*. Norman: University of Oklahoma Press, 2016.
Scott, James C. *The Moral Economy of the Peasant: Rebellions and Subsistence in Southeast Asia*. New Haven and London: Yale University Press, 1976.
———. *Weapons of the Weak: Everyday Forms of Peasant Resistance*. New Haven and London: Yale University Press, 1985.
Seed, Patricia. *To Love, Honor, and Obey in Colonial Mexico: Conflicts Over Marriage Choice, 1574–1821*. Stanford: Stanford University Press, 1988.
Serulnikov, Sergio. *Subverting Colonial Authority: Challenges to Spanish Rule in Eighteenth-Century Southern Andes*. Durham: Duke University Press, 2003.
Smidt, Andrea J. "Bourbon Regalism and the Importation of Gallicanism: The Political Path for a State Religion in Eighteenth-Century Spain." *Anuario de Historia de la Iglesia* 19 (2010): 25–53.
Spores, Ronald. "Differential Responses to Colonial Control among the Mixtecs and Zapotecs of Oaxaca." *Native Resistance and the Pax Colonial in New*

Spain, edited by Susan Schroeder, 30–46. Lincoln and London: University of Nebraska Press, 1998.

Stavig, Ward. "Conflict, Violence, and Resistance." In *The Countryside in Colonial Latin America*, edited by Louisa Schell Hoberman and Susan Migden Socolow, 213–234. Albuquerque: University of New Mexico Press, 1996.

Stein, Stanley J. and Barbara Stein. *Silver, Trade, and War: Spain and America in the Making of Early Modern Europe.* Baltimore: Johns Hopkins University Press, 2000.

———. *Apogee of Empire: Spain and New Spain in the Age of Charles III, 1759–1789.* Baltimore: Johns Hopkins University Press, 2003.

Stern, Steve, ed. *Resistance, Rebellion, and Consciousness in the Andean Peasant World, Eighteenth to the Twentieth Centuries.* Madison: The University of Wisconsin Press, 1987.

Stresser-Péan, Guy. "Ancient Sources on the Huasteca." Vol. 11 *Handbook of Middle American Indians, Part 2, Archeology of Northern Mesoamerica,* edited by E.Z. Vogt, 582–602. Austin: University of Texas Press, 1969.

Suárez Argüello, Clara Elena. *Camino real y larga: la arriería en la Nueva España.* Mexico: CIESAS, 1997.

Taylor, William B. *Drinking, Homicide, and Rebellion in Colonial Mexican Villages.* Stanford: Stanford University Press, 1979.

Tilly, Charles. "Revolutions and Collective Violence." *Handbook of Political Science.* vol. 3, edited by Fred I. Greenstein and Nelson W. Polsby, 483–552. Reading MA: Addison-Wellesley Publishing Co, 1975.

———. *From Mobilization to Revolution.* Reading, MA: Addison-Wesley Publishing Company, 1978.

Torquemada, Juan de. *Primera-[tercera] Parte De Los Veinte I Vn Libros Rituales I Monarquía Indiana: Con El Origen Y Guerras, De Los Indios Occidentales, De Sus Poblaçones Descubrimiento, Conquista, Conuersion, Y Otras Cosas Maravillosas De La Mesma Tierra: distribuyidos en tres tomos.* Madrid: N. Rodriquez Franco, 1723.

Tutino, John. *From Insurrection to Revolution in Mexico: Social Bases of Agrarian Violence, 1750–1940.* Princeton: Princeton University Press, 1986.

Van Young, Eric. *Hacienda and Market in Eighteenth-Century Mexico: The Rural Economy of the Guadalajara Region, 1675–1820.* Berkeley: University of California Press, 1981.

———. "Conflict and Solidarity in Indian Village Life: The Guadalajara Region in the Late Colonial Period." *The Hispanic American Historical Review* 64: 1 (1984): 55–79.

———. "Moving Toward Revolt: Agrarian Origins of the Hidalgo Rebellion in the Guadalajara Region." In *Riot, Rebellion, and Revolution: Rural Social Conflict in Mexico*, edited by Friedrich Katz, 176–204. Princeton: Princeton University Press, 1988.

———. "Agrarian Rebellion and Defense of Community: Meaning and Collective Violence in Late Colonial and Independence Era Mexico." *Journal of Social History* 27: 2 (1993): 245–269.

———. *The Other Rebellion: Popular Violence, Ideology, and the Mexican Struggle for Independence, 1810–1821.* Stanford: Stanford University Press, 2001.

Velasco Toro, José. "La política desamortizadora y sus efectos en la region de Papantla, Veracruz." *La palabra y el hombre* 72 (1989): 137–162.

Vinson III, Ben. "The Racial Profile of a Rural Mexican Province in the 'Costa Chica': Igualapa in 1791." *The Americas* 57: 2 (2000): 269–282.

———. *Bearing Arms for His Majesty: The Free Colored Militia in Colonial Mexico*. Stanford: Stanford University Press, 2001.

———. "La categorización racial de los afromexicanos durante la época colonial: una revision basada en evidencia referente a las milicias." *Memorias de la academia Mexicana de la historia* 44 (2001): 27–53.

———. "Los milicianos pardos y la relación estatal durante el Siglo XVIII en México." In *Fuerzas Militares en Iberoamérica, Siglos XVIII y XIX*, edited by Juan Ortiz Escamilla, 47–60. Mexico City: Universidad Veracruzana, El Colegio de Michoacán, El Colegio de México. 2005.

Vizcarra, Catalina. "Bourbon Intervention in the Peruvian Tobacco Industry, 1752–1813." *Journal of Latin American Studies* 39: 3 (2007): 567–593.

Wada, George and James C. Davis. "Riots and Rioters." *Western Political Quarterly* 10: 4 (1957): 864–874.

Walton, Timothy. *The Spanish Treasure Fleets*. Sarasota: Pineapple Press, 1994.

Williams García, Roberto. "Etnografía prehispánica de la Zona Central de Veracruz." *Revista Mexicana de Estudios Antropológicos* 13: 2 and 3 (1952–1953): 157–162.

Zilli, Juan. *Historia sucinta del estado de Veracruz*. Xalapa: Universidad Veracruzana, 1943.

Index

Italic text is used for terms of Spanish origin. Place names are in Mexico, unless stated otherwise.